CONSTITUTIONAL
LITERACY

Constitutional Conflicts

A Series by the Institute of Bill of Rights Law

at the College of William and Mary

Edited by Rodney A. Smolla and Neal Devins

CONSTITUTIONAL LITERACY

A Core Curriculum for a Multicultural Nation

Toni Marie Massaro

DUKE UNIVERSITY PRESS   *Durham and London*   1993

© 1993 Duke University Press

All rights reserved

Printed in the United States of America on acid-free paper ∞

Typeset in Dante by Keystone Typesetting, Inc.

Library of Congress Cataloging-in-Publication Data

appear on the last printed page of this book.

Contents

For my Mother and Father,

Billie D. and Anthony P. Massaro

—first Teachers—

with love and gratitude

Acknowledgments

This book reflects in subtle and important ways the abiding influence of my parents, brothers, and sisters. They taught me to care about the themes in this text and to appreciate how people of good faith might divide over them yet still seek common ground.

I also owe my colleagues at Arizona who participated in a faculty seminar on Part II herein and who otherwise took an interest in this work. My dean, Thomas Sullivan, did all a dean should do and more, including review an early, unpruned version of the manuscript. Jamie Ratner helped me to focus Part II and to make my peace with the book's inevitable omissions. Thanks also go to Junius Hoffman, Robert Glennon, Dan Dobbs, Kay Kavanagh, David Wexler, Ted Schneyer, and Lynn Baker of Arizona and Elizabeth Rapaport of Duke for their encouragement.

Participants at a faculty seminar at Stanford Law School offered extremely helpful criticisms of Chapter 6, for which I am very grateful. I thank in particular Dean Paul Brest, Tom Grey, Deborah Rhode, Mark Kelman, and Michael Wald for their various forms of intellectual inspiration and personal support.

Jeffrey Mirel and Daniel B. Yeager suspended their own work in order to provide thoughtful, extensive, line-by-line critiques of the manuscript. The work is much better than it would have been without their careful criticisms, although I must add the usual disclaimer that neither they nor any other readers should be blamed for its limitations. Donald Brooks, Matthew Leavitt, and Rosa Sabater also took valuable time to review specific chapters and to offer helpful comments. Two anonymous readers for Duke University Press gave much-needed feedback that prompted important changes in the text.

My students are the book's raison d'être and have been the source of immense professional pleasure. Elizabeth Dallam, Stephen McManus, Lisa

D'Oca, Joseph Parkhurst, Kirsten Oberholtzer, and Sarah Works provided superb research assistance, and my seminar students at Stanford and Arizona offered wonderful intellectual companionship that made the process of thinking and writing more vital, less monastic, more fun.

A splendid team of secretaries at the University of Arizona College of Law provided outstanding work and consistent support. Many thanks to Barbara Clelland, Norma Kelly, Angela Badilla, and B. J. Hartford.

Special and warm thanks go to Rachel Toor of Duke University Press for bringing this book to life and for making the publication process so painless. I also am indebted to Jean Brady, Managing Editor at Duke Press, and to Timothy P. Niedermann who prepared an extremely careful and thoughtful edit of the manuscript.

My life-long friends Jacquelyn Fox-Good and Timothy Good afforded special insight into the Hirsch material and the continuing gifts of their intellectual curiosity, their exemplary commitment to teaching, and their supreme fairness. They prove to me that teaching conflicting ideas capaciously and judiciously can happen.

Barbara Allen Babcock was an inspiration. She performed throughout this process the multiple roles of mentor, editor, wise counsellor, and dear friend. I—and many others—are lucky indeed that she chose the classroom over the courtroom, and the scholar's life over that of a national-level politician.

And, finally, I thank Genevieve Leavitt, who offered at every turn of this effort the right response: a shove when the work was moored, a ballast when it lurched, and a compass when it wandered from its charted course. Thanks to her good humor and reorienting sense of what is truly core, I added more laugh lines than worry lines along the way.

1   Introduction

Each age must write its own books.—Ralph Waldo Emerson

A remarkable event drew national attention to America's educational institutions in 1987. Two academic books—E. D. Hirsch's *Cultural Literacy* and Allan Bloom's *Closing of the American Mind*—spiraled to *The New York Times*'s best seller list. The surprising appeal of these books struck many observers as a sign of profound, widespread dissatisfaction with American education. This dissatisfaction has only deepened since.

Hirsch, a humanities professor at the University of Virginia, decried the loss of a shared set of cultural facts, images, and allusions that enables people within the culture to communicate effectively. He proposed that we regain this cultural literacy by teaching a national, core list of facts to all American elementary and high school students and amplified his proposal with his own list and the subsequent, more elaborate, *Dictionary of Cultural Literacy*.

University of Chicago professor Bloom took aim at our elite universities, which, he wrote, no longer teach the classics and instead leave the student adrift on a sea of superficial and naive moral relativism. He favored redirecting the nation's brightest college students toward the study of classical philosophy and away from the mistaken notions of Pragmatists and other relativists.

Despite the many differences between their proposals and underlying philosophies, the two professors struck a common chord, which was reflected in the popularity of their books and in the dialogue about their central claims. Many people in the final decades of the twentieth century agree that something basic and abiding is missing from their own educations, and from those of their children. Some of these people favor dramatic, national-level curricular changes to help address that deficiency. A search for coherence thus has become a central curricular, if not cultural, concern.

This modern coherence movement has been fueled by a parade of studies and reports that trumpet the dismal performance of American students on tests of history, geography, literature, reading, and math. Most frightening of these announcements is the number of American high school graduates who cannot identify the differences between Marxism and capitalism, locate Europe on a map, or name the century in which the Civil War was fought. Coupled with these reports are complaints that the teachers themselves are underqualified and thus unable to impose more rigorous standards of basic literacy, let alone to lead the students in advanced study. Professionalization, say some critics, has led to overprotection of teacher job security at the expense of teacher quality.

Apprehension about knowledge deficits among teachers and students has been enhanced by a worsening economy and by the growing sense that the United States has lost its competitive advantage over Japan, Germany, and other nations. Like the launch of Sputnik in 1957, the blast-off of the Japanese economy in the 1980s has quickened our national resolve to "do something" about our educational system.

Accompanying our current, acute economic woes are the agonizing, chronic problems of racial, gender, ethnic, and socioeconomic inequality. A perceived increase in racial hostility, a depressingly wide if not growing gap between minority student performance and that of white peers, and escalating and controversial demands for more pluralistic, multicultural education have sparked angry conflicts over curriculum, over student-discipline policies, over values instruction, and over funding equalization schemes. On college campuses, charges of "political correctness" and "McCarthyism" meet countercharges of "Eurocentrism," "racism," "heterosexism," and "sexism."

By 1990, the perceived crisis in American education had spawned several reform proposals that only shortly before would have had little chance of success. For example, the movement for "choice" among competing public and even private elementary and secondary schools, regardless of where the parents lived, became a priority of the Bush administration's *America 2000* blueprint for this country's educational future. Similar proposals for competition among public schools and for vouchers that parents could apply to tuition at private sectarian schools previously had been rejected by most educators and other observers as fatal to the mission of common, public schooling, to desegregation, and to separation of church and state. The Bush proposals, however, were surprisingly popular, and choice alternatives were adopted in some states.

The historically intense resistance to national standards of education likewise softened, and the *cri de coeur* of coherence advocates was echoed in the Republican administration's call for a national core curriculum and American Achievement Tests. Moreover, this coherence agenda had bipartisan support, as liberals and conservatives in both national parties expressed concern that American public schools not abandon the melting pot ideal. Arthur Schlesinger, Jr., and other commentators expressed their fear that racial politics were compromising the integrity of the public school curriculum and threatening to "disunite" the United States. These observers denounced experimental programs such as African-American academies with Afrocentric curricula as a form of "ethnic cheerleading" that would only deepen racial divisiveness. In their view, race-conscious measures politicize education and wrongly reinforce the notion that race is determinative, and the outbreak of ethnic violence in Bosnia and elsewhere stood as a grim warning that race-consciousness is always dangerous social policy. Instead, they urged, the nation should rally behind an account of American history that stresses our commonality rather than our particularities and that respects the positive contributions of Western liberal thought to human rights, cultural criticism, and the cause of human liberty.

This rising interest in nationally-defined common standards has been accompanied by a paradoxical surge in interest in decentralizing power over the schools. Critics argue that bureaucratization and centralization of school authority at the state and district levels has deadened local interest in self-determination and reform; layers of needless administrative authority and enforced standardization have stymied innovation, added expense, and removed any incentive for particular schools to experiment, compete, and excel. Competition, decentralization, and local control have become rallying cries of many reformers. Ironically, these decentralization and deregulation appeals often come from the same people who lament that the nation lacks a unifying center and who hope that a rigorous, nationally uniform curriculum will provide that center. Apparently, they assume that local communities would voluntarily obey national definitions of curricular content.

This book chronicles the call for a national curriculum and tries to place it into historical and constitutional perspective. This book is inspired by the belief that these school-based debates about Western civilization, national standards, local control, and multi-culturalism are highly relevant to many social and constitutional problems beyond the schoolhouse gate. In school and nonschool settings alike, American policy makers face the difficult questions of whether race or cultural consciousness is ever good public policy—whether official emphasis on race, ethnicity, gender, or other particularities inevitably produces more hostility and divisiveness than respect for human difference. Likewise, school and nonschool officials must reconcile the sometimes sharp tension between national solidarity and individual dissent, between majoritarian rule and subcultural pluralism.

Although curricular innovation by itself is unlikely *either* to effect cultural coherence and harmony—as the core curricularists hope—*or* to effect cultural disunity and hostility—as many who oppose a multicultural curriculum fear—the curriculum battle, writ large, clearly does reflect an undeniably critical national dilemma: how best to accommodate the cultural, racial, ethnic, and other differences within this heterogeneous national culture. As such, the curricular wars raise concerns that are, or should be, of interest to all Americans.

Part I of this book describes the educators' opposing views about a core curriculum and outlines the long pedigree of similar controversies over the form and the content of common schooling in the United States. The discussion makes plain that democratization of schooling and increasing cultural diversity within the school population have presented educators throughout the twentieth century with a complex curricular challenge: how to meet the educational needs of a wide range of students whose home cultures and career aspirations differ significantly. The modern curriculum debate is a continuation of a century-long struggle to meet these diverse needs.

Part II attempts to rephrase the educators' debate in constitutional terms. It discusses in particular the constitutional principles of freedom of religion, freedom of speech, and equality and argues that these are critical components of our national character that should inform any national curriculum proposal. The final chapter describes the features of an American curriculum that respects these constitutional principles.

This book aims to present both sides of the curriculum debate fairly, because proposals that slight the arguments of either are doomed from the outset. Both the history of efforts to construct an American culture through education and our constitutional practices make evident that Americans, ironically, are bound most distinctively by dissents—by a common faith in the right to break away from cultural consensus. Our *unum* is our *plures*. As such, any national curriculum proposal that fails to recognize our pluralism and conflicts along with our common commitments surely will be rejected by many Americans as a distorted portrayal of the national character and experience. That is, public education must respond both to E. D. Hirsch's sensible claim that we need a common knowledge base in order to communicate and to Stanley Fish's critical observation that "it is difference all the way down." This book outlines the first principles of a national curriculum mindful of both insights.

PART I

Formal
Schooling and
the American
Paideia

2 The Rise of Formal Schooling and the American *Paideia*

Every government degenerates when trusted to the rulers of the people alone. The people themselves therefore are its only safe depositories. And to render them safe, their minds must be improved to a certain degree.—Thomas Jefferson

Without undervaluing any other human agency, it may be safely affirmed that the Common School, improved and energized, . . . may become the most effective and benignant of all the forces of civilization.—Horace Mann

INTRODUCTION

The modern call for a national curriculum reflects an enduring vision of public education as a means of melding the diverse mix of American cultures into one national culture. That vision, and resistance to it, are as old as the nation itself. "Americanization" programs of the early twentieth century, evangelical Protestant initiatives of the mid-nineteenth century, republican-spirited proposals for common education of the eighteenth century, and Puritan schooling of the seventeenth century all were inspired by a related sense of the link between formal schooling and a common cultural identity.

In each era, the content of the common lessons, and the peril of failure to learn those lessons, were defined differently. For the early white colonists, the common text was the Bible, and the peril of ignorance was vulnerability to "that old deluder, Satan."[1] For statesmen such as Thomas Jefferson, who urged fellow Virginians to adopt his proposal for common, public schooling, the lessons were defined in terms of a different objective: to render the children safe from the peril of tyranny by despots.[2] In Jefferson's view, intelligent self-government and public schooling were inextricably bound.

During the mid-1800s, a coalition of several reformers supported public, common schooling for still different reasons. Some of these reformers favored public schools as an alternative to the then waning church influence over public character and as instruments for promoting an American *paideia* (an education designed to produce both a broad and enlightened outlook in the student and an ideal common culture) that was Anglo-Saxon Protestant in character and that stressed virtuous character, patriotism, and wisdom.[3] Others, such as Horace Mann—the most powerful nineteenth century advocate of public schools—viewed common schools as engines for social harmony. They felt schools should act explicitly as mechanisms for softening the sharp edges of capitalism and for offering to the children of poorer workers, especially immigrant workers, a means of assimilating into the American society and economic structure.[4]

Common schooling in common subjects and common values thus always has been a critical component of American progressivist dreams, but the ideal structure for the delivery of that education and the ideal content of these common lessons have always been contested. Moreover, the disagreements have tended to reflect deep-seated political, religious, and philosophical conflicts among the various progressivist movements.

Many contemporary Americans seem unaware that public schooling, as we now know it, is a relatively recent achievement that had a long and difficult birth. They likewise seem unaware that the perception that America faces imminent cultural disintegration and the notion that a core American curriculum might fend off that disintegration and restore a common culture have long pedigrees. Skepticism about such a curriculum and conflict about its content are old concerns.

For example, seventeenth and eighteenth century intellectuals disagreed vigorously about whether education should emphasize the classics, ancient languages, and rationalism—a position embraced by many Federalists—or instead should stress geography, the sciences, and modern languages, as republican-style educators advocated.[5] Some eighteenth century Americans also disagreed, as do many twentieth century Americans, over whether and to what extent the national government should play an active role in shaping the content of public education. George Washington and Benjamin Rush argued early on that a national college should be established to teach an American curriculum, though their proposal lacked broad-based support and was never adopted.[6]

The modern college-level battles over the "great books" and Western civilization courses, too, are echoes of old conflicts, which were waged with considerable force in the early and mid-1800s and which, in turn, echoed the earlier, seventeenth century battles between the "ancients" and the "moderns." The gloomy sense that our lower-school children are less educated in the basics than were their parents, and than society safely can endure, thus plagued our ancestors much as it plagues us today. And even the Allan Bloomian apprehension that college undergraduates lack the specific philosophical commitments and moral rigor of past generations is not peculiar to the late 1900s. On the contrary, his colleague, Mortimer Adler, wrote an essay in the 1940s that described undergraduates of that era in identical terms.[7]

The following, decidedly brief history of efforts to forge cultural core values through a common education offers both encouraging and discouraging news about the modern crisis. The encouraging news is that the current claim that we are barreling into an abyss is overstated. At worst, it is a slow crawl. At best, there may be no abyss after all. The discouraging news is that, in the century since the great experiment of widespread public schooling was inaugurated, education still has failed to "render them safe," to effect social harmony, to assure widespread literacy, or to fulfill in a strong sense the various other progressive dreams of the advocates of past generations. These failures should make us skeptical of excessively ambitious claims about public education as an instrument of positive social transformation. They shore up what should be an obvious claim: public education *alone* cannot cure poverty, cultural entropy, anomie, inequality, or other social or economic pathologies.

This overview of the rise of compulsory schooling in America does not try to plumb the full, complex range of social, economic, and other forces that a complete history of education would include[8] but simply to highlight our enduring conflicts over the competing tugs of unity and difference. The aim here is to illustrate the provenance of the core curriculum debate and to demonstrate the link between aggressive Americanization initiatives and racial, ethnic, and religious politics. The modern debate echoes the various intellectual forces that drove curriculum reform at the undergraduate level in the 1920s to 1940s. The unavoidable conclusion from this is that no attempt to forge a core set of American values that fails to take account of our cultural pluralism ever has been, or likely ever will be, a *compelling* call for solidarity among all American peoples.

THE RISE OF COMMON, PUBLIC, COMPULSORY SCHOOLING

The colonists who settled in what became the United States brought with them Western European educational traditions along with their other cultural practices and beliefs. These educational traditions, more than those of the Native Americans, shaped the practices that conventional histories of public education describe as the precursors to modern public education.

In general, the colonists regarded education of the child as the responsibility of the child's family, especially the child's father. Education of youth was hierarchical, Protestant, privately funded, informal, and home-centered. The Massachusetts Bay Colony in 1647 passed legislation that required each township to provide for a teacher to instruct the children,[9] but formal, compulsory schooling outside the home was unusual during the early colonial period. On the contrary, formal schooling was regarded as "the last rather than the first resort of a colonial parent or master."[10]

In the late 1700s, however, intellectual support for compulsory, publicly funded schooling increased. The most significant statement of these eighteenth century arguments came from Thomas Jefferson. Jefferson proposed that all free, white children in Virginia receive at least minimal, uniform instruction in certain basic subjects, at public expense if necessary.[11] Unlike the early Massachusetts legislation, the Jefferson proposal was based principally on the argument that, in a democracy, citizens require education in order to exercise intelligently their right of self-governance.[12] The Massachusetts legislation, in contrast, had been based on the argument that education was necessary to protect children from the beguiling importunings of Satan.[13]

Whether the evil of ignorance lay in vulnerability to Satan or in vulnerability to despots, the idea thereafter began to take hold that education was of critical importance in protecting children from evil and in perfecting American society. Yet many observers who believed in education were unconvinced that this education should be conducted by the state or that it should be funded by public money. Indeed, Jefferson was unable to convince fellow Virginians of the wisdom of his modest version of public schooling, and his proposal never was enacted. More ambitious proposals of the era, some of which aimed for a uniform system of national education, likewise failed to take hold.[14] Schooling other than college instruction remained, for decades thereafter, predominantly a matter of family, church, or other private and local concern.[15]

One powerful and enduring source of resistance to a common school system was organized religion, members of which believed that secularized education would weaken the influence of church and the Bible over the children and the community.[16] Here and in Europe, opposition to public schooling also was based on a secular fear of the normalizing effect of compulsory education. To place the educational reins in the hands of government, critics argued, or to insist that all children receive the same type of education, would be to deaden autonomy and sow the seeds of tyranny.[17] These commentators disapproved of efforts to imitate the civic-oriented, uniform education policy of ancient Sparta and believed that compulsory schooling proposals paid inadequate attention to the shortcomings of the Spartan model.

These secular objections to the most aggressive accounts of the republic's interest in shaping its citizens through education echoed more general, liberal anxieties about an overly powerful government. These are well-captured in the grim warning of libertarian John Stuart Mill that, "A general State education is a mere contrivance for moulding people to be exactly like one another: and as the mould in which it casts them is that which pleases the predominant power in the government . . . it establishes a despotism over the mind. . . ."[18]

Yet even strong individualists such as Mill—past and present—recognize the need for at least minimal public control over the content of the education that all children must receive, even over parental objections.[19] Mill himself proposed that all children undergo annual, government-enforced, public examinations on "objective" facts in specified areas, "so as to make the universal acquisition, and what is more, retention, of a certain minimum of general knowledge virtually compulsory."[20] If the child were unable to pass these examinations, and if there were no excuse for that failure other than parental neglect,[21] then the government could punish the child's father. The government itself could undertake to provide instruction in the basic subjects, but only as one experiment among many ways of providing education to the children. Parental choice, constrained by testing in certain basic subjects, was the salient feature of the Mill education model.

The differences between this Mill minimalist account of compulsory education and the accounts of other, more ambitious reformers show that the terms *common, compulsory,* and *public* education are ambiguous and have always been controversial. To different reformers, *common* has meant common to all children; to all free, white children; to all free, white, male children; to all children whose parents elect the common school alternative; or some variation of the foregoing. *Compulsory* has meant that all children must be educated, whether at home or elsewhere; that all children must be educated in a formal school; or that all children must attend a formal school unless they can adduce specific justifications for their excusal. *Public* has meant that the schooling is funded entirely by public money; that it is free only to indigent children; that it is partly funded by public money; that the government not only funds the education but also provides it; or a permutation of any of these. Thus, although both Thomas Jefferson and John Stuart Mill—to take two important examples—favored compulsory education, they hardly agreed on the precise form, content, or ends of that education.

Our current, relatively uniform construction of the terms *compulsory* and *public* education developed very gradually. Not until the end of the nineteenth century were state acts prevalent that compelled all children to attend formal schools and that authorized the use of public money to fund public schools.[22] Even then, many people resisted the movement, and some in particular objected to the transfer of significant authority and financial responsibility for education to the state government. States that adopted compulsory-schooling statutes consequently often ceded principal power over the curriculum and the operation of the schools to the local communities.

This American resistance toward compulsory, formal schooling stemmed in part from the colonial tradition of education as an informal, sectarian, and home-centered process. But it also had roots in American constitutionalism. The United States Constitution nowhere mentions education in the list of functions properly assumed by the federal government. Rather, control over education is a power "reserved to the states," under the Tenth Amendment. Unlike other functions assumed by the states, however, education was considered by many in the nineteenth century more properly to be a highly localized, community-centered enterprise. Moreover, the division between public, secular and private, sectarian education remained blurred. As such, it was not until the twentieth century that state-level power over public schooling, and a corresponding deemphasis of local and of sectarian control of education, gained enough popular support to become the prevailing practice.[23]

Most accounts of the rise of public education during the late 1800s cite the work of Horace Mann in Massachusetts as singularly influential.[24] Mann believed passionately in the value of public and common education for the children of Massachusetts and defended his proposal in flowery, millenialistic terms.[25] In particular, he was convinced of the benefits of education for social equality, perhaps because his own socioeconomic status had been elevated by his educational opportunities.[26] Mann stated that "without undervaluing any other human agency, it may be safely affirmed that the Common School, improved and energized, as it can easily be, may become the most effective and benignant of all the forces of civilization."[27] Whether this unbounded faith in public, common schools as a vehicle for eliminating gross disparities in social goods was warranted continues to be hotly contested. But modern theorists who view public schooling as a vehicle for equalizing economic opportunities still rely on arguments that echo Mann's nineteenth century social reform aspirations.

Of course, Horace Mann could not have succeeded where Thomas Jefferson had failed without the complex set of cultural changes that gave widespread support to his call for public schooling. These changes included rapid industrialization and urbanization in the Northeast, the rise of government social welfare programs, conflicts between Protestants and Roman Catholics, the desire of organized labor to remove children from the work force, a humanitarian movement to improve conditions for the poor, and a more generally felt desire, based in part on fear of newcomers, to assimilate into one culture the massive waves of immigrants that poured into the United States in the late 1800s and early 1900s.[28]

Many nineteenth century reformers came to view common, public schools as vehicles for achieving social reform, though they defined reform in different ways. For example, some evangelical Protestants wished to homogenize and perfect American education according to Protestant values and to spread that ideal education to the world. Other reformers favored uniform schooling because they imagined that assimilation through such schooling would promote social efficiency. In particular, they hoped to defuse potential social and political unrest[29] and to efface cultural differences among workers, especially between newer immigrant populations and more established ethnic communities.[30] What many of these nineteenth and early twentieth century accounts of public education shared was a hope that through common, public schooling, national solidarity might be better secured and core national values more effectively transmitted.

The growing American ideal education (*paideia*) initiative of the late 1800s and early 1900s met resistance, however, from several fronts. First, the evangelical Protestants were internally divided about the proper content of this American *paideia*; this eventually undermined and finally ended their campaign.[31] Second, some members of the groups that reformers sought to assimilate into a standard, national identity resisted those efforts.[32] Perhaps the most vocal of these resisters were American Catholics, who so opposed the Protestant emphasis of mid–nineteenth century education and its overt anti-Catholic bias that they eventually created an independent system of parochial schools rather than expose their children to the ostensibly secular public school curriculum.

Still other forces, such as regional differences of opinion about the morality of slavery and philosophical differences about the ideal form and content of education likewise undermined the efforts to frame one authoritative American canon.[33] Within states, significant curricular variations often existed among the schools that reflected the different ethnic, religious, and socioeconomic compositions of individual communities.[34] Even within a single school, students sometimes received different instruction depending on their vocational aspirations, abilities, or intention to attend college.

Despite this resistance, compulsory schooling came to dominate the educational landscape during the early 1900s. By 1918, every state had adopted a compulsory school act. In the 1920s and 1930s, states began enforcing these requirements in earnest. By 1920, Cremin reports, "over ninety percent of American children between the ages of seven and thirteen were reported as enrolled in school,"[35] and the vast majority of them were enrolled in public elementary and secondary schools. Moreover, the content of this education became reasonably, though never completely, coherent. As Cremin describes it, the common core curriculum conveyed

> a Christian *paideia* that united the symbols of Protestantism, the values of the New Testament, *Poor Richard's Almanac*, and the *Federalist* papers, and the aspirations asserted on the Great Seal. It was a national *paideia*. . . .[36]

That is, a national *paideia* eventually did emerge and was taught in the nation's schools, but over the strong objections of some of the nation's peoples.

THE TWENTIETH CENTURY AND PATTERNS OF PUBLIC EDUCATION

Though compulsory public schooling became the norm in the United States, the form, content, and philosophy of that public schooling has continued to change throughout the twentieth century. Among the reasons for these changes were the following particularly influential occurrences.

First, international conflicts tended to inspire changes in curricular focus. World Wars I and II, the Korean conflict, the Cold War, and the Vietnam War each had distinctive repercussions for American education. World Wars I and II inspired skepticism about political education in some educators, while for others the wars stood as sober reminders of the need for training in democratic values. During the Cold War era, apprehension about the military and technological superiority of the Soviet Union prompted nationwide efforts to emphasize and reward student achievement in math and science. The catalyst for this was the launch of the Soviet Sputnik satellite in 1957, which gave rise to the term *Sputnik era* in educational history. The Vietnam War, fought during the 1960s and 1970s, gave rise to significant domestic unrest, protest against the government, and widespread ambiguity about the proper international role of the United States. Students during this era were exceptionally willing to question and even to defy adult authority and often employed a vocabulary of constitutional rights to advance their criticisms of the older generation. Some educators responded to this with proposals for more diversified, student-centered curricula and greater student control over significant aspects of school operation.

Second, the metropolitanization of America had a profound impact on the structure and organization of schooling. Urban centers became the hubs of American industry and hence the source of economic opportunities. Workers gravitated to the urban centers, greatly increasing the population of the urban public schools. Large, city-wide school systems—such as the New York City school system—had administrative needs that had no counterpart in earlier or nonurban school settings. One consequence was the development of centralized administrative bodies that resembled large bureaucracies. For some aspects of school management, in at least some cities, local solutions began to appear both inadequate and inefficient. Another consequence was that "individuals came to be defined more by the facts of race, class, ethnicity, religion, and occupation than by the place they happened to live, and to be regulated more by the rules and policies of governments, professions, and formal institutions than by the unspoken conventions of localities."[37]

Third, the emergence of multiple, standardized tests of intelligence and academic achievement affected educational philosophy and child placement. Educators sought to assess, label, rank, and sort students on the basis of these ostensibly objective measures of merit. Michael Apple has interpreted this rise in standardized testing as a response to the "breakdown of a once accepted economic and moral order."[38] As he has put it, "[t]he language of science and technology seemed a way to reconstitute this order."[39]

Fourth, the Progressive movement in education, associated with the philosopher and educational theorist John Dewey, destabilized traditional patterns of educational philosophy and practice, and inspired curricular, pedagogical, and school organization changes. Indeed, some educators now regard this movement as the principal cause of the curricular confusion that erupted in the mid- to late 1900s and thus as the most important curriculum development of the twentieth century.

A fifth, monumentally important development of the 1900s was the civil rights movement, which wrought tremendous revisions in education policy and practice that bear on the modern core curriculum debate. The watershed decision in 1954 of *Brown v. Board of Education*, and a host of cultural and legal initiatives thereafter, led to the demise of the "separate but equal" concept of education. Equal access to education for racial and ethnic minorities, females, and students with special educational needs thereafter became national priorities.

The rethinking of racially segregated schools sparked a penetrating, more pervasive critique of American society. Building on the work of the Progressives, the civil rights movement attacked traditional definitions of equality and achievement and conventional accounts of American political and social history. The result was the emergence of counteraccounts, a heightened consciousness regarding the ways in which conventional histories could slight or distort the experiences of minorities, of women, and of other nondominant subgroups and greater emphasis on the plural aspect of cultural identity.

The failure of the states to secure educational equality for black school children also prompted unparalleled federal intervention into state and even local educational affairs. The initial result was violent opposition and resentment of federal power. But as time eased at least some of the fiercest opposition, national sentiment moved toward greater respect for the role of the federal government in assuring fair delivery of educational services. Twentieth century citizens came to accept a more interventionist role for the federal government in education than eighteenth century Americans would have dreamed possible, though resistance to this intervention remains a powerful instinct, especially in regions most affected by busing of schoolchildren to achieve desegregation.

The impact of federal legislation and federal constitutional law on public school curricula, organization, management, financing, and even school location has been profound and pervasive. Throughout the twentieth century, American public education has been slowly transformed into a professionalized, and in many ways standardized, business—a business with a virtual monopoly power over the education industry. Efforts to make public education more uniform and efficient have often resulted in centralized, state-level authority over significant aspects of public education, such as textbook selection, teacher training and certification, financing, and employment practices. Although local community control remains an important aspect of school governance, state and federal regulation of the operations of local school districts has expanded dramatically. By the late 1970s, all public schools were subject to a complex array of local, state, and federal statutory mandates, as well as to the commands of state and the federal constitutions. In addition to these formal governmental mandates, the informal pressures of the market have exercised increasing power over the content of public education.

Three of these twentieth century developments deserve more extended consideration, as their relevance to the modern call for a national curriculum is often overlooked or underplayed. The first is the struggle between Protestants and Catholics over the content of public schooling at the elementary and high school levels during the mid-1800s. The second is the Americanization movement of the early 1900s. The third is the mid-1940s battle over the scope, content, and aims of liberal post-secondary education in general and over the educational philosophy of John Dewey in particular.

RELIGIOUS WARS AND THE RISE OF THE
PRIVATE / PUBLIC SCHOOL COMPROMISE

The rise of formal, publicly funded schooling and its underlying assimilation ideal triggered inevitable conflicts among religious sects that desired curricular space for their parochial beliefs. Of particular significance were conflicts between Catholics and Protestants waged during the nineteenth century.

In the 1840s, the potato blight in Ireland and population shifts in the Germanic regions of Europe caused a tremendous surge in immigration to the United States. Between 1845 and 1855, three million immigrants entered the United States, most of whom were Catholic.

The influx of these Catholic immigrants kindled intense anti-Catholic sentiment. Indeed, the Catholic-Protestant clash became so intense that it inspired the rapid rise of a nativist political party in which membership was restricted to native-born Protestants.[40]

The Catholic-Protestant hostilities reared their heads in education. Catholics rebelled, particularly in Northeastern cities, against use of the King James version of the Bible in publicly funded schools, against the curriculum's alleged promotion of "socialism, Red Republicanism, Universalism, Infidelity, Deism, Atheism, and Pantheism,"[41] and against the "open slurs" against Catholicism included in textbooks of the mid-1800s.[42] In terms that echo the arguments of modern multiculturalists and some Protestant fundamentalists, the nineteenth century Catholics objected that the public schools were imposing an alien culture on their children.

Yet public school officials' attempts to accommodate Catholic demands proved futile, in part because the nature of these demands made compromise impossible. Purging the textbooks of anti-Catholic bias proved unsatisfactory because the Catholic leadership insisted that "the religious liberty of Catholic schoolchildren could be protected *only* in a school where Catholic religion was taught."[43] In any event, Protestant influence over the curriculum was so pervasive that the "nonsectarianism" that the common schools came to embrace was a form of "sectless Protestantism,"[44] which was difficult to excise from the school program. Finally, Catholics would not accept the alternative of presenting a range of religious viewpoints to all common-school students. As Diane Ravitch explains:

> A school which attempted to teach all creeds or no creed at all was repugnant to them. Devout Catholics did not want their children exposed to other religions, nor did they want their children educated in a school which put error and truth on equal footings.[45]

The public schools in conflict with these devout Catholics thus had little choice but to deny their requests, lest the schools become explicitly Catholic institutions.

Frustrated by their inability to control the curriculum, Catholics turned their efforts toward developing an independent system of parochial schools and attempting to direct their tax money to these institutions. The response of public officials, however, was to deny the direction of public education funds to any religious society. Thus the policy emerged in New York City in the mid-1800s that its common schools would be "free and open to all" but "devoid of religious sectarianism."[46]

The result was that Catholics not only felt compelled to create an independent school system designed to promote Catholic values, they had to fund that system without public support. The current system of so-called double taxation of parents who choose to send their children to private schools and the deletion of religious instruction (as opposed to instruction about religion) from school curricula grew out of the fierce political battles in which American Catholics were the eventual losers.

"AMERICANIZATION" AND THE PUBLIC SCHOOLS

Significant episodes of immigration to the United States by Western Europeans, Eastern Europeans, Pacific basin natives, Mexicans, and a variety of other groups into the early 1900s inspired a strong movement toward a common American education on the ground that it would promote the acculturation objective of public schooling.[47] Immigration transformed the public school population into a multicultural array of rituals, religions, languages, family traditions, and other practices. Public education struggled during this period, with uneven and contested success, to reconcile the goal of enculturating all students into a common set of values and practices with the goal of protecting the individual—and hence her community of origin—from unreasonable domination by the majority.

Some immigrants, of course, embraced fully the ideal of Americanization and were enthusiastic about adopting the American culture and the English language. Among others, however, resistance to the assimilation agenda was profound[48] and even led some groups to disobey altogether the requirement of formal education of their children.[49] Still others resisted by demanding curricular changes, bilingual instruction, excusal programs, changes in personnel, and other measures that would give voice to their differences and better preserve their cultural distinctiveness.

Few of the early twentieth century observers, including those who were critical of the Americanization movement, denied that schooling necessarily and correctly serves an assimilative function, in that elders must instruct youth in what the elders believe is the most important, salient cultural knowledge. To *assimilate* means simply to absorb into a cultural tradition. In at least this rather weak sense, observers accepted that *any* education is inescapably an assimilative enterprise.

But not all reformers of the early 1900s construed the assimilation task of public schools in this weak, culturally bound, and relatively noninvasive manner. Rather, some reformers viewed American public schools as effective tools by which the dominant, "native" community could compel other immigrant or nondominant communities to observe its nativist norms, to accept existing economic, social, and political arrangements, and, implicitly, to abandon any competing traditions and practices the immigrants may have possessed. Used in this more invasive sense, assimilation was a coercive and very controversial goal of the public schools.

The justification that the strong assimilationists offered for this aggressive account of acculturation was their sense that the flood of immigrants threatened national unity, and even national security. Indeed, widespread apprehension about the disuniting of America[50] and about racial and ethnic factionalization[51] began as early as the Civil War,[52] and by the turn of the century, the anxieties about cultural outsiders had become so pronounced that some observers were convinced that the country's stability was in serious jeopardy. One nineteenth century educator compared the massive influx of immigrants to the United States to the influx of Goths and Huns to the Roman Empire.[53] He and many of his contemporaries were convinced that public, common education was necessary to Americanize these newcomers and to prevent a comparable crumbling of the American empire.[54]

The spirit of the assimilation-through-education movement of the late nineteenth and early twentieth centuries plainly was not pluralistic or inspired by a vision of a multicultural community. The prevailing sentiment about American immigrants is better captured by the following remark, made by one nineteenth century observer: "What kind of American consciousness can grow in the atmosphere of sauerkraut and Limburger cheese?"[55]

This attitude was not confined to the local level. In 1911, the United States Immigration Commission published a multivolume study that intensified efforts to Americanize immigrants. The federal officials characterized Americanization as a "national problem" and advised that public funds be directed to national education programs that might alleviate the "problem."[56]

This pervasive early twentieth century anxiety over Americanization became, as one commentator observed, an "hysterical taking of stock" of American personality and being.[57] Exaggerated fears about the social impact of wide-scale immigration gave rise to ugly racial theories, as "[i]mmigration, formerly more than welcomed as an economic boon, was now scrutinized as a eugenic menace."[58] These racial theories often assumed the superiority of white, Northern European people.[59] Standardized testing, which became popular during this era, offered ostensibly scientific proof of the racial superiority claims of those groups that tended to perform best on these examinations—white, Northern Europeans.[60]

Some historians view the Americanization movement of the late 1800s and early 1900s and the concomitant rise of standardized, bureaucratized education—especially in the large urban centers of the East—as causally connected. They believe that the rise of public common schools was inspired by the existing population's fear and disdain for foreigners and by its desire to acculturate rapidly the increasing numbers of immigrant children.[61] That is, public education as we know it was designed to preserve the status quo and to stabilize social and economic conditions in a manner that favored a white middle and upper class. The assimilation motives, these historians argue, were hardly ecumenical. On the contrary, the immigrant communities were expected to abandon their cultural traditions and languages in favor of the dominant community's ways. Assimilation was intended to be, and was, a vehicle for subcultural repression and even subcultural death.

Several of these historians claim that assimilation-through-education also was a purposeful means of repressing economic reforms. Michael Apple argues that, "[n]ot just in 1850, but even more between 1870 and 1920, the school was pronounced as the fundamental institution that would solve the problems of the city, the impoverishment and moral decay of the masses, and, increasingly, would adjust individuals to their respective places in an industrial economy."[62] That is, public schools were used to preserve the existing social, political, and economic order and to promote acceptance of its inequalities.

Not all nineteenth or early twentieth century reformers, however, favored an invasive, aggressive version of assimilation-though-education or the explicit use of formal schooling to preserve the status quo. Rather, both the "melting pot" metaphor and the implicit assumption that immigrants should shed their foreign manners, beliefs, and languages in favor of a white, Anglo-Saxon, Protestant norm were contested from the start.[63]

Historians have traced the term *melting pot* as a description of American culture to Crèvecoeur, a French observer of the American personality, who remarked in 1782 that American society was a new blend of being—not merely a slightly modified England. The term did not come into common usage, however, until 1908, when Israel Zangwill's play, "The Melting Pot," first was performed.[64] Once popularized, the metaphor drew immediate criticism from commentators who felt that immigrants should preserve their institutions and ways of life rather than merge into an amalgam of cultures defined as "American." Notable among these assimilation resistors was Horace Kallen, whose writings in the early to mid-1900s have influenced many writers since who likewise reject a strong assimilation role for public schools.

Kallen believed that the strong cultural assimilation implied by the "melting pot" image, and enforced by Americanization zealots, was both biologically unrealistic and psychologically unsound, inasmuch as diversity is a basic principle of human existence.[65] He argued that the true American culture was the very antithesis of the racially and ideologically homogeneous culture envisioned by groups like the nativists of his era.[66] Instead, Kallen observed,

> [i]t is founded upon variation of racial groups and individual character; upon spontaneous differences of social heritage, institutional habit, mental attitude and emotional tone; upon the continuous, free and fruitful cross-fertilization of these by one another. Within these Many . . . lies the American One.[67]

In Kallen's view, democracy and cultural pluralism are inextricably bound. The proper American metaphor thus should be a "mosaic" of cultures, not a "melting pot."[68] "Hyphenated Americans," he argued, were inevitable, and, terms such as *Italian-American* should not be terms of reproach,[69] as they had become in the early twentieth century.

The contrast between the Kallen attitude toward assimilation and ethnicity and that of the strong assimilationists of the early 1900s demonstrates how abiding the tension has been between theorists who favor one national culture and those who favor multicultural diversity. Throughout the century, these competing pulls of common culturalism and multiculturalism have caused educational policies to swing toward and away from the poles of strong, national assimilation and strong, local pluralism. For example, during the mid- to late 1800s, German organizations demanded that German language classes be included in the public schools for German-American students. In San Francisco, this effort initially led to the formation of so-called cosmopolitan schools, which embraced the notion that these immigrant children should be taught in their parents' native language and that schools should adapt to the parents' ethnic diversity rather than seeking to homogenize diverse cultures.[70] Later, however, this bilingual, bicultural approach was replaced with a program in which most instruction was in English and only a small portion of the day was devoted to foreign language instruction.[71] In other states, the pendulum later swung even farther away from bilingualism and an emphasis on cultural diversity, such that, in 1923, the state of Nebraska criminally prosecuted a Lutheran school instructor for teaching the German language to an elementary school pupil.[72] Although the United States Supreme Court overturned the conviction, the Nebraska statute and its defense all the way to the United States Supreme Court display the extent to which some Americans regarded education in English and in "American ideals" as critical to national well-being.[73]

Unlike the nationalism of earlier eras, however—such as the republican exuberance of Thomas Jefferson's call for common education or even the mid-nineteenth century rhetoric of Horace Mann—the nationalism of the early to mid-twentieth century became panicky, defensive, and coercive. Forced flag salutes and loyalty oaths, laws against foreign language instruction, and a spate of overtly assimilationist texts that lauded American values over those of foreign nations[74] reveal that the Americanization programs early in this century were part of a conscious and concerted assault on nondominant immigrant community practices, traditions, languages, and ideals. The spirit behind this call for cohesion was not the anthropologically inevitable need to transmit cultural values to the young and assimilate them into dominant cultural practices. Nor was it an outcome-neutral effort to melt all communities into one complex American alloy. Rather, it was a prophetic, even missionary effort, inspired by the conviction that American practices—defined according to white, Anglo-Saxon, Protestant, liberal democratic standards—were superior to their foreign counterparts, and that these superior American practices were imperiled by the military power of foreign nations and by the presence within American society of a large population of immigrants who ostensibly were loyal to foreign governments and not committed to American ideals. The melting pot of these reformers' imagination—unlike that of Horace Kallen—was not one in which all ethnic, religious, and racial communities would shape the amalgam but one in which foreign mannerisms would burn away and the residue would be an "American"-talking, "American"-acting, flag-saluting, industrious, responsible, clean and civic-minded, democratic man.

The coincidence of the aggressive Americanization efforts of the early to mid-1900s and the large waves of immigration during those years makes vivid the link between national unity appeals and issues of racial and ethnic equality. Given this history, and given the strong relationship between past calls for a set of American core values and fear of cultural outsiders, modern thinkers should not be surprised when a contemporary call for a national core curriculum sparks resistance from some African-Americans, Jewish Americans, Native Americans, Asian-Americans, and other non-Anglo-Saxon Protestants. Scrutiny of the history of appeals for American solidarity throughout this century reveals the hidden and sometimes explicit conditions of that "solidarity"—conditions that have required some cultural groups to sacrifice much in the way of cultural distinctiveness, language, tradition, and customs, while other groups have suffered little or no change or sacrifice. Skepticism about the motives of those who advocate national solidarity, in view of this history, prompts some intellectual and political leaders of American racial, ethnic, and religious minorities to resist the call for national coherence on curriculum. Those leaders favor instead a "discreet separateness"[75] as the preferred means by which to render *their* children safe. The American *paideia*, to them, offers only more false assurances of equality, pluralism, and respect for religious, ethnic, and racial differences.

Indeed, critical theorist Michael Apple has observed that the historical American commitment to maintaining a sense of community based on cultural homogeneity and values consensus has tended to reflect *only* the values of those with social and economic power.[76] As such, he argues, the modern call for cultural coherence "may pose the same threat to contemporary workers, women, Blacks, Latinos, and American Indians as it did to early twentieth century Blacks and immigrants from Eastern and Southern Europe"[77] and thus will encounter similar resistance and even occasional outright defiance. That is, unless education reformers take seriously the *plures* part of the *unum* then this most recent call for national coherence and common identity is not likely to be heeded by Americans who find in its history evidence of unreasonable nativism and who fear its repetition.

"GREAT BOOKS" AND COMPETING CURRICULAR
VISIONS IN THE TWENTIETH CENTURY

A third, particularly important piece of the historical backdrop to the modern core curriculum debate is the early to mid-twentieth century discourse regarding college-level distribution requirements. Although the college debates obviously concerned education of a more mature and intellectually sophisticated population of students than that of the public elementary and secondary schools, they nevertheless reflected concerns in American education that transcended the college context. Moreover, the college-level discussions were somewhat prompted by changes in high school education and the type of graduate high schools had begun to produce. Likewise, as college instruction changed, high school and even elementary instruction changed, to the extent that these institutions sought to prepare some of their students for advanced study.

The twentieth century witnessed a dramatic increase in the number of students who attended secondary and post-secondary schools. At the turn of the century, only eight percent of the age-eligible population attended high school. An even smaller percentage attended the nation's colleges and universities. Students who did attend post-secondary schools typically were from the middle or upper socioeconomic class, and those who attended the nation's elite institutions typically were white, male, Anglo-Saxon Protestants.

Throughout the century, however, and especially after World War II, the number and diversity of students attending high school and college steadily increased. The changes in the composition of the student body at both levels of education inevitably had an impact on the content of instruction as the origins and the destinations of the students became more diverse. Attempts to meet changing student needs prompted some secondary schools to diversify their curricula and to add explicitly vocational courses for those students who were not college-bound. Criticism of these curricular innovations as "fads" and as mistaken departures from instruction in basic subjects in favor of "costly luxuries" were expressed as early as 1893.[78] This curricular diversification clearly threatened the common school ideal.

At the college level, the larger number of students from diverse backgrounds translated into entering classes of students with educational backgrounds that differed substantially from that of past entering classes and that often differed substantially within a given entering class. No longer could professors assume that all entering students had been exposed to a common, fairly constant curriculum of precollege subjects and texts. Nor could they assume that the students shared a common cultural background in the strong sense that they could have assumed this in prior eras.

During most of the nineteenth century, the elite colleges and universities had resisted the demands of utilitarianism, democracy, and professionalism. Students learned moral philosophy that was "Aristotelian in origin and English and Scottish in modification."[79] This education "lacked democratic pretensions; it located virtue and wisdom not in the people but in an educated few fit to be their leaders. And it carried the reassuring message that knowledge could be ordered, unified, and contained."[80] During the later part of the century, however, high schools began to offer modern languages, applied sciences, agriculture, domestic science, and manual training.[81] This was *not* the traditional college preparatory curriculum. Undergraduate institutions thus faced a curricular dilemma: if they adhered to their standards of earlier decades, they could not compete for these diversely trained high school graduates; yet if they modified their standards and began to offer "remedial" education to fill the students' educational gaps, they sacrificed other institutional concerns.[82] The rise and democratization of the American high school therefore put higher education in "curricular disarray."[83] By 1901, educators at all levels no longer could agree about what was essential.[84]

The unsurprising result was the emergence of studies, scholarship, and committee reports that sought to redefine the role of the university and of elementary and secondary schools in a changing culture, and the curricular implications of these modified duties. In fact, at least thirty colleges and universities adopted general education programs between the turn of the century and the 1940s.[85] The risk of vastly oversimplifying the broad and complex range of the educational theories of this era, and of their philosophical justifications, is immense. Nevertheless, one can observe at least three distinct and particularly influential bodies of thought about the proper content of college—and by implication, lower school—education: the Deweyan Progressive approach, the Chicago Aristotelian approach, and the Harvard anthropological approach.

DEWEY AND THE PROGRESSIVES

John Dewey, and the Progressive education movement of the early to mid-1900s with which he is associated,[86] condemned the traditional school methods of the late nineteenth and early twentieth centuries. First, Dewey believed that education of the child could transform society and thus be a positive instrument of social reform. As such, he deemphasized the cultural reproduction function of education, which traditional nineteenth century methods tended to stress, in favor of a cultural revision function: schools should improve, not merely solidify and transmit, existing social arrangements. Dewey maintained that all of education, like all of experience, not only borrows from the past, it modifies the future.[87] To best realize this future-modifying potential, a teacher must assure that the educational experiences are ones that "create conditions for future growth," rather than inhibit growth.[88]

Second, Dewey believed that education and the child's experiences should be inextricably bound. Effective and meaningful learning entails the application of the scientific method to one's own immediate experience.[89] In the case of a small child, the educational experience should relate to the world she actually inhabits and should be linked to the one she will enter after her formal schooling. It also should engage the child and compel her to interact with the material. To divorce the school experience from the child's life experience, and to make school a noninteractive process of funneling information from the adult instructor into the child, is to render education stale, irrelevant, and rote. Instead, the progressive educator would argue, teach the child mathematics by creating a facsimile store or bank in the classroom—have the child learn to make correct change, to add up a bill, to balance a checkbook. Or, if the child is the daughter of a farmer, use examples that draw on her knowledge of agriculture and farm life. In short, teach to the child, not to the curriculum.

Third, the Deweyan Progressives believed in the democratic arrangement of authority within the school. Democracy, argued Dewey, makes possible a better quality of experience than nondemocratic social arrangements in that it respects individual freedom, offers wider access to experience for all, and encourages decency and kindness in human relations.[90] Traditional education was often autocratic and harsh. Dewey regarded this type of instruction as miseducative and experience-repressive. Because the principal objective of education should be to create the conditions for future growth[91] and because only a democratic social arrangement will maximize the conditions for future growth, the school should be run democratically. The child should learn the democratic habits of responsible social cooperation and adaptation[92]—that is, the rules of communal living—at school, as well as beyond formal schooling.

As to the question of which subjects to include in a progressive education, Dewey remarked as follows:

> There is no such thing as educational value in the abstract. The notion that some subjects and methods and that acquaintance with certain

facts and truths possess educational value in and of themselves is the reason why traditional education reduced the material of education so largely to a diet of predigested materials. According to this notion, it was enough to regulate the quantity and difficulty of the material provided, in the scheme of quantitative grading, from month to month and from year to year. . . . If the pupil left it instead of taking it, if he engaged in physical truancy, or in the mental truancy of mind-wandering and finally built up an emotional revulsion against the subject, he was held to be at fault. No question was raised as to whether the trouble might not lie in the subject-matter or in the way in which it was offered. The principle of interaction makes it clear that failure of adaptation of material to needs and capacities of individuals may cause an experience to be non-educative quite as much as failure of an individual to adapt himself to the material.[93]

Dewey thus did not debunk subject matter coverage per se, as some of his critics wrongly suggest. But he surely did accord it dramatically less significance than educational theorists who regarded certain texts or materials as intrinsically worthwhile, independent of contextual factors such as the intellectual readiness of the child, her family and social context, her likely work setting, her cultural background, or changes in the world since the texts were written. Moreover, he specifically rejected education that stressed memorization or rote learning over critical thinking and development of trans-substantive skills that the child could adapt to changing situations throughout her life.

Dewey summarized his sentiments about the limited value of factual literacy as follows:

What avail is it to win prescribed amounts of information about geography and history, to win ability to read and write, if in the process the individual loses his own soul: loses his appreciation of things worth while, of the values to which these things are relative; if he loses desire to apply what he has learned and, above all, loses the ability to extract meaning from his future experiences as they occur?[94]

The early Progressive movement in education, like all broad intellectual currents, contained distinctive strands. In general, however, all Progressives agreed on the potential of education to change social and political arrangements. That is, they viewed education as sufficiently independent of prevailing social, economic, and political forces that it could modify rather than merely reproduce these forces. But they disagreed about which educational forces should play the leading role in effecting these changes. John Dewey insisted that reconstructed schools should be the principal levers. In contrast, his contemporary, Jane Addams, saw schools as playing only a limited role: settlements and other similar, community-based institutions would be the main catalysts of social change.[95] Addams believed that educating the community would in turn change the child, and thereby change the environment. Dewey preferred to change the child, who then would change the community. All Progressives, however, believed that dialectical relationships existed among the child, the community, and the educational process.

DEWEYAN INFLUENCE ON CORE CURRICULA AT COLUMBIA, CHICAGO AND HARVARD

In many respects, the modern core curriculum controversy tends to divide commentators along lines that were drawn between Dewey Progressives and his contemporary critics. Sociologist Daniel Bell has described these lines of disagreement and has identified three distinctive attitudes about a core college curriculum that emerged at Columbia, the University of Chicago, and Harvard during the first half of the twentieth century.[96] Bell's account credits Dewey as the inspiration for the Columbia model of undergraduate education that emerged after World War I and as having sparked or influenced the opposing visions of liberal education at Chicago and Harvard. Appreciation for the differences among these three approaches to a college-level curriculum yields insight into the philosophical differences that tend to divide modern commentators on the question of whether a core curriculum is sound educational policy at any level. In essence, the central tension within the debates lies between a belief that school should adapt to or even foster social change and a belief that schooling is primarily acculturative and designed to preserve social stability.[97]

The Columbia Model

According to Bell, Columbia College "never had a doctrinal commitment, like Chicago's and Harvard's (at least in theory, if not always in practice), to a *single* theory or substantive formulation of educational philosophy."[98] Bell offers several reasons for this difference, including the influence of John Dewey. In particular, Columbia embraced Dewey's belief in the continuity of experience and in the process of learning, rather than in a curriculum centered either on "eternal verities," a hierarchy of knowledge, or on a body of so-called great books or great ideas as the organizing conception.[99] Rather, Columbia viewed the ideal curriculum as one that is adaptable either to the specific needs of the existing student body (as in the implicit notion of "acculturating" the ethnic-group student to Western traditions), to the changing conceptions of what the central problems of society are (particularly in the Contemporary Civilization courses), or to the shifting states of knowledge in the several fields themselves.[100]

The Columbia philosophy thus was rooted in the principles of change and adaptation and made the emerging future, rather than the settled past, the main focus of student inquiry.

The Chicago Model

Columbia's philosophical embrace of change and adaptation differed starkly from the University of Chicago's emphasis on eternal verities during the tenure of President Robert M. Hutchins, who believed that without some organizing "theology or metaphysics a unified university cannot exist."[101] In selecting books for its humanities curriculum, the University of Chicago emphasized classification and analytical processes—that is, "the identification of genres, the principles of genre, the nature of rhetoric, and the theories of criticism which might or might not be relevant to different kinds of work."[102] The Chicago approach was Aristotelian in that it attempted to "find the controlling principles of 'classification' in the definition of subjects or of disciplines within fields."[103] According to Bell, this approach tended toward an "aristocratic critique of the democratic—perhaps one should say populist—foundations of American education."[104] One purpose of this aristocratic critique was to uncover the eternal truths, which betrayed the Chicagoans' assumption that such universals exist and can be identified. As Hutchins put it, education should "draw out the elements of our common human nature. These elements are the same in any time or place."[105]

The Harvard Model

Harvard's general education philosophy, as it was framed in a 1945 report—the famous "Redbook"—described the ends of education in yet another way. The report set forth a formal statement of educational philosophy that was intended to influence both post-secondary and secondary education. In it Harvard declared that the purpose of a general education was to afford all citizens "some common and binding understanding of the society which they will possess in common."[106] By stressing the need of all Americans to share in this core, the Redbook rejected aristocratic aims in favor of democratic concerns. The problem facing education, according to this 1945 account, was that American high schools no longer were providing—as they had in 1870—a common core of learning for all students.[107] The Harvard response to this loss of a cultural center was for schools to expose all students to the great works, which it defined as those that have had the greatest influence over time. A humanities curriculum designed along these lines would, claimed the report, help to unify what had become a "centrifugal culture."[108] In particular, the students should receive an American history curriculum that is very fact-intensive as preparation for the work of citizenship.[109]

These three attitudes toward general education reflected distinct visions of knowledge and truth. Under the Chicago vision, books were chosen on the basis of presumptively foundational principles of classification and universal themes. The works were taught as illustrations of an intellectual pattern or genre. The well-educated student was one who could classify, identify, and analyze hierarchical relationships among ideas according to controlling principles. The task of isolating these universals, however, did not need to be performed by all members of the culture. On the contrary, the work might best be performed by educational elites who appreciated the sophistication of the task. Moreover, the controlling principles were not rooted in American custom per se but in transcultural, historical truths.

Under the Harvard vision, books were chosen on the basis of cultural consensus and traditional, abiding influence. The aim was not to tease out "universalisms" but to acculturate students and to draw them into conversations with writers whose works had tended to shape Western thought. The well-educated student was one with a firm grasp of the best, time-tested, inherited intellectual knowledge and one who knew the particulars of American history that were essential to good citizenship and democratic participation.

The Columbian educational vision was more pluralistic and pragmatic in its aims, methods, and justifications. Books were chosen for several, sometimes disparate, reasons, depending on changes in student populations, subject matter, and other social forces. In general, however, a well-educated student was one who understood the principle of "conceptual inquiry,"[110] which was an intellectual tool to apply to all experiences and problems. The student should be aware of certain baseline historical facts; but she also should appreciate "the nature of evidence, the reason why a scholar chose some facts rather than others, and the guiding conceptual frameworks that lie behind the selection of evidence."[111] Armed with the insight of conceptual inquiry, the student would be prepared to analyze whatever new experiences lay beyond formal education and to adapt to shifting states of knowledge.

These three tendencies—the Aristotelian / aristocratic, the American cultural / democratic, and the pluralistic / pragmatic—were contradictory in significant respects. They reflected disagreements about knowledge, truth, history, the nature of experience, the relevance of contemporary life, and the ideal preparation for the future. They also betrayed different attitudes about culture, citizenship, and the extent to which cultural or other contextual factors determine human personality and meaning.[112] The Chicago approach was least impressed by the nineteenth and early twentieth century emphasis on historicism and relativism. The Harvard approach was most explicitly anthropological, in the sense that it made acculturation into great Western and American values and practices the stated, governing purposes of a common education and justified the selection of materials principally upon culture-specific, stable definitions of greatness. The Columbia approach was most accepting of the contingency of knowledge and value claims and was expressly pragmatic, dynamic, and fluid.

Despite these philosophical and methodological differences, however, all three schools agreed on the need for a shared vocabulary and a common store of facts and allusions. Indeed, they often taught the same books, though in quite different ways. Moreover, as a practical matter, all three methods placed the primary burden of developing basic language and factual competence on elementary and secondary schools, not colleges.

Of particular importance to contemporary reflections on education is that the historical efforts to fashion an ideal curriculum were inspired by the reformer's perceptions that education of the early to mid-1900s was in crisis. Indeed, educators then were concerned with the same alleged decline in factual competence that has consumed modern commentators. In 1945— one half-century ago—teachers already were lamenting that high school graduates no longer had a common core of educational experiences.[113] The 1945 critics viewed 1870 as the golden era of secondary education. It is profoundly ironic, then, that many critics writing now view the 1940s and 1950s as education's "good old days." Such critics might do well to heed the words of one historian, who concluded that historical efforts to unify and standardize general liberal education "ran out of steam" because some of the university professors

> did not speak the language of the country which they addressed. . . .
> General education . . . was not an expression of the dominant culture. It
> spoke for a counterculture that acted as if it were *the* culture, it was an
> expression of the "establishment."[114]

CONCLUSION

Changes in the secondary school and college-going populations since the "golden eras" of 1870 and 1945 have complicated attempts to define a unitary curriculum for all students. As the 1945 Harvard report acknowledged, in 1870 high schools were attended mainly by well-to-do children, who were taught narrow and rigid curricula, and who had a common cultural and religious background.[115] Since 1870, however, the American high school has changed dramatically from a preparatory school for college-bound elites to a school open to all students and designed to prepare a more diverse student population for very diverse lives. Demographic changes caused some educators in the early 1900s to refashion their curricula to meet the different vocational needs of their students. The Harvard report criticized these efforts at diversification and vocationalization on the ground that they splintered the curriculum and thus splintered the population into diverse groups that were unable to communicate with each other.

Modern commentators likewise object to the splintering of the curriculum and maintain that a return to a basic, narrower curriculum is in order.[116] As the current educational discourse makes plain, however, the puzzle of how best to accommodate changes in the composition, function, and structure of American education remains unsolved in 1993. If anything, some of the problems that confronted the 1945 educators have become more acute and intractable in that the "centrifugal forces" (as the report put it) of cultural pluralism, modernity, and rapid obsolescence of knowledge have grown stronger in the intervening decades. Moreover, student bodies no longer consist of predominantly white, middle class students. Faculty in influential colleges and universities likewise have become more diverse, which in some cases has translated into course offerings that depart substantially from the traditional core curriculum.

On the other hand, the changes in the administrative and structural features of public elementary and high school education since 1945 may make a unitary, national curriculum easier to implement than it was in earlier times. Schooling in the United States has transformed from an intensely local, family- and church-centered enterprise into a centralized, bureaucratized, and relatively standardized concern—run less by the community in any strong sense of the word than by educational professionals, bureaucrats, and administrators. Local influence over school policy dissipated substantially after World War II, as Congress exercised its purse-strings power to compel schools to respond to national standards regarding such matters as bilingual education, gender and race equality, mainstreaming and special services for students with special educational needs, access to school property for extracurricular activities, and Head Start programs for at-risk schoolchildren. These developments, coupled with a period of judicial activism in overseeing local board decisions regarding school funding schemes, student and teacher discipline, mandatory classroom exercises, and other matters of constitutional concern have in some ways rendered atavistic the traditional slogan that education is a matter of local concern.

The post–World War II centralization of school authority makes it possible for fewer people to make curricular decisions for larger numbers of students.[117] For example, some state-level boards of education are authorized to choose the textbooks for all public schoolchildren within their state. Moreover, a handful of states with the largest school-age populations have a disproportionate influence on the textbook market such that a few large states—California and Texas, especially—may determine the available choices of textbooks for the country as a whole.[118]

Despite this increased centralization and federalization of education, however, some modern observers insist that the incoherence in American education that worried the drafters of the Redbook in 1945 has worsened considerably since. They claim that cafeteria-style course offerings in American high schools and colleges proliferated in the 1960s, and academic standards declined, such that large numbers of students began to leave formal schooling without common, basic skills or common, basic factual competence in literature, history, geography, and mathematics. Some argue that the absence of common learning imperils our cultural unity and that nationally defined standards of education must be established and enforced. In some forms, these arguments resemble those of early twentieth century commentators who believed in assimilation-through-schooling. In other forms, the arguments echo the college curricular debates from the 1920s to the 1940s. In still other forms, the debates turn on concerns that divided Protestants and Catholics in their intense struggle over the religious content of public schooling. The following chapter describes the strands of arguments made by commentators who claim that the coherence of American education declined to a dangerous level after World War II and presents their proposed solution to this decline: a national, core curriculum.

3 The Modern Call for a National Core Curriculum

If the American Way of Life had to be defined in one word, "democracy" would undoubtedly be the word, but democracy in a peculiarly American sense. On its political side it means the Constitution; on its economic side, "free enterprise"; on its social side, an equalitarianism which is not only compatible with but indeed actually implies vigorous economic competition and high mobility. Spiritually, the American Way of Life is best expressed in a certain kind of "idealism" which has come to be recognized as characteristically American. It is a faith that has its symbols and rituals, its holidays and its liturgy, its saints and its sancta; and it is a faith that every American, to the degree that he is an American, knows and understands.
—Will Herberg

Serious education must assume, in part, an adversarial stance toward the very society that sustains it—a democratic society makes the wager that it's worth supporting a culture of criticism. But if that criticism loses touch with the heritage of the past, it becomes weightless, a mere compendium of momentary complaints.
—Irving Howe

INTRODUCTION

Modern education reformers have responded to the perceived deficiencies in the educational system with a host of proposals,[1] one of which is that all American students be exposed to a common core curriculum.[2] On college and university campuses, the core curriculum proposals have centered on distribution requirements for undergraduates at institutions such as Stanford University.[3] At the elementary and secondary school level, the discussions have focused on the claims of commentators, such as E. D. Hirsch, Jr., Chester Finn, and Diane Ravitch, that our children suffer from basic factual deficiencies that render them culturally illiterate.[4] Some of these critics favor national curriculum standards and national tests in certain basic skills areas, which would complement the existing standardized tests such as the Iowa Basic Skills test, the SATs, the ACTs, and other nationally administered measures.[5]

Although a national curriculum surely would not determine student behavior, beliefs, or even knowledge in the strong way that some commentators wish or fear, it surely would affect instruction and thus would influence students. The content of any core curriculum therefore is of considerable practical moment. This content also is politically significant because it inevitably reflects the drafters' definition of the minimal conditions of membership in the national community. In this light, contemporary arguments over a core curriculum, whether in the nation's colleges and universities or in its primary and secondary schools, are not merely peripheral skirmishes over membership in an elite community of scholars or students; rather, they are central debates about membership in national public life.

The heat cast by these disputes makes clear that Americans disagree strongly about the meaning of their national community and about the role of public education in forging a national identity. Ambivalence about conscious attempts to shape national solidarity, diverging estimations of the salience of subcultural identity, and dissent about the meaning of equality are major fault lines within the debate.

This chapter presents the best of the arguments in favor of a core curriculum, using E. D. Hirsch's proposal as a vehicle for contrasting the various purposes and philosophies of the core curricularists. Not all people who believe in a common curriculum believe in it for identical reasons; likewise not all agree on its ideal content. They do agree, however, on the need for common knowledge and join forces with Hirsch in advocating that all American schoolchildren receive at least some common lessons in history, government, language studies, mathematics, and other curricular pillars.

Theorist Amy Gutmann recently remarked that "[t]he greatest challenge facing public education in America today is its pluralism."[6] A growing number of thinkers agree and also believe that we must meet this challenge by seeking common curricular ground.

THE HIRSCH PROPOSAL

Relying on an array of recent statistical studies, his own experiences as a university professor, and accounts of other teachers, E. D. Hirsch, Jr., has advanced the provocative claim that Americans are becoming culturally illiterate.

Hirsch maintains that strong evidence now exists that literacy has declined sharply in the United States,[7] along with the amount of shared knowledge that can be taken for granted when communicating to others.[8] In particular, students' knowledge of civics declined between 1969 and 1976[9] and has continued to decline since. According to Hirsch, this decline in common knowledge threatens our ability to communicate with one another, our ability to compete in a global market, and our democratic system of government.

Reading literacy requires that the reader possess certain background knowledge, in addition to other skills.[10] For example, a reader unfamiliar with the American court system would have enormous difficulty understanding a newspaper account of a federal appellate court ruling, even if she were an excellent reader in other respects. Students today, says Hirsch, lack much of this basic background knowledge and thus cannot decode many materials that are critical to public communication, to the ability to function in the workplace, or to the ability to cast meaningful votes.

Hirsch emphasizes that in modern society, cultural literacy is becoming more important because much specific, job-related knowledge is rapidly becoming obsolete.[11] The workplace has changed in that fewer industrial jobs are available that require low or weak literacy or minimal pre-job training. Many of these tasks now are performed by computerized machinery, which has shrunk the market for unskilled labor. Moreover, in an increasingly international economic and political world, only highly literate societies can prosper economically.[12]

Cultural literacy likewise is particularly critical, he argues, to the American system of government. As Hirsch expresses it, "The civic importance of cultural literacy lies in the fact that true enfranchisement depends upon knowledge, knowledge upon literacy, and literacy upon cultural literacy."[13]

He traces the decline in shared knowledge to mid-twentieth century educational theorists' experimentism, and their adoption of content-neutral methods of teaching children. In particular, Rousseau- and Dewey-inspired educators began to embrace a doctrine of educational formalism, which "assumes that the specific contents used to teach 'language arts' do not matter so long as they are tied to what the child already knows. . . ."[14] The educational formalists' failure to use reading as an opportunity to teach traditional materials of literate culture was "a tragically wasteful mistake" that has caused a fragmentation of students' educational experience, a deemphasis of memorization of core cultural facts, and even a loss of a cultural center.[15]

The curriculum fragmentation came in several forms and was often justified by a misguided, romantic insistence on the need to respect the child's individuality. Vocational education, tracking, a proliferation of boutique-type course offerings, and other attempts to match the education to the child tended to stratify students along racial, gender, and socioeconomic lines and also meant that subject matter mastery often took a back seat to the concern that the child have a "good experience."[16] This strong emphasis on a child-centered definition of a "good experience" and on the child's individuality, says Hirsch, was both unrealistic and counter-productive. As he puts it, "Children can express individuality only in relation to the traditions of their society, which they have to learn. . . . Americans in their teens and twenties who were brought up under individualistic theories are not less conventional than their predecessors, only less literate, less able to express their individuality."[17]

To recover this touchstone of shared traditions, American schools should adopt a curriculum that stresses national over local information.[18] For example, all schools must teach about Abraham Lincoln but not Jeb Stuart,[19] about the Pilgrims but not Father Marquette. Schools should resist the call for a splintered, multicultural curriculum on the ground that Americans have not even achieved *mono*literacy[20] and therefore are not prepared for *multi*literacy. Although nothing in this approach prevents local communities from supplementing the lessons of national literacy with matters of local literacy, these local matters should be subordinate to matters of national concern.[21]

Hirsch translated his theoretical argument into concrete, practical suggestions. He and his collaborators compiled a list of things every literate American should know, which they developed into a dictionary of cultural literacy and designed classroom materials to implement the cultural literacy program. The materials draw most heavily on traditional national texts—such as the Declaration of Independence, the Gettysburg Address, and the Constitution[22]—but they also include some recent works, such as the "I Have A Dream" speech by Dr. Martin Luther King, Jr.[23]

Recognizing that his materials would be unacceptable to people who favor a more pluralistic, less conventional, and less Western-European-centered canon, Hirsch responded in the following stern language:

The acculturative responsibility of the schools is primary and fundamental. To teach the ways of one's own community has always been and still remains the essence of the education of our children, who enter neither a narrow tribal culture nor a transcendent world culture but a national literate culture. For profound historical reasons, this is the way of the modern world. It will not change soon, and it certainly will not be changed by educational policy alone.[24]

Thus, while sympathetic to some of the multiculturalists' concerns, Hirsch argues for a stress on cultural unity in order to provide the nation's school-children with a common base of national cultural knowledge. To the extent that some education multiculturalists reject this goal, Hirsch dissents.

CORE CURRICULUM SUPPORTERS

Several influential education theorists and policy makers, including Diane Ravitch, Chester Finn, Lynn Cheney, and William Bennett, concur with the Hirsch propositions that common knowledge is critical and that this knowledge base has withered. They point to numerous reports, such as the well-known *Nation at Risk*,[25] that support the claim that some high school graduates lack basic reading and mathematics skills and basic knowledge of history, government, literature, and science. Among these studies' most notorious findings is that some college students are unable to distinguish Marxist philosophy from the principles of American constitutionalism.[26] Another sobering statistic, which received exceptional media play, is that more than forty percent of the college seniors surveyed could not identify when the Civil War occurred.[27]

The Hirsch proposal thus appealed to many writers. In particular his refusal to defer to the arguments of multiculturalists appealed to people's inclination that our public institutions, including our educational institutions, should refer to our common characteristics, not to our diverse cultural identities.[28] The call for a common curriculum represents, to some listeners, an important corrective to the excesses of educational particularism and a timely reaffirmation of the American melting pot ideal.

Yet, while many people endorse curriculum proposals like Hirsch's, they do so for very different reasons. Hirsch manages to appeal to several ideologically different camps because he restricts his argument to the areas of widest cultural agreement and because he justifies his quite conventional list in ostensibly nonsubstantive terms—that is, not on the ground that his list is intrinsically good, but on the ground that we need some list, any *reasonable* list,[29] and we might as well use the one that this culture already has devised, subject (of course) to modest, ongoing revision. Also, Hirsch only expects a culturally literate person to catch the allusions, not to pledge allegiance to them. She should know, for example, the story of George Washington and

the cherry tree and be aware that this American fable reflects both a traditional cultural respect for honesty and a national tendency to mythologize
the founders. She need not believe the story, the myth, or that the culture in
fact respects honesty.

Some commentators reject this anthropological, nonsubstantive justification for the list but are willing to endorse the proposed list because it is
loaded with terms that they agree are important to learn. For example, many
educational conservatives believe that a traditional education—with an emphasis on adult-centered values, democracy, respect for authority and tradition, discipline, and attention to foundational skills and knowledge—is superior to Dewey's romantic emphasis on child-centered values, undirected
learning, and experimental processes. If any place exists for such undirected
adventures in education, they argue, it is in college. At the elementary and
secondary level, the child should be acculturated into the dominant American values through traditional and rigorous training, not only because these
happen to be the culture's values, but because they are sound values. In
particular, American children should be taught about American liberal democracy and its roots and should learn to respect this political system,[30] lest
they lose their ability to govern themselves. The commentators invoke
Thomas Jefferson's warning that failure to educate citizens renders them
vulnerable to political despots. Given that the Hirsch list emphasizes terms
that relate to American constitutionalism and basic civics and given that
Hirsch approves expressly of Jefferson's linking of literacy and democracy,[31]
educational conservatives find much to their liking in his proposal.

The values implicit in the Hirsch list likewise appeal to many Protestant
fundamentalists to the extent that they correspond with the fundamentalist
emphasis on the Bible, the Constitution, and patriotism. The Hirsch list tilts
in the direction of a secularized version of Judeo-Christian ethics[32] because
the traditional American creed is built, in part, on doctrines that also inspire
Christian fundamentalism. As such, the list offers an acceptable beginning,
though clearly no endpoint, to the fundamentalists' evangelical mission.[33]

Objectivist philosophers such as the late Allan Bloom,[34] too, would approve of the Hirsch list, but for still different reasons. Greatly simplified, their
view is that merit, truth, and reason are not hopelessly historically-bound,
subjective, and nonneutral concepts. As such, they believe that to claim that
any one canon of literature is as good as any other or to deny the power of
reason is dangerous nonsense. Without grounding principles, truth and
virtue have no meaning. *Merit* becomes an empty term that is replaced by
politics, *power*, and *perspective* as the governing principles of value or achievement. The good life—which education seeks to transmit and to foster—

likewise loses meaning, and curricular choices become arbitrary exercises of cultural authority rather than thoughtful selections based on neutral, ahistorical principles.

The objectivists deny that the traditional canon is simply an arbitrary assertion of white, male, Western European power over minority dissent. Some of them, such as Mortimer Adler, defend a traditional Great Books curriculum in terms that assume the existence of at least some "unifying truths." Moreover, they insist that the path to reason is smoothed by exposure to a so-called Great Books canon. As such, they likely would applaud Hirsch-like reform of elementary and secondary school education and would extend his insight to higher education by reviving distribution requirements that assure that all undergraduates are exposed to the central teachings and texts of Western civilization.

The cultural literacy movement also appeals to many economic and political realists. In essence, Hirsch is saying that, in our culture *as it stands*, people must learn "the list" in order to survive and thrive. Familiarity with the canon already is a basis on which cultural privileges are assigned. He does not defend his selection of terms on the list in normative terms; rather he simply is arguing that the list *already exists*, written or unwritten, and thus should be taught to everyone.

The realists agree with Hirsch that, in the immediate future, major revisions of the canon are unlikely, perhaps even undesirable. In the meantime, they concur that we should make this canon explicit and maximize opportunities for all children to become familiar with it. Indeed, the Hirsch approach of compiling an actual list and teaching it nationwide may advance in particular the interests of disadvantaged groups because it requires that all children be exposed to it. If jobs, social status, and other social goods truly depend upon one's familiarity with the dominant terms, texts, and values, then educators who teach instead local, subcultural canons will disable their students from competing effectively for these public goods. As such, nationalizing and standardizing the curriculum might discourage this practice and might empower disadvantaged groups more than any strongly multicultural, pluralist, or localized approach to the curriculum could.

This practical defense of a core curriculum is likewise attractive to many business representatives, who complain that the nation's schools are failing to produce an adequate supply of literate, competent workers. Several of these leaders recently have taken an active role in reforming American education and in some cases have applied significant private money to the development of innovative programs in public schools.[35] The concern that drives the business interest in education is that American businesses cannot compete in an international economy without a highly trained, literate pool of qualified workers. A decline in literacy will compromise the nation's ability to protect American economic interests from foreign challenges. To the extent, therefore, that the Hirsch proposal links cultural literacy with literacy and defines cultural literacy in national rather than local terms, the proposal may serve the needs of multinational and national businesses, which seek a literate workforce able to move freely throughout the nation and the globe as business opportunities dictate. Standardization of a common vocabulary among potential employees would further their interest in workers who can communicate with all segments of these national or international organizations without translators or other intermediaries familiar with multiple subvocabularies, practices, or mores. Cultural fragmentation of the sort Hirsch condemns is, among other things, inefficient. Business tends to value efficiency and thus is likely to approve of the efficiencies inherent in the Hirsch model.

The Hirsch proposal also finds support among many parents who seek concrete guidance about how best to secure or boost their children's intellectual, social, and economic futures. If the list is one that culturally literate Americans "should know," then these parents may prefer that schools teach this information and may try to supplement the school curriculum by tailoring family activities to advance these educational objectives. Parents who believe that admission to college, especially to an elite institution, is important tend to react favorably to concrete statements about what precisely their children should learn to prepare for these schools. A University of Virginia humanities professor's insight into what post-secondary institutions expect carries some weight. Parents who wish to open opportunity's door for their children tend to take seriously the remarks of educational insiders such as Professor Hirsch.

These parents' notion that knowing "what is on the test" is the key to higher education access is hardly foolish. Many tests, such as the SATS, ACTS, GRES, MCATS, and LSATS, already regulate access to colleges, to graduate schools, and to a vast array of other educational and economic opportunities. Parents who are familiar with the tests likely perceive that they tend to test a particular type of knowledge—one that is not sensitive to subcultural variations, often involves extensive memorization, and tends to be traditional and national, not local. But, however comfortable the parents might be in rejecting a traditional education as meaningless for themselves, they may be unwilling to impose that conclusion on their children. Parents whose own educations fall short of the cultural literacy mark may feel unqualified to second-guess the advice of educationally privileged professionals or to commit their children to their own level of education. Parents who have had the advantages of education in elite institutions may want their children to receive similar advantages. Thus, if learning the list determines or influences access to higher education and if higher education determines access to economic and other important opportunities, then parents who are concerned about their children's futures will care about the list.

Another cluster of Hirsch sympathizers includes people who believe that a strong sense of belonging to a community is important to human happiness. This sense of belonging depends, they note, upon having a shared language, shared rituals, myths, values, knowledge, and customs. To teach all American schoolchildren a common American creed, as traditionally defined, would inspire a stronger sense of our national community[36] and might help to hold us together.[37] Critical to these communitarians is that the Hirsch list reflects *traditional* cultural values, but unlike the educational conservatives, they favor the list because it reasonably reflects these American cultural traditions, not because the American traditions are superior to other cultures' traditions. In other words, they agree with Hirsch's anthropological justification of the traditional curriculum.

Perhaps the most vocal group of commentators who favor a traditional core curriculum, however, are people who oppose the perceived trend toward multiculturalism as a primary value in education because of its strong emphasis on race and ethnicity. In particular, they abhor multicultural education strategies that teach the standard works—such as Shakespeare, Milton, or Hawthorne—through the prism of radical cultural criticism[38] or replace them with nontraditional texts. They also condemn efforts to admit as students or hire and promote as instructors members of racial or other outgroups whose credentials are, according to conventional criteria of merit, less impressive than those of white, male applicants.

These commentators' most serious criticism is that multiculturalist efforts treat race and ethnicity as determinative, defining forces.[39] The danger they perceive in multiculturalism is that it fosters, rather than erodes, separatism and intergroup tensions. They feel that cultivation and reinforcement of subcultural differences in the public schools will reverse the historic and distinctive theory of America—which has been, argues Arthur Schlesinger, Jr., "not the preservation and sanctification of old cultures and identities, but the creation of a new national culture and a new national identity."[40] These critics fear racial separatism in education,[41] such as the effort in some urban areas to establish African-centered schools, wherein the teaching staff would consist primarily of black men who would serve as role models for the male, black, and Hispanic students.[42] Equally worrisome are efforts to inculcate Afrocentric values, such as the attempt of the Indianapolis school system to use an Afrocentric approach to history, as this Afrocentric approach often becomes a form of "ethnic cheerleading," teaches bad history, and is likely to foster resentment among racial groups.[43] Racial hostility, these critics continue, is only encouraged when professors reinforce the view that race and ethnicity are determinative and may pose insurmountable obstacles to interethnic and interracial understanding; the modern experiences of Quebec and Bosnia counsel against celebration of cultural difference rather than cultural unity. As one writer expressed it, "The chief risk . . . is that [such a curriculum] can promote tribalism and downplay the value of discovering common cultural ground. The very idea of the melting pot, of assimilation, indeed of a common American identity, is under fire in some academic circles."[44]

A related, media-amplified criticism of multicultural education initiatives is that the reformers have overpowered dissenters and weak-willed administrators and are transforming American colleges and universities into "politically correct" regimes. A particularly provocative indictment of this tendency came in 1991 from young Dinesh D'Souza, then a recent graduate of Dartmouth College.[45] D'Souza charged that college and graduate school education had been captured by left-leaning social activists. The civil rights demonstrators of the 1960s, he warned, had become the insulated, tenured professors of the 1990s,[46] who now were foisting their personal versions of political correctness,[47] along with their postmodernist predilections, on an overwhelmed minority of conservative, centrist, and Western culture–oriented colleagues and an unwitting student body.[48] According to this view—which arose in the early 1990s out of the controversy over attempts to discipline those who used racial slurs and other forms of "hate speech" on college campuses—liberal values such as academic freedom and unfettered discourse now were threatened by a "victim's revolution" of feminist, critical race, and other radical scholars.[49]

The college curriculum in particular has been politicized, say these critics, in ways that threaten critical inquiry and that silence voices that challenge aspects of the "pc" agenda. The results of this development have been not only disorganized or fragmented curricula but also a concerted assault on the central contributions of liberal Western philosophy, including freedom of expression[50] and other cherished liberal values.

This last objection to multiculturalist education thus bleeds into another, which is that it is a wrongheaded and dangerous denial of the positive contributions of Western traditions.[51] Neutrality among competing versions of the good life, some declare, is a central tenet of Western liberalism. To abandon this neutrality, even for the worthwhile end of eradicating discrimination, is a grave mistake. Moreover, the Western civilization canon is exceptionally well-suited to the task of inculcating in schoolchildren the instinct for cultural criticism, as well as an appreciation of difference, toleration, and respect for individual autonomy. Reading the Great Books will not stultify minds into an unreflective embrace of the status quo; on the contrary, the readings included in the traditional Western canon contain the best arguments against it.[52] After all, say defenders of these texts, both Dewey and Aristotle appear on the list—as do Marx, Mao Tse-tung, and Mill.[53] Even those who feel excluded by the traditional canon thus can find much to treasure within it.[54] In stark contrast, the methods and the materials of some modern multiculturalists undermine critical thought in that they reject neutrality as a goal, embrace particularism, and attempt to impose politically correct attitudes on detractors.[55]

Finally, the opponents of a multicultural curriculum complain, the information that multiculturalists would teach instead of the traditional curriculum is simply incorrect or relatively trivial. In the effort to boost racial, ethnic, or gender pride, the multiculturalists exaggerate or misstate facts. For example, Cleopatra was not black[56]—contrary to the claims of some Afrocentric texts.[57] Similarly, the stretch to include some pre-eighteenth century female authors causes fanciful or shallow works to be treated as works on par with far more brilliant, significant classics. The result is an absurd trivialization of greatness and the substitution of quotas and cross-representativeness for merit as the grounds for selecting educational materials. The only standard supplied by multiculturalism, say these observers, is a proportional diversity of ethnic, racial, gender, religious, or sexual background. Lost are the universal standards of reason, beauty, merit, truth, or any other transcendent measure of human achievement.[58]

A final group of core curriculum sympathizers are people opposed to subcultural challenges of the dominant list on expressly racist, sexist, or other repressive grounds. The traditional list, even with its cultural revision caveat, soothes people whose interests are threatened by advancements since the 1950s of members of racial and ethnic minorities, women, and other historically marginalized groups. The traditional core curriculum, taught in the conventional manner, reasserts the rules most comfortable to those whose interests coincide with the canon. Most of the authors of the traditional texts and the leading historical figures included in the Hirsch list and in Great Books proposals tend to be white, male, and Western European. People who believe that Western European, white males are superior to other groups and who favor a system that celebrates these figures' lives, therefore prefer the traditional canon to one that gives equal attention to African novels, female biographies, South American poetry, Asian philosophy, or Native American environmentalism.

In sum, many people resonate to the Hirsch call for curricular coherence, though for many different reasons. They accept that reading literacy depends partly on cultural literacy and that a general, nationally defined literacy may make more sense than a specific, locally defined one, given the nationalization and even globalization of so many conditions of modern life. Because the Hirsch proposal does not foreclose the possibility of local differentiation and because it does not demand that teachers instill loyalty to the list, as opposed to mere recognition of its terms, the proposal can accommodate a diverse range of interests without sacrificing the central goal of coherence. Its national focus diffuses the impact of any particular subculture and thus may respect diversity more than any one insular, local focus could. Moreover, Hirsch does not commit himself to a particular philosophical, religious, or strongly political position. His orientation is liberal democratic, of course, but in its most capacious form. And although his proposal is instrumental, the end is a form of baseline literacy, not a refashioned modern man or woman. The baseline that he proposes would be useful to a wide range of occupations and to intelligent self-governance. It also might provide a modest degree of cohesion within the educational process, which is an acceptable goal to many people.

Indeed, a national core curriculum, defined as minimally and as traditionally as Hirsch's, seems so benign and sensible to some observers that they find it difficult to understand why anyone would object. In particular, they cannot imagine why anyone would object to an education that assured that high school graduates knew basic principles of the government that would control much of their lives. If, for example, our graduates are as gravely deficient in basic civics as Hirsch claims, then something clearly must change. Worse, if they cannot read, express themselves in writing, or locate Europe on a map, then they are utterly lost. Since much of the Hirsch proposal seems dedicated to assuring this sort of bare, real-world survival knowledge, the proposal could only be opposed by dreamers, radical separatists, or people willing to sacrifice a generation of children in pursuit of their utopian aims.

CONCLUSION

To state the many reasons why a range of contemporary thinkers might approve of a national curriculum is not to suggest that all of them make sense or that they accurately characterize the multiculturalists' education agenda. As the next chapter makes clear, many thoughtful observers believe that a national list would produce more bad than good. It is extremely interesting, however, to note the extent to which so many modern observers seem to endorse the concept of a nationally defined literacy. This is simply remarkable, given our long national history of favoring local control over education, including the curriculum. For conservatives, especially religious conservatives and others who are committed to family-centered values and to strong local community control over the upbringing of children, the proposal of a national list with room for "cultural revision" should produce more apprehension than the national core curriculum concept seems to. That is, the modern climate is distinctive in that it seems peculiarly receptive to federal-level definitions of literacy and community.[59] As Chester Finn has noted, recent opinion surveys reveal that the public is in favor of "seismic" changes in the basic rules of education.[60] One such study revealed that 70 percent of the respondents favored requiring public schools to conform to national achievement standards and goals. Sixty-nine percent favored requiring public schools to use a standardized national curriculum. And a whopping 77 percent said that they favored requiring public schools to use standardized national testing programs to measure the academic achievement of students.[61]

This is, even to people who have watched the education pendulum swing toward and away from local control, an incredible set of statistics. Indeed, as Hirsch himself points out,[62] many of the changes that he recommends already have been implemented in some schools across the country. These changes, and the public support that they represent, put into context the recent proposals that urge the adoption of national achievement tests.[63] National standards proposals are an outgrowth of continuing dissatisfaction with the "centrifugal forces" that first were described in the 1945 Harvard report. Frustration with a host of social problems, including the apparent failure of public schools to graduate students who can read and write, have turned many people toward Washington for a traditional and coherent plan of attack. Moreover, the sudden and sweeping movement toward democracy in Eastern Europe, as well as the outbreaks of ethnic violence in the Balkans and elsewhere, have given the modern call for national solidarity a substantial boost in popularity, and has lent greater force to the call of a traditionally defined, national core curriculum, with its emphasis on democratic, "American" values. For all of these reasons, increasing numbers of people seem willing to endorse national lesson plans for the nation's schoolchildren.

4 Critiques of the Call for Coherence

I find that many who talk the loudest about the need of a supreme and unified Americanism of spirit really mean some special code or tradition to which they happen to be attached. They have some pet tradition which they would impose on all.—John Dewey

It's not a matter of being for or against Western civilization. We are all victims of it. It's time to consider that the classics may, in fact, make more sense to us as records of blindness to the plight of the world's majorities, than as sublime masterpieces. . . . That doesn't mean, however, that we don't need to read and analyze them. It means that we need to keep our eye on the ball.—Michele Wallace

INTRODUCTION

Not everyone has been caught up in the tide of enthusiasm for a revitalized American identity fostered by a national core curriculum. On the contrary, a significant number of commentators remain opposed to a national standard of cultural literacy. The strands of their opposition to a core curriculum, like those of support for it, are several and varied.[1] In general, however, the opponents tend to object to the "listness" of the Hirsch plan and its objectification of knowledge, the tendency of his tradition-centered proposal to perpetuate the social status quo, the way in which Hirsch minimizes the concerns of cultural and religious pluralism, the extent to which his proposal fails to address the deeper conditions of inequality and misplaced educational priorities, and the centralization of power over educational policy inherent in any national core curriculum proposal. Many opponents also demur that there already *is* a list, which already is taught—at least to students in wealthier school districts and elite post-secondary schools. To them the core curriculum debate is much ado about the wrong social problem, and reformers might better spend their energy popularizing an appeal for school and family financial equalization plans or other aggressive means of lifting poorer students from the bog of severe inequalities and deprivation. This chapter examines the best of these arguments against the core curriculum, with particular emphasis on multiculturalists' criticisms of Hirsch-like reform.

MULTICULTURALIST CRITIQUES

A national identity of the sort that Hirsch and others would like to reclaim or forge is relatively easy to describe. The geographical contours of the culture in question are the borders of the United States. The relevant texts are those that have tended to shape Western thought since the ancient Greek times forward. The political values that receive the greatest weight are those of democracy "American-style."[2] The moral and ethical values that it celebrates are of a secularized Judeo-Christian form, coupled with industriousness, honesty, and tolerance of others. The primary figures are of Western European descent. The controlling legal concepts are from the English legal tradition. The language of the culture is English.

Multiculturalism, in contrast, has nearly as many definitions as it has proponents.[3] True to the pluralism implied by the embrace of cultural difference, the multiculturalists do not speak in one voice in their critiques of a national curriculum. In general, however, they reject a monocultural account of America's past and regard national monoculturalism as an inappropriate ideal for the American future. To them, assimilation is both an unrealistic and undesirable governmental objective—at least as an affirmative, paramount, and mandatory policy.

PHILOSOPHICAL PREMISES

Multiculturalists favor robust cultural pluralism,[4] which, in its most radical and disturbing form, may include cultural separatism. The underlying belief is that, to the extent that a basic principle of human existence is diversity, assimilation is destructive of human personality.[5] The homogenization of mass society and the mistaken striving for unifying public truths deny both the way in which cultures tend to produce unique truths or values[6] and the important link between morality and cultural community.[7]

To fail to respect cultural distinctiveness and cultural identity, however, is to produce neurosis, crime, delinquency, and alienation.[8] "Immoral" acts become more frequent because morality is the acceptance of restrictions, which must be tied to social group identity in order to be meaningful.[9] As

Seymour Itzkoff stated in 1969, "Morality does have a locus—the cultural community."[10] Loss of cultural community therefore means the loss of a moral center.

Some multiculturalists thus view laws that require that all children receive a uniform education as impermissible intrusions on subcultural autonomy and favor unconditional exceptions for "home education" or excusal from all or part of the standard curriculum. Within the public school system, multiculturalists favor diversified, highly contextualized curricula that "not only partak[e] of the . . . standards of knowledge of the Western world, but also of the cultural and historical experiences unique and special to the [cultural backgrounds of the students]."[11] This might mean, for example, black-run schools in black communities[12] and Afrocentric curricula for African-American children.[13]

Inherent in this position is a belief that, if school culture is not tailored to the student's home culture, then the child either will be alienated from the school culture or will become alienated from the home culture.[14] Either outcome may destroy self-esteem, cause psycho-emotional harm, or otherwise impair the child's personal or educational well-being.[15] Multiculturalists regard these potential harms as more serious than the potential harm of cultural pluralism. In their view, national curricularists like Hirsch underestimate the cost of enforced assimilation for members of genuinely distinctive subcultures and misperceive the importance of a more intimate cultural identity to the child's, as well as society's, well-being. Emphasis on a national, impersonal, and standardized culture may exacerbate the anomie that already is pervasive in modern society, in that such a broadly-defined community cannot substitute for the vastly more meaningful, intimate, and salient bonds of subcultural communities. The model of national government that they prefer, therefore, is a federation or commonwealth of multiple cultural communities,[16] rather than one national, cohesive community.[17]

Multiculturalists tend to reject universalism[18] and to embrace openly anthropological relativism.[19] They believe that morality is rooted in a particular culture's history, conventions, practices, and beliefs and cannot be subject to one transcultural standard or hierarchy.[20] The search for a "unitary common good" simply is not part of many multiculturalists' agenda.[21]

In its strongest and most controversial form, multiculturalism advocates granting subcommunities plenary acculturative authority over their youth. Radical theorists defer to parochial idiosyncracies to a degree that even some other multiculturalists reject. In effect, strong multiculturalists favor unconstrained cultural pluralism, regardless of whether some of these cultures are intensely ethnocentric, monocultural, or intolerant of outsiders.

More moderate multiculturalists, however, approve of constrained plural-ism, under which limited assimilation to a national culture is acceptable, provided it is noncoercive and does not overpower the assimilative pulls of the various subnational communities. Like the strong multiculturalists, the moderate multiculturalists condemn the Anglo-Saxon bias of the traditional definition of the American national culture, and argue for a more inclusion-ary, pluralistic national identity.[22] Thus, although they might not reject the "melting pot" metaphor as an appropriate theoretical description of an *ideal* national culture, they deny that the national culture that Hirsch and others propose matches the melting pot ideal. On the contrary, these multicultural-ists argue that the traditional national culture is strongly Western European and is dismissive of Mexican, Native American, African, Asian, and other non-Western European influences. As one multiculturalist writer put it, "[T]he melting pot . . . is in reality a myth."[23] Given the misleading nature of the "melting pot" metaphor, these multiculturalists prefer other terms—such as *mosaic*.[24]

All multiculturalists point out that the late nineteenth century educa-tional "golden age" that reformers often invoke to measure the decline of our cultural literacy was not golden after all, and was an era in which few people other than social elites attended the secondary or post-secondary schools. Moreover, the era was tainted by the intentional exclusion of blacks, women, poor, and other disadvantaged classes of students.[25] During the 1870s, for example, only 3 percent of all students went to high schools.[26] Racially segregated schools were not held unconstitutional until 1954.[27] In-deed, as late as 1963, ninety-nine of every one hundred Southern blacks remained in all-black schools.[28] Educational equality between girls and boys has yet to be achieved.[29] Too, gross economic disparities among various public school districts never have been held to be unconstitutional under the federal Constitution,[30] though some state courts have begun to require funding equalization as a matter of state law.[31] As such, the golden age of literacy was golden only for a handful of economically and otherwise priv-ileged students.

Moreover, if literacy is defined as mastery of a list of traditional cultural information, then a full explanation of the decline in literacy must consider that that information has never been equally available to all members of society. Nor have all groups had an equal opportunity to shape the list, to criticize the dominant interpretation of what counts as academic or intellec-tual achievement, or otherwise to assure that their perspectives were part of the dominant story. Yet failing to take this pattern of exclusion into account when evaluating the decline in cultural literacy, or merely mentioning it in passing instead of making it a central concern within educational theory and curricular planning, perpetuates the exclusion. In particular, this omission deceives people into accepting conventional measures of intellectual, academic, and other achievements as "objective" and "neutral,"[32] without regard for the ways in which historical and contemporary biases consistently infect such measures.[33]

Finally, the multiculturalists observe, the future is decidedly pluralistic. As of the turn of the millennium, over fifty percent of all students in the United States will be members of so-called minorities.[34] At present there are "twenty-three million Americans over the age of five who speak a language other than English at home."[35] Multiculturalism thus is an educational necessity, not a passing fad or a social luxury. To stress traditional cultural reproduction and stasis over cultural pluralism and flexibility is as shortsighted in education as is stressing local over global forces in economics or environmental sciences. The Margaret Mead observation that we have become "immigrants in time"[36] has yet to be taken seriously enough by policy makers, especially by those who use 1870, or even 1945, as a reference point for education in the 1990s.

EDUCATION STRATEGIES

Multiculturalists favor several strategies to promote diversity in public education. First, they endorse programs that assure that the school culture respects and accommodates the child's home culture.[37] In effect, they favor bicultural education for all children from nondominant cultures insofar as it is feasible.[38] One writer has defined *biculturalism* to mean that "the child is allowed to explore the mainstream culture freely by using those preferred modes he brings to school from his home and community. . . . [T]his . . . clearly requires a bicultural educational environment in any school confronted with the responsibility of providing equal educational opportunities for children whose home and community differ culturally from the mainstream."[39] Public and private school programs that tailor their curricula to bridge the gap between home and mainstream culture play an important role in multicultural education.

Multiculturalists also demand that subnational cultures play a central, not peripheral, role in shaping school programs, practices, and procedures. They would, for example, reject as an inadequate fulfillment of multicultural goals a one-shot, optional course on Mexican history in a school that enrolled numerous Mexican-American students. Most, however, also would reject an educational program that made no effort to introduce all students to the national culture. By providing access to both cultures—national and subnational—the school better enables the child to choose whether to assimilate into the national culture and to what extent. Likewise, the school validates the child's home culture and thus reduces the alienation that sometimes occurs when the school culture and home culture are extremely dissimilar.[40]

Multiculturalists are not content, however, to change only the content of education for children whose native culture departs from the national monocultural ideal. They also seek to revise the curriculum of all American students to reflect the contributions of outgroups whose histories have been trivialized, misstated, or omitted. Thus, for example, stories of the colonists should be told in a manner that reflects that the land they "discovered" already was occupied. Accounts of the lives of the Founding Fathers should be expanded to include uncomplimentary facts, where appropriate, such as that some were slave owners.[41] And the revised texts that amplify African-American history should be taught to all children, lest non-African-American children be raised in ignorance of this history. Indeed, James Baldwin describes this move as necessary for all students—white students and students of color—to have an accurate sense of their own identity. He states as follows:

> If, for example, one managed to change the curriculum in all the schools so that Negroes learned more about themselves and their real contribution to this culture, you would be liberating not only Negroes, you'd be liberating white people who know nothing about their own history.[42]

Only through such pervasive, culture-wide revision of the dominant, traditional story can educators respond to Baldwin's claim that "[w]hat passes for identity in America is a series of myths about one's heroic ancestors."[43] Part of the multicultural agenda, therefore, is to pursue and present a richer, more nuanced, and less sanitized truth about America to all schoolchildren.

A third, and more controversial, aspect of the multiculturalists' agenda is to teach this revised American history progressively and politically. Multiculturalists would describe the omissions or distortions of the dominant histories and anthologies as the product of conscious and subconscious discriminatory attitudes and practices within American society. They would teach children that racism, sexism, and other forms of prejudice consistently make it more difficult for some group members to compete equally for economic and social goods. Unless the facts of group-status discrimination are acknowledged, they say, then the harmful effects of discrimination cannot be ameliorated. American education must face up to these painful and dangerous facts and assign responsibility for them to the human agents who contributed to them, rather than denying them, minimizing them, or otherwise fostering the impression that the inequities within society are inevitable, natural consequences of life, or a function of a merit-based distribution of social goods.

The multiculturalist teacher thus sees herself not merely as the conduit of historical knowledge but as the facilitator of future change. Educators, she believes, should elevate consciousness about discrimination to further a specific substantive end—a world in which difference does not occasion subordination. To secure this ideal future, the educator must develop in the students an acute and accurate sense of past and present obstacles to it.

To dislodge the hardened habits of tradition and to expose more people to the insight that the received tradition reflects inadequately the interests of some Americans, teachers must engage in aggressive consciousness-raising.[44] One means of effecting the changed perspective that multiculturalists stress is storytelling. Novels, poetry, scholarship, and essays that make vivid the psycho-emotional costs of educational and other practices that devalue members of nondominant racial and ethic communities, women, gays, or members of other outgroups may provide students with a richer sense of what it means to be discounted or affirmatively repressed than any discussion of abstract rights or principles of justice. Narratives, some multiculturalists believe, trigger the "click" that alters consciousness permanently, which in turn paves the way to empathic appreciation of another's experience[45] and to greater tolerance.

Multiculturalists regard this "click" as essential to human solidarity and genuine understanding of the heart of multiculturalism and as the only secure means of reducing intergroup hostility and violence. Only by engaging people's deepest empathic capabilities, by listening to the "sorrow songs" of others,[46] can the nation's multiple cultures transcend the often polarized and confrontational politics of race, ethnicity, gender, sexual orientation, and religion. Given the historical treatment of some groups, however, this listening must come first, and predominantly, from whites, and especially from white males. As David Mura has put it,

> In the realm of culture in America, white European culture has held the floor for centuries; just as with any one-sided conversation, a balance can only be achieved if the speaker who has dominated speaks less and listens more. That is what conservative cultural critics are unwilling to do; for them there is no such thing as collective guilt, much less the obligation that such guilt bestows.[47]

Some multiculturalists interpret the growing resistance to multicultural education[48] as a defensive refusal to cede the floor and to accept the responsibilities of past and present discrimination. Educators who feel threatened by multiculturalism, who lack the experience that precedes understanding and the commitment and interest critical to empathic understanding based on vicarious experience, have made hyperbolic accusations that *all* multiculturalists endorse separatism and would usher in a new and destructive age of "tribalism."[49] Such educators wrongly conflate all multiculturalists, trivialize the significance of past oppression and present patterns of discrimination, and exaggerate the extent to which multiculturalists have captured higher education and transformed the dominant curriculum.[50] Their sharply worded backlash, say some multiculturalists, is a reaction to the shift of only modest, though genuine, power to previously powerless groups.[51] This loss of turf, not fidelity to philosophical principles or a well-intentioned effort to protect liberal education from the subverting and dangerous influence of partisan politics, is the real root of much of the animosity toward multicultural education. The disagreements thus are not, as they sometimes appear to be, about whether Cleopatra was black[52] but are about white male anger about the preferential treatment that non-whites and women ostensibly receive in admissions to schools, in hiring and promotion, and in other respects. These alleged advantages, coupled with a dramatic increase in the numbers of non-white and female students, teachers, administrators, and other educational policy makers, threaten educators whose personal career or educational interests are not advanced by multicultural programs.

Other multiculturalists, however, are more sympathetic to some of the emotional, adverse reactions to multiculturalism. They acknowledge that the confrontational rhetoric and tactics of some radical multiculturalist scholars and activists have offended even some long-time liberals and civil rights allies who resent overquick resort to damning labels such as racist, sexist, homophobic, or fascist and the cavalier dismissal of neutrality as an ideal, even if it is not always a realistic goal. Nevertheless, even these moderate multiculturalists reject the empirical claim that often accompanies the objections to confrontational tactics, which is that the tide really has turned such that minorities and women now control the education industry. Rather, they believe that the necessary reforms have barely begun and that many of the programs of the 1960s and 1970s that people today condemn as "ineffective" failed, not because they were ill-conceived wastes of public resources, but because they were underfunded and underenforced.[53] Moreover, modern-day "tribalism" and ethnic segregation, they maintain, spring less from the modest multicultural inroads into education or from radical rhet-

oric than from poverty, persistent discrimination, and the increasingly intractable socioeconomic stratification of American society. Teaching Maya An-
gelou to all sixth graders or an Afrocentric curriculum to inner-city African-
American male school children, they point out, hardly threatens our national
solidarity or security. That one-fifth of the nation's children grow up in
poverty, however, clearly threatens both. The multiculturalists insist that
antidiscrimination and full equality must precede all other national and local
educational priorities because all other rights and liberties depend on equality for their meaningful fulfillment.

Given their baseline commitment to the substantive principle of equality,[54] multiculturalists tend to judge procedural and structural aspects of
education contextually. In general, they prefer decentralization and community control,[55] because this tends to reduce the conforming force of standardized, broader-based regulations. Nevertheless, local control can—in some
contexts—mean cultural homogeneity and repression of difference. In these
situations, most, but not all, multiculturalists favor whatever organizational
structure best promotes the substantive end of nonsubordination.

CRITICAL EQUALITY THEORISTS

Multiculturalists often join forces with another, overlapping group of commentators—critical equality theorists. The proponents of critical equality are
bound by the conviction that equality is the baseline condition of a just
society[56] and by the belief that, until equality is achieved, all other rights are
chimerical. They decry the unequal distribution of educational resources
among various groups and regions and argue that redressing such inequalities should be the paramount educational priority.[57] To achieve equality,
curricular changes are essential—though hardly sufficient—in order to empower historically disfavored groups and correct for the distortions and
dismissiveness of past curricula. Critical equality advocates share the multiculturalists' view that systemic and pervasive discrimination and a cultural
bias in favor of Western European practices and values—not merit, nature,
or differential attitudes or effort—often explain the gap between white and
nonwhite educational and economic achievement levels.[58]

Like most multiculturalists, the critical equality theorists are not necessarily opposed to a national cultural ideal as one *part* of each American's
cultural identity. Indeed, critical theorists expressly hope that respect for
equal rights of all group members would become part of the American
national character. Unlike the multiculturalists, however, the critical equality
theorists are not defined by a commitment to the importance of communal

bonds to human personality or to the preservation of cultural distinctiveness.[59] On the contrary, they often worry that small communities, even more so than larger, more cosmopolitan ones, can be highly insular, repressive, and inegalitarian.[60]

Many of the critical equality theorists, such as Giroux and McLaren, denounce the "conservative discourse of schooling" that ascended in the 1980s, arguing that it mischaracterized the progressive educational movements of the 1960s and 1970s in an effort to discredit those movements' strong democratic objectives.[61] They maintain that the "back-to-basics and rigor" reform movement of the 1980s merely multiplied injustice in the name of excellence.[62] In fact, they argue, those who claim that schools are meritocratic institutions that foster equality of opportunity and outcome engage in "a quaint oversimplification which masks schooling's socially and culturally reproductive dimensions."[63] As such, the term "excellence" is

> reduced to a code word for legitimating the interests and values of the rich and the privileged. Within this perspective, remedial programs which try to extricate the lowly from their benighted condition label such students as "deprived" or "deviant" youth. This labeling not only serves to entrap students within the contours of a professional discourse, doubly confirming the legitimating power of school practices, but also serves to reproduce intergenerational continuity by defining who are to become members of the elite class and who are to occupy the subaltern class.[64]

The critical equality theorists fear that the stress on excellence and rigor that became the hallmark of educational reform of the 1980s undermines the goal of equality and redefines the ends of public schooling solely in terms of what promotes economic growth and competitiveness of the student in the marketplace.[65] Job skills and authoritarian education, they warn, will become more important than liberal and creative arts, and cultural uniformity will become more important than cultural pluralism.[66] Reformers wrongly will assume that culture can only be understood through the Great Books or through a process of cultural restoration called cultural literacy. Under this approach, the critics claim,

> cultural and social difference quickly becomes labeled as deficit, as the Other, as deviancy in need of psychological tending and control. At stake in this perspective is a view of history, culture, and politics committed to cleansing democracy of its critical and emancipatory possibilities. Similarly, in this perspective, the languages, cultures, and histor-

ical legacies of minorities, women, blacks, and other subordinate groups are actively silenced under the rubric of teaching as a fundamental act of national patriotism.[67]

Many of the critical equality theorists are philosophical descendants of John Dewey and his Progressive allies, in terms of their rejection of pedagogical methods that stress rote memorization and a nonindividualized, nationally uniform curriculum. They believe that if mastery of Hirsch's list becomes an important measure of academic performance then other, more important skills of critical analysis will atrophy. And if public schools increasingly are obliged to compete with one another for students, then teachers will feel compelled to teach to the list rather than to pursue other goals. The list will overdetermine the content of the curriculum and the selection of pedagogical methods. As such, the proposed revival of standardized lessons, with little regard for an individual child's educational, family, or cultural background, will undermine the humanistic, emancipatory, and democratic virtues of post-Deweyan progressive reforms.

In some formulations, this egalitarianism is linked to a class perspectivist critique of advanced capitalism. These writers argue that capitalist business interests and the educational agenda are destructively intertwined.[68] The force of capitalism, they claim, so dwarfs any counterforce of education that education cannot overcome or substantially reverse or subvert it. Indeed, educators cooperate actively and enthusiastically with business and industry to hold, train, and sort students in ways that best serve the market.[69] State educational policies, therefore, are expressly designed to legitimate capital accumulation and to preserve the power of the capitalist class.

To other critical equality theorists, the force of capitalism is seen as less overwhelming. These critics recognize the strong influence of the dominant economic class on educational policy but deny that the government simply defers to this influence in all respects. Rather, "[t]he capitalist State and its educational system are . . . more than just a means for co-opting social demands, or for simply manipulating them to satisfy dominant class needs."[70] That is, a dialectical relationship exists among state educational officials, social reformers, and business and industrial interests.[71]

All critical equality theorists, however, share the perspective that schools should participate in the struggle for cultural justice and should seek to advance civil rights and democratic public life.[72] In particular, schools should assume active responsibility for achieving genuine equality rather than promote passive acceptance of current conditions of inequality. Thus, their critical agenda—that is, a thorough-going critique of the rhetoric of schooling, the explicit and hidden curriculum in the public schools, the pattern of distribution of educational resources, the pattern of educational outcomes, and the locus of school authority—is closely linked to their normative agenda: greater democratization of society and fairer distribution of social and economic goods.

ANTI-UNIVERSALISTS

Also opposed to a unitary, national canon—though not nearly as much as their detractors imagine—are the anti-universalists, who, Allan Bloom claims, have invaded the humanities departments of our elite colleges and universities. The unifying characteristic of these thinkers is a rejection of universal notions of "timeless truth" or "the nature of the good."[73] They would deny the Robert Hutchins-type notion that, before we can evaluate whether American education is in bad shape, we must identify "first principles" or historical truths against which we can evaluate the state of our educational souls.[74] Instead, they believe that what are called first principles really are "just a set of abbreviations of, rather than justifications for, a set of beliefs about the desirability of certain concrete alternatives over others; the source of those beliefs is not 'reason' or 'nature' but rather the prevalence of certain institutions or modes of life in the past."[75]

This rejection of universal truths leads these commentators to dispute the claim that the canon should be read as something other than an historical product.[76] The canon is not, they argue, grounded on any neutral, ahistorical foundation.

Their rejection of an ahistorical truth, however, does not lead all of these writers to reject the argument that students should be exposed to the traditional canon. On the contrary, even their most powerful spokesperson— Richard Rorty—concedes the usefulness of both a Hirsch-like reform of precollege education and even of a two-year Great Books curriculum for undergraduates.[77] Some thus are willing to defer to the old canon as an acceptable curricular baseline on the ground that it represents this culture's dominant historical practice. But most would endorse a college-level core curriculum only because they perceive that modern high schools are producing students with deficits in the curricular baseline. Once these deficits are cured, they favor the concept of "university as flea market"[78] over that of a university joined by a strong consensus about its function and mission. That is, most anti-universalists identify two educational moments in a student's life: a primary, acculturative stage, in which the student is exposed to the culture's best judgment about what is useful and important through that culture's abiding texts; and a secondary (college-level) stage, in which the student is "left free to shop around in as large and noisy a bazaar as possible."[79]

Some of these theorists would go farther, of course, and urge that even at the elementary and secondary school levels, students should be allowed to roam freely and not be constrained by some adults' historically contingent estimations of the good life. Most, however, deny that such freedom is feasible or desirable for elementary-level schoolchildren and believe it is only slightly more appropriate for high schoolers.[80] In essence, therefore, the curricular battle between the anti-universalists and their philosophical opponents is over who has the better claim about the proper post-secondary, not elementary or secondary school, experience and over the way in which educators should present the traditional core curriculum. They are not in total disagreement with Hirsch or his proposal.[81]

Where they do depart from Hirsch is in their response to the moderate multiculturalist critique of the traditional list. Although some anti-universalists might be content to teach the old list, despite its exclusions, most would be willing to expand the list to add the voices of women, African-Americans, and others to give fuller and more accurate expression to the whole culture's best provisional guesses about the good life. Modern anti-universalists define *literature* broadly to include "just about every sort of book which might conceivably have moral relevance—might conceivably alter one's sense of what is possible and important."[82] This redefinition inevitably includes far more works than the traditionally defined set of texts and, if it were used as the basis for a core curriculum, would mean a far more inclusive and wide-ranging canon.

Anti-universalists are likely to share John Dewey's relative skepticism about subject matter coverage and factual literacy as driving principles of sound education. To them, the ideal society, and hence the ideal education, would be one in which "everybody [has] a chance at self-creation to the best of his or her abilities."[83] That is, individual self-creation would be a paramount goal rather than the cultivation of strong and pervasive collective aspirations. Perhaps most importantly, the product of this education would be "someone who [meets] doubts about the culture, not with Socratic requests for definitions and principles, but by Deweyan requests for concrete alternatives and programs."[84]

In sum, the anti-universalists would certainly reject a unitary core curriculum for all upper-level undergraduates. For lower-level students, some might approve of a core curriculum defined in national terms but would reject the claim that the core curriculum should be taught according to the Aristotelian / Chicago-style tradition. Moreover, in defining *Great Books*, they likely would interpret *great* more ecumenically than would the anti-relativists. Though many of them approve of an acculturating stage in a child's education and some even endorse Hirsch-like reform of pre-college education, none endorses dogmatism or presentation of the core materials as historical truths. These thinkers believe that students should be prepared for adult lives in which they approach problems with Deweyan requests for concrete alternatives. As such, they believe that teachers should teach the core curriculum in a manner that trains students to frame these Deweyan requests rather than to memorize answers to standard questions.

STRONG INDIVIDUALISTS

A fourth, overlapping group of commentators who would tend to oppose a unitary core curriculum, at least beyond the primary stage of education, consists of the strong individualists. The paradigmatic strong individualist is John Stuart Mill.

In *On Liberty*, Mill outlined his ideal educational scheme for all children. The scheme was one in which the father was responsible for ensuring that the child received an education, subject to state punishment if he failed to fulfill this obligation. The father could not, however, choose whatever content he desired for the education; the father would be obliged to ensure that the child learned certain basic "facts" so that the child could pass an objective examination regarding these "facts."[85] Beyond this minimal and neutral shared vocabulary, however, the child was not subjected to any majority-driven definition of the good life or of a proper education, lest the child's autonomy be unduly compromised.[86]

In many respects, the Hirsch proposal urges precisely the same sort of fact mastery that Mill viewed as an essential component of a child's education. As such, Mill might have approved of the Hirsch list and of the recognition-but-not-affirmation method of teaching the list. But his anxiety about government or majoritarian suppression of individuality would have made him deeply skeptical of consensus-driven definitions of the core facts. In particular, he feared government-run (as opposed to government-enforced) education, for the following reasons:

> A general State education is a mere contrivance for moulding people to be exactly like one another: and as the mould in which it cases them is that which pleases the predominant power in the government, whether this be a monarch, a priesthood, an aristocracy, or the majority of the

existing generation; in proportion as it is efficient and successful, it establishes a despotism over the mind, leading by natural tendency to one over the body.[87]

Indeed, the bureaucratization and standardization of public education that has occurred since Mill's death likely would have shocked his sensibilities. As such, a modern Millian might accept the Mill theoretical model of some compulsory education, even in a liberal society, but vigorously deny that contemporary education falls short of providing this minimal core.

This claim is borne out by the work of several prominent liberal individualists, who are Millian in perspective. These writers accept that children cannot choose freely the content of their educations. They likewise accept, in theory, the need for some common ground among all schoolchildren of a liberal society.[88] They nevertheless tend to be critical of the current system of education on the ground that it achieves far too much, not too little, standardization and allows far too little room for family control over the content of the child's education.[89]

In recent years, the liberal individualist critique of state-run education has become particularly powerful. Libertarians have redoubled their long-standing efforts to deregulate education and to maximize family autonomy in the education arena through choice proposals and voucher plans that would provide families with control over which school their children attend and offer economic incentives to opt out of public education.[90] The most radical of these proposals tend to merge with those endorsed by the strong multiculturalists, though the strong individualists favor them for different reasons than the multiculturalists. In these proposals, the strong individualists would permit a child's parents to opt out from any compulsory, state-enforced education. As such, they are in partial sympathy with the multicultural separatists, and with some Christian fundamentalist separatists, who favor parental freedom to choose their child's education. The individualists favor this autonomy, however, on the ground that it maximizes individual choice and pluralism and that the child's parents are the best proxies for the child's own inarticulable interest.

All but the most radical individualists, however, concede the need for some exposure to the items that Hirsch lists as core. Thus, although many favor decentralization of school authority, they do not favor deregulation to the extent that students reach maturity without certain baseline skills and common cultural knowledge. Thus, whether an individualist endorses the Hirsch list depends primarily on her estimation of the force of the empirical claim that this minimal baseline currently has eroded to a dangerous degree.

For example, most strong individualists likely would agree that all American schoolchildren should learn basic principles of American government. They might dispute, however, claims that most schoolchildren lack this knowledge. Moreover, the individualists might disagree about how much civics, or other knowledge that Hirsch cites as core, is essential. In general, however, the strong individualist would define that core curriculum minimally, non-aspirationally, and as objectively as possible.

This means that a strong individualist would be inclined to draft a shorter list than the one Hirsch proposes. Moreover, the individualist might favor devoting less of the formal school program to the national list than Hirsch recommends. Finally, the individualist likely would favor providing as many opportunities as possible for all people to modify and supplement or otherwise influence the list, in order to promote pluralism and individual autonomy. Complete autonomy from cultural norms and from exposure to the dominant list is not, to most individualists, desirable, as such freedom actually may subvert central liberal-individualist values by permitting escape into repression or denial of the principle of individual autonomy.[91]

EMPIRICAL SKEPTICS

A final important group of national curriculum skeptics are people who object to the empirical claims that the teaching of cultural literacy, defined in Hirschian terms, has so declined that a national core curriculum deserves first-tier educational reform status and who doubt that teaching a core curriculum will rebuild cultural literacy. These commentators cite studies that indicate that the traditional list of so-called Great Books has always dominated American public and private school curricula,[92] though access to this cultural information has never been equal for all social groups.[93] Moreover, even if literacy *did* decline during the 1960s and early 1970s, this decline began to be addressed in the late 1970s and the early 1980s. Thus, most of the reforms that Hirsch claims are necessary already have been implemented,[94] with little impact on the literacy or cultural unity Hirsch hopes to foster.

Worse, they warn, any movement toward a back-to-basics approach "immediately [will] translate into minimal competency testing legislation."[95] This will mean an undue emphasis on testable, measurable skills and knowledge, and on memorization rather than reasoning.[96] This also will misdirect educational reform toward a "teaching-to-the-tests," and highly instrumental approach to education[97] and will precipitate a drift to a mediocre mean and minimum competency rather than to excellence and elevated standards.[98]

These commentators regard the swell of approval for Hirsch-like reform as based on a mistaken view of what schools actually are doing. People who are underinformed about the state of education find proposals like Hirsch's seductive because they promise order, implementable goals, accountability, and—most of all—the illusion of rapid improvement in American education and American society. Yet the past ten years of reform show that many of the proposed modifications already have been made and are not curing our educational woes. In short, a *paideia* is no panacea.

Reformers must look elsewhere, these critics argue, for answers to the perceived crisis in American education. Whether that answer lies in decentralization, vouchers, deregulation, higher pay for teachers, greater funding for programs servicing at-risk children such as Head Start, or some combination of these or other reform proposals is unclear. But teaching to the list, by itself, won't resolve the perceived crisis in education. Indeed, intense focus on the core curriculum and the multiculturalism critique has distracted commentators away from concrete issues that require more money, more pervasive social change, and far more energy to address than defining or assailing a list.

By framing the educational crisis in curricular terms, Hirsch and others have prompted mostly abstract, rhetorical, and highly polemical skirmishes but little positive reform. In the meantime, the high school drop-out rate for some minority groups exceeds 30 percent,[99] an estimated twenty-seven million Americans lack basic literacy skills, and fifty million more are unable to read well enough to function in the work place.[100] The blame for these staggering statistics, say these critics, cannot possibly lie with Jean Jacques Rousseau, John Dewey, pedagogical fashions of the 1960s, multiculturalism, deconstruction, or a creeping nihilism. First, although Deweyan *rhetoric* about child-centered education may pervade educational theory, educational *reality* is more adult-centered, nondemocratic, nonindividualized, and nonromantic than critics admit. For example, as early as 1918, there already were over one hundred standardized achievement tests in the main elementary and secondary school subjects.[101] After World War I, standardized testing mushroomed and has come to be a pervasive and stable feature of modern education.[102] Moreover, the tests have come to be used not only as indices of educational strengths and weaknesses but as determinants of access and placement.[103] As such, the claim that education lacks standardized, national measures of achievement is sheer folly.

Nor is power over the content of education more scattered or splintered than in earlier times. In 1947, there were approximately ninety-five thousand school districts in the United States. By the 1970s, the number had decreased to approximately sixteen thousand,[104] thereby increasing centralization and standardization of schooling since the "golden years" of early twentieth century America. To establish national-level control of the curriculum would further centralize this authority, to be sure, but this is not a clearly desirable outcome if the goal is to reestablish 1940s-style education. One first would have to determine who would compose the national-level decision making body and would have to justify their extensive, highly centralized authority. This justification for federal curricular power must consider that the existing standardized achievement tests, coupled with the relatively small number of different textbooks that actually are used nationwide, are not already resulting in cultural literacy. If these existing national influences are inadequate prods to curricular coherence, then why would a formal national curriculum, which under current proposals would be voluntary, be more effective?

These critics also remark that, if the pedagogy of the 1960s is the root of the cultural literacy problem, then the culturally illiterate ones should not be Allan Bloom's college-age students or E. D. Hirsch's seventeen-year-olds. Rather, they should be people in their thirties and early forties, who were in elementary or high school in the 1960s, but those people are not the focus of either professor's theories. Multiculturalism likewise cannot explain the new "fact gap." The multicultural movement is a new and very modest phenomenon in elementary and high school curricula, which was eclipsed in the 1980s by a much stronger back-to-basics movement.[105]

Finally, if creeping nihilism is the root of the problem, one wonders why we should fear anything so much that creeps so slowly. Essays written about students in the 1940s[106] expressed concerns about the impact of value relativism identical to those expressed by some modern writers. Thus, the "death of reason" as a guiding force either was foretold prematurely or has been given excessive weight as a cause of our educational malaise.

In short, some critics suggest that the facts simply do not support the Hirsch theory of cause and effect. We may well suffer from acute cultural illiteracy, but this is not the principal source of the failures of modern education. Nor is a widely taught list of items that "every American needs to know"—the subtitle of Hirsch's book—the answer to our as-yet unidentified *real* problem.

CONCLUSION

In the past thirty years, the multiculturalist critics of the traditional canon have succeeded in influencing the curricula and education policy in colleges, high schools, and elementary schools. Just how much progress they actually have achieved, however, is a matter of considerable debate.[107]

The critics maintain that too much has *not* changed[108] and that, contrary to their opponents' claims, discrimination and inequality remain serious social problems both within and beyond education. College campuses are not enclaves of feminism or arch-liberalism, as some alarmists assert. Rather, conservatism and centrism are alive and well,[109] and the insights of the civil rights movement remain obscure to, or entirely lost on, many educational policy makers, educators, and their students. Many people still fail to perceive that the conventional measures of educational achievement, worker productivity, and other important social, economic, and political achievement are based on male, Western European, heterosexual, Protestant, capitalist norms. The mistaken assumption of the neutrality of this norm is so pervasive that it goes unrecognized. Policies based on these traditional, unstated norms thus are still often viewed as neutral and meritocratic, whereas policies that reject these norms in favor of alternatives are perceived as political. Likewise, anyone who challenges the traditional canon is accused of politicizing education, whereas defenders of the canon can claim to be resisting politicization, rather than protecting entrenched political interests.[110]

Serious consideration of these normative and empirical reservations about Hirsch-like reform of precollege education and about Bloom-like revision of undergraduate education reveal the complexities of the national curriculum debate. The critiques destabilize many of the assumptions on which the call for a national curriculum is based and make any resolution of the matter seem problematic.

How, then, should the controversy be resolved? Taken together, what do the history of curricular reform in the United States and the contemporary, lavish commentary about whether to adopt a national core suggest about an appropriate national policy? Is there, or should there be, a national *paideia*— an ideal national public culture—which all American education should promote?

Part II responds to this question by referring to our constitutional philosophy and practice. It concludes that any national core curriculum must reflect both the core curricularists' interest in cultural solidarity and their critics' interest in cultural pluralism, because both interests are integral to our national constitutional character. Part II then goes on to explain what it means, in practical application, for a curriculum to respect both concerns.

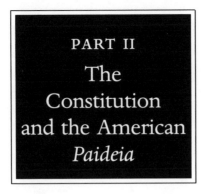

PART II

The
Constitution
and the American
Paideia

5 Constitutional Commitments
   and Conflicts

Among this country's community-defining symbols, none is more visible or more influential than the law, and especially the law of the Constitution.
—*Kenneth Karst*

INTRODUCTION

The call for a national core curriculum has ignited a firestorm of commentary. Part I explained this combustion in historical, education-specific terms. Part II recasts the debate over national standards in constitutional terms.

An apt preliminary question, however, is why add a constitutional perspective to an already multiperspectived, discipline-freighted debate?

The first and most obvious reason to consider constitutional materials is that the Constitution and the Bill of Rights would be vital components of any curriculum designed to convey knowledge of the nation as a whole. National standards regarding social studies, to name one curriculum pillar, unquestionably would include coverage of these political documents, their history, and their differing interpretations. Likewise, national standards surely would include coverage of the efforts by African-American men and women to secure the indicia of equality under federal law, especially constitutional law. That is, constitutional law is a central part of the national story.

A second, obvious connection between the Constitution and any national education proposal is that whether the federal government can or should play a role in forging education standards depends on an assessment of the limits of federal government power—a constitutional as well as practical political matter. Indeed, the extent to which any branch of government can impose mandatory schooling requirements is, at root, a constitutional question.

The most important reasons to consider a constitutional perspective on the national curriculum controversy, though, are more subtle. One is that Americans tend to define themselves and their assumed rights in reference to constitutional principles more than any other tenets.[1] For example, those who resist a common curriculum often appeal directly to constitutional principles in support of their goals and invoke, in particular, the Bill of Rights mandates of freedom of religion, freedom of expression, and equal protection under the law. Discussions of whether our public institutions should be secular rather than sectarian, should permit a range of views or should be restrained, or should promote racial or gender equality all typically occur against the backdrop of our constitutional commitments. There are, of course, many other ways meaningfully to address these same collective and individual interests. But in the United States, we most often talk about them using constitutional language as our common vocabulary, rather than the vocabularies of philosophy, sociology, or other disciplines, and often speak as though the Constitution were a guarantor of those interests. The Constitution and its vocabulary offer a particularly accessible and engaging framework for the core curriculum debate in that constitutional language transcends disciplines, sects, political affiliations, and dialects.

Moreover, the commitments set down in the Constitution are believed to have specific pedagogical implications. They imply a preference for methods of instruction that inspire critical deliberation, are tolerant of diverse viewpoints, and respect individual autonomy. As such, they shape American educators' choices about what to include in the curriculum, perhaps especially in materials that touch on politics, religion, race, and gender.

Still another reason to stress the connection between the curriculum debate and the Constitution is to correct people's mistaken view that the tugs of nationalism and individualism and of solidarity and pluralism only concern the courts. Constitutional principles, many people wrongly assume, are the province of lawyers and judges, not ordinary citizens; these same people often interpret constitutional law narrowly to mean solely the results reached by the courts, especially the United States Supreme Court.

Yet constitutional consequences and responsibilities extend far beyond the very limited category of cases in which sitting judges declare that specific government action offends the Bill of Rights. The Supreme Court rarely overturns education officials' decisions,[2] especially curricular decisions. The current Court in particular is unlikely to second-guess such decisions. Constitutional values nevertheless are implicated whenever educators decide that American history should emphasize Western European, male authors, that classroom discussions should refer to particular religious beliefs, or that all children should learn about AIDS, birth control, or homosexuality. Likewise, constitutional values clearly are involved when parents request that their children be excused from all or part of the common curriculum. That is, constitutional interests are not exhausted by the narrow category of cases in which a judge holds that these interests give rise to a legally enforceable right.

The Court's deference to educators' judgments about these sensitive issues is based in part on its confidence that the American majority can reasonably be trusted to consider the interests of ideological, religious, racial, ethnic, and other minorities when drafting general rules. That is, respect for freedom of speech, cultural pluralism, and even—at times— separatism is a national value that American school officials and voters are expected to understand and possess. The Court assumes that most American citizens are prepared to participate in this ongoing struggle to reconcile our competing constitutional interests. Whether American education actually prepares its students to assume the duties of democratic citizenship, includ- ing the duty of identifying and respecting constitutional values, therefore is crucial. This text is, among other things, an appeal to American educators to make every effort to prepare our students for active, critical participation in the constitutional conversation. For, as Sanford Levinson eloquently has noted, "[T]he United States Constitution can meaningfully structure our polity if and only if *every* public official—and ultimately *every* citizen— becomes a participant in the conversation about constitutional meaning, as opposed to the pernicious practice of identifying the Constitution with the decisions of the United States Supreme Court or even of courts and judges more generally."[3] This widespread participation can only occur, however, if we are better educated than we currently seem to be in the relevant history, principles, and values.

THE CONSTITUTIONAL BALANCE BETWEEN
ASSIMILATION AND DISSENT

Laws of general application inevitably threaten the interests of minorities in heterogeneous societies like the United States. We confront, perpetually, the dilemma of our differences.

Responses to the difference dilemma often proceed from one of several baseline perspectives on the role of law in a pluralistic society.[4] Disagree- ments about which one should inform American public policy can become quite vigorous, as the core curriculum debate proves.

One basic perspective is assimilationist. Given our cultural pluralism, one might assume that, in the absence of compelling counterindications, majority preferences should dominate such that our dominant cultural practices, enforced by formal law, should be observed by all citizens. The primary benefit of such assimilation is thought to be protection of "a treasured common life which constitutes a civilization."[5] For example, one might insist that all citizens should respect the principle of equality on the ground that it is a national value worth preserving at the expense of any subcultural dissent. Likewise, assimilationism might mean that all children should be exposed to a common curriculum taught in a common language, despite their parents' desire to insulate their children from dominant cultural knowledge and practices. The assimilationist instinct is profound and abiding within American culture and is most powerful, and potentially most offensive, when general laws are directed at assimilation of the nation's youth.

A second perspective is pluralist.[6] This approach demands that laws of general application should respect subcultural group perspectives and, insofar as possible, make allowances and exceptions for cultural practices that depart from the majoritarian norm. Thus, for example, religious and multiculturalist separatists should be excused from compulsory school laws when these laws threaten the groups' interest in preservation of their distinctive ways of life, regardless of the national collective interest in a common education base for all children.

A third perspective is individualist.[7] The emphasis under this approach is on individual, not group-based, interests when adopting general laws. Like pluralism, individualism construes broadly the opportunities for people within the national culture to think and act in a distinctive, nonstandard fashion. Both pluralism and individualism emphasize the destructive aspects of assimilation and the culturally positive benefits of variation, diversity, and multiplicity. And both present strong challenges to the scope and uniform application of compulsory school laws.

American constitutional law has reflected, on different occasions, all three interests. Its most common stance is assimilationist, but in significant moments it has been strongly pluralist, even in the context of schooling, where assimilationist instincts are most powerful. That all three interests are significant to national policy generally and that American public schooling in particular must effect a balance among them is best illustrated by the Court's 1925 decision, *Pierce v. Society of Sisters*.[8]

In 1922, Oregon passed a Compulsory Education Act that required every parent or guardian to send children between the ages of eight and sixteen to public school. The act made no exception for parents who wished to send their children to a private school, regardless of the quality of that private instruction.[9]

Two private educational institutions—the Society of Sisters and Hill Military Academy—filed an action seeking to enjoin the state from enforcing the act.[10] Their argument was that to compel all parents to send their children to public schools interfered with the right of parents to control the upbringing of their children and the right of schools and teachers to engage in a useful business or profession. The act violated the Fourteenth Amendment in that it denied the plaintiffs their liberty and property without due process of law.[11]

The Court agreed with the plaintiffs and held that the 1922 act

> unreasonably interfere[d] with the liberty of parents and guardians to direct the upbringing and education of children under their control.... The fundamental theory of liberty upon which all governments in the Union repose excludes any general power of the State to standardize its children by forcing them to accept instruction from public teachers only. The child is not the mere creature of the State; those who nurture him and direct his destiny have the right, coupled with the duty, to recognize and prepare him for additional obligation.[12]

The Court also held that the educational institutions' rights had been infringed because they were engaged in an enterprise that was not inherently harmful and because the state act would have destroyed their businesses.[13]

In ruling that the Oregon act was unconstitutional, however, the Court noted that states can regulate all schools, including private sectarian ones, and can demand that all children attend a school that satisfies valid state regulations. This power includes the power to require that all teachers be "of good moral character and patriotic disposition," that studies "plainly essential to good citizenship" be taught, and that "nothing be taught which is manifestly inimical to the public welfare."[14] The state simply cannot demand that these studies take place in a public school.

Pierce seeks to accommodate the assimilation, pluralism, and individualism interests by establishing a right of parents to send their children to an accredited private school while upholding states' broad power to regulate schools to assure that all children are exposed to lessons essential to good citizenship. The opinion weighs the dominant culture's interest in "conscious social reproduction" against the collective and individual interest in critical deliberation.[15] By doing so, it confronts an essential paradox of education in a liberal democratic state: education seeks to promote neutrality among competing versions of the good life while trying to instill in students the principles of the liberal democratic state, among them the nonneutral preference for critical deliberation.

The Court sought to mediate between these paradoxical desires by adopting a midground approach. It did not give parents absolute control over their children's education, contrary to what some parents and minority communities still believe to be the correct balance of state and individual liberty interests. Parents of nondominant communities do not have free license to insulate their children from the influences of the secular popular culture and possess no constitutional right to cultural separatism of the sort endorsed by some strong multiculturalists, religious fundamentalists, and libertarians.

The Court's refusal to permit unchecked parental secession[16] from state education laws betrays a fairly widespread belief that unmodified pluralism and freedom from communal obligations is unworkable, even dangerous, public policy. Ours is, in design if not always in practice, a liberal democratic state, not a purely liberal or a purely majoritarian democratic one. Our liberal leanings incline us to permit maximal dissent, disruption short of violence, and the right to depart from any state-imposed version of the good life. Families, as proxies for the best interests of the individual child and future adult right-bearer, should be given maximal (though not total) power to determine family beliefs, values, and practices. The government should be, insofar as possible, neutral with respect to alternative versions of the good life. Our democratic leanings, however, draw us back and demand that the liberal instinct be bounded by rules that protect all families, all individuals, and democracy itself. As stated earlier, even libertarian John Stuart Mill acknowledged the need for some common lessons that the state could demand that all children receive. Moreover, the liberal interest in critical deliberation and respect for dissent may be defeated if families are permitted to secede from education that inspires critical thought. Recognizing the peril of allowing complete secession from common lessons, *Pierce* offered parents only a qualified constitutional right to direct their children's education.

Yet *Pierce* likewise refused to give the state full control over the students' education. Despite the weighty collective interest in assuring that all youths receive uniform instruction in "good citizenship" in a setting subject to state observation and control, the Court refused to uphold the Oregon legislation. By doing so, the Court preserved parents' option to send their children to institutions that may be segregated, ideologically and culturally separatist, and committed to values that conflict with some liberal democratic aspirations. For example, sectarian schools—both then and now—do not offer competing accounts of the genesis of man, of the role of women, or of human sexuality. Thus a decision to allow children to attend such schools was and is a decision to permit ideological segregation and to allow some teachings that are not compatible with some public values.[17] Though the Court cabined this subversive potential by insisting that the state can prevent instruction that is inimical to the public good, it surely recognized that detecting subversive activity of that type would be virtually impossible. That is, the *Pierce* compromise is neither costless nor uncontroversial.[18]

The Court likewise rejected the Millian solution of narrowly restricting states' authority such that they could require, at most, that all children receive instruction in certain "objective" facts dictated by the state. The Court could have demanded that the state role in education be limited to that advocated by some modern school voucher advocates such that each family would receive public money with which they could purchase the education program they prefer. Instead of restricting state control to this bare minimum, however, the Court acknowledged the state's right to become deeply involved in education not only by running its own schools but also by demanding that private schools meet standards that exceed minimal fact presentation and include inculcation of the values of "patriotism" and "good citizenship." Nothing in *Pierce* required states to impose these more expansive standards, of course, but nothing in *Pierce* limited their ability to do so either.

In sum, the states, not the courts, pour content into the critical and capacious phrases, "studies plainly essential to good citizenship" and studies "manifestly inimical to the public welfare." If a state wishes to impose core curricular requirements on all schoolchildren, it may do so, provided it does not bar them from learning those lessons in a private school setting. And if the state wishes to assimilate all children into patriotic values, democratic practices, and civic responsibilities, it may, subject to modest restrictions.

The Court since *Pierce* has repeated that states' power to define these values and to acculturate its youths through formal schooling laws is very strong but not limitless. For example, states cannot make it illegal to teach schoolchildren subjects *in addition* to the state-imposed curriculum. The Court struck down a Nebraska statute that made it a misdemeanor to teach any subject in a language other than English until after the student passed the eighth grade.[19] The rationale was that mere knowledge of a foreign language—in this case, German—could not reasonably be regarded as harmful. The statute was prompted by World War I anxieties about foreign powers and, like *Pierce*, reflected the deeply xenophobic tendencies of many early twentieth century Americans. Again, however, the Court acknowledged the powerful state assimilationist interest, which included fostering "a homogeneous people with American ideals prepared readily to understand current discussions of civic matters,"[20] though the Court concluded that Nebraska's means of achieving this desirable end exceeded the state's legitimate powers.[21]

Likewise, a public school district cannot compel Jehovah's Witness school-children to salute the American flag, on pain of discipline for "insubordination," despite the state's interest in national unity.[22] In terms highly relevant to the modern call for national curricular coherence, the Court stated as follows:

> As governmental pressure toward unity becomes greater, so strife becomes more bitter as to whose unity it shall be. *Probably no deeper division of our people could proceed from any provocation than from finding it necessary to choose what doctrine and whose program public educational officials shall compel youth to unity in embracing.*[23]

Yet despite this stirring rhetoric against compelled unity, the Court actually held that states need provide only minimal room for dissent. This World War II-era flag salute decision involved an obligatory "stiff-arm," open-palm salute to the flag, which closely resembled the Nazi salute to Hitler. The Court in 1943 surely understood the symbolic importance of permitting American students to opt out of such a compulsory patriotic ritual, in order to distinguish American society from that of European fascist regimes. The Court did nothing, however, to prevent a school from compelling that the Jehovah's Witnesses attend classes in American history or civics, even if the express purpose of such classes were to inculcate "the ideals, principles and spirit of Americanism,"[24] or be present when others saluted the flag. Rather, the Court barred only the most flagrant, ritualistic forms of indoctrination and, even then, only when they entailed compelled *affirmation* of the patriotic beliefs rather than mere *exposure* to them. Indeed, many schools still perform the classroom ritual of a daily flag salute and pledge of allegiance, though students and teachers who dissent may not be required to participate. As the Court emphasized, "National unity as an end which officials may foster by persuasion and example is not in question."[25]

The Court has acknowledged the assimilationist interest in "awakening the child to cultural values, in preparing him for later professional training, and in helping him to adjust normally to his environment."[26] It has approved of public schools acting as "an 'assimilative' force by which diverse and conflicting elements in our society are brought together on a broad but common ground"[27] and has afforded schools broad discretion to control the content of their curricula and to choose which cultural values they wish to promote.[28] The current Court, in particular, believes that education is "primarily the responsibility of parents, teachers, and state and local school officials, and not of federal judges"[29] and will intervene only when a school curricular decision has "no valid educational purpose" and "directly and sharply" implicates constitutional interests.[30]

Until the recent departures of Justices Brennan and Marshall, however, the extent to which courts should defer to educators' decisions was controversial within the Court and often resulted in split rulings and conflicting rationales. The source of the disagreements was the justices' competing visions of the degree to which pluralism and individualism should check the state's right to transmit public values within the public schools. The following sections discuss the Court's efforts to balance these competing interests in three crucial contexts: freedom of religion, freedom of expression, and equal protection challenges to government policy, including school policy.

RELIGIOUS PLURALISM AND THE COMMON CURRICULUM IDEAL

The most intractable conflicts between an assimilationist ideal and its pluralist and individualist counterweights arise when religious parents insist either that their children be excused from general education regulations or that the school curriculum reflect their religious beliefs. In essence, these parents seek protection from what they regard as a dominant alien culture that undermines parental authority, subcultural autonomy, and religious pluralism. Their legal objections to secular authority take two forms: one is that laws of general application, including school laws, burden the free exercise of their religion; the other is that the government has been captured by other religious groups, such as secular humanists, to the extent that government is establishing a religious culture contrary to their own and coercing their children to assimilate into it. The following sections elaborate on these objections and describe the Court's fluctuating, often conflicting, responses to both types of claims.

SECESSION AND EXCUSAL REQUESTS

Religion-based resistance to common standards occasionally manifests itself as open defiance of general laws. Religious parents refuse to comply with compulsory school laws; religious workers defy workplace rules inconsistent with their beliefs; and religious citizens defy criminal laws that compel them to act contrary to deeply held convictions. In defense of their recalcitrance, believers assert that the government regulation in question violates the free exercise clause of the First Amendment and the American commitments to religious pluralism and individual autonomy.

In 1972, Amish families in Green County, Wisconsin, launched this type of challenge to the Wisconsin compulsory education laws. The families had refused to send their children to school—public or private—after the eighth grade, on the ground that secondary education would

> place[ ] Amish children in an environment hostile to Amish beliefs with increasing emphasis on competition; in class work and sports and with pressure to conform to the styles, manners, and ways of the peer group, [and] also . . . [would take] them away from their community, physically and emotionally, during the crucial and formative adolescent period of life.[31]

In *Wisconsin v. Yoder*, the Court held that this potential threat to the Amish way of life justified the parents' refusal to comply with the attendance laws; Wisconsin had to excuse the Amish children from attendance requirements imposed on other Wisconsin school-age children.

The Court began its opinion by restating the *Pierce* compromise. The states can, the Court noted, impose reasonable regulations for the control of education. But the state's interest in preparing young people for meaningful participation in political and social life must be weighed against the parents' or other caretaker's interest in directing the upbringing of the child and observing the tenets of their religion.[32] As applied to the Amish and to their limited request that their children be excused only from secondary education, the balance tipped toward the parents.

Yoder, at first glance, appears to be a significant victory for religious pluralism and for individual autonomy. Yet on closer inspection, it establishes only a narrow exception to compulsory education laws. The Court remarked, with approval, that the Amish keep to themselves, do not "eliminat[e] jobs that might otherwise be held by adults,"[33] are productive and law-abiding, and "reject public welfare."[34] Also, the members of this insular group of pacifist farmers requested only that their children be excused from secondary-level education. As such, the religious pluralism respected in *Yoder* was highly qualified and relatively nonthreatening. Indeed, in no subsequent decision has the Court concluded that any other religious person could be excused from any other general criminal statute on the ground that compliance with the act interfered with his or her religious beliefs.

Nevertheless, *Yoder* struck an important cultural chord in protecting the Amish community's separateness. As Justice Burger stated, "Even their idiosyncratic separateness exemplifies the diversity we profess to admire and encourage."[35] What Americans *profess* to admire and encourage is surely an important part of our national character. *Yoder* reflects the diversity-affirming part of our character and expresses the common belief that religious autonomy must, on occasion, trump the interest in common standards.

There is, of course, another side to our character—one that has prevailed more often in the Court and in other public decision-making settings and that reflects an often compelling collective interest in denying religious persons' right to be excused from general obligations. The recent case of *Employment Division v. Smith* best expresses that other side.

In 1990, the Court addressed whether the state of Oregon could criminalize sacramental use of peyote by members of the Native American Church. Oregon's general laws regarding use of controlled substances made no exception for peyote, unlike the laws of several other states. Smith argued that his free exercise of religion interest overcame the state's interest in regulating use of peyote.[36]

The Court disagreed and held that the Free Exercise Clause allows "application of a neutral, generally applicable law to religiously motivated action."[37] It distinguished *Yoder* on the ground that *Yoder* involved both free exercise of religion and the *Pierce*-based parental right to direct the upbringing of one's children. In the absence of such a "hybrid" right or specific evidence that the law was intended to discriminate against religious practices, the interests of the political majority trump those of the dissenting religious person or community.[38]

Many religious and cultural pluralists regarded *Smith* as scandalous because the Court interpreted freedom of religion in a way that greatly curtails the ability of religious people to defy general laws on religious grounds.[39] Not only to Native Americans but also to other people who regard defiance of general standards as critical to perpetuation of their alternative ways of life and to their religious autonomy, the opinion was deeply disheartening. The full force of the decision and its strongly statist tone are most vivid in the following passage from Justice Scalia's majority opinion:

> The government's ability to enforce generally applicable prohibitions of socially harmful conduct, like its ability to carry out other aspects of public policy, "cannot depend on measuring the effects of a governmental action on a religious objector's spiritual development." . . . to make an individual's obligation to obey such a law contingent upon the law's coincidence with his religious beliefs, except where the State's interest is "compelling"—permitting him, by virtue of his beliefs, "to become a law unto himself,". . . .[40]

Although doubtless aware that deference to political processes can result in laws that take inadequate account of the beliefs, practices, and sensibilities of nondominant communities, Justice Scalia argued that this "unavoidable consequence of democratic government must be preferred to a system in which each conscience is a law unto itself or in which judges weigh the social importance of all laws against the centrality of all religious beliefs."[41] His response was fortified by his apparent confidence that a society that prides itself on constitutional values, such as freedom of religion, is likely to be solicitous of those values in its legislation.[42] In other words, Justice Scalia and a majority of the Court trust the American people and their elected officials to take religious pluralism into account when writing and enforcing general laws.

Quite naturally, this trust is not shared by all—especially not by people whose religious interests are most often overlooked by the majority. Many multiculturalists and religious fundamentalists believe that the majority does not and will not accommodate their concerns. Some of them so object to the practices and values of the dominant culture that they demand an unbounded right to secede from all general rules, to develop their own curricula, or to raise their children at home with no instruction in dominant cultural practices.

Yet excusing citizens from general obligations, including schooling, when-ever those obligations conflict with their religion clearly imperils other important public purposes. The exodus of such people ultimately could compromise the very interests that make the request for excusal compelling. For example, to allow parents to educate their children at home exclusively within their religious tradition can, and sometimes does, mean that the children will be taught that women are subordinate to men, that Jews are a people to be despised, that African-Americans are inferior, and that homo-sexuals are doomed to hell. Faith, in religious terms, can require that the believer suspend critical judgment or conventional methods of scientific proof in favor of spiritual conversions, biblical authority, or deference to a higher power.

People who doubt the potentially violent collision between secular consti-tutional values and some religious people's convictions give neither set of values due respect. Clearly, to invoke pluralism as a reason to permit unfet-tered secession by religious families from public lessons is to ignore that this may permit escape into lifestyles that teach intolerance of other practices or beliefs. It therefore conceivably could produce adults who, if given political power, would reject pluralism as a common aspiration. Consequently, the Scalia emphasis on state power to enforce generally applicable standards of conduct reflects a critical part of our constitutional character—a part that can prove essential to the preservation of individual liberty and to communal ends. Likewise, however, an emphasis on democratic values without boundaries can undermine individual liberties and the common interest in pluralism and diversity.

Yoder reflects an important constitutional interest when it defers to a minority religious group, even when the group seeks to withdraw their children from part of the primary stage of acculturation and thus may compromise their children's future ability to assimilate into the dominant secular culture. It is the high-water mark of tolerance for religious difference in American constitutional law.

Yet *Smith* reflects an important constitutional counterweight—deference to majority-imposed standards of conduct even when they conflict with central practices of a religious minority and even when the state interest in the majority-imposed standard is fairly weak. *Smith* is the low-water mark of tolerance for religious difference in American constitutional law.

Smith and *Yoder* both are good law at present. The vast terrain between them enables a wide range of theorists to claim constitutional authority for very different accounts of compulsory education. Commentators can plausibly argue that either moderate, if not strong, pluralism or national core curricularism is consistent with our constitutional heritage.

This means, among other things, that religion-based objections to common education requirements cannot be deflected as easily as some core curricularists or secularists might hope. If the justification for a core curriculum is to assimilate American schoolchildren into an American culture, then one must consider that our national culture respects idiosyncratic subcultural separateness even when it means a separate education. Thus, religious parents' desire that their children be excused from exposure to the core curriculum must be given due consideration.

All students who are not allowed to opt out of the core, however, should be taught about the conflicting concerns that animate *Yoder* and *Smith*. They should recognize that our collective ends often may conflict with religious subcultural practices and that the Court's unwillingness to disrupt general laws stems in part from its assumption that American citizens will take these subcultural differences into account when voting on public measures. Awareness that both *Yoder* and *Smith* represent key aspects of our dominant cultural practices may sensitize policy makers, including reformers, to the commitment to religious pluralism within the national *unum*. An *American* education, if defined in part by our long-standing constitutional traditions, can ignore neither instinct.

CHALLENGES TO THE CURRICULUM

In their most interesting and provocative challenges of public education, some religious parents seek not to be excused from general school laws but to transform the curriculum. They argue that what is now taught in public schools is itself a form of religion—secular humanism—and thus violates the Establishment Clause,[43] because to make education relentlessly secular is to make it *anti*religious, not merely religiously neutral or areligious. In their view, the strict separation of religion from public schooling that evolved during the 1900s and that was reinforced by Supreme Court decisions in the 1960s through the 1980s has wrongly substituted the religion of secular humanism for that of Christianity. Their goal is to win back the public schools as part of a broader campaign to reinfuse Christian values into American public life. They do not wish to secede from but to revive this public life.

They define *secular humanism* as "the prevailing, overarching intellectual system, in which 'Man' instead of God has become 'the measure of all things.' The result of this profound transvaluation is moral and cultural relativism.

> . . . [A]n indifference to biblical absolutes has been engendered over the centuries by such diverse media as modern science, Enlightenment philosophy, and Nietzschean nihilism and, more recently, hallucinogenic drugs, surrealistic art, and rock music. The result was Communism and Nazism in Europe and the culture of drugs, abortion, homosexuality, and nontraditional sex roles in the United States. From this same perspective, the most powerful vehicle of secular humanism today is the public school."[44]

The religiously based objection to secular humanism simply cannot be reconciled, however, with modern public schools' notions about a proper secular education. Since the mid-1900s, the public schools' primary strategy has been to avoid religion, as traditionally understood, as much as possible.[45] Principles or facts that only are "believable only on the basis of a sectarian religious faith"[46] are omitted from the curriculum. In this way, the public schools seek to avoid political turmoil and to respect their constitutional obligation not to "establish" any religion by subsidizing religious practices or beliefs with public funds or public support. The schools' rationale, best expressed by Amy Gutmann, is that "secular standards constitute a better basis upon which to build *a common education for citizenship* than any set of sectarian religious beliefs—better because secular standards are both a fairer and a firmer basis for peacefully reconciling our differences."[47]

This secularization of public schooling became mandatory national policy in a series of Supreme Court cases that involved prayer[48] and creationism[49] in the public schools. No other decisions better illustrate the sharp tensions between some believers and those citizens who believe that religion is best left outside the public schoolhouse gate.

During the 1960s, secularist parents challenged the practice in some public schools of reciting a prayer in the classroom. The Court, in some of its most controversial cases, concluded that even when a classroom prayer is "optional"[50] or is nondenominational in nature[51] it constitutes impermissible government encouragement of religion.[52]

Resistance to the school prayer rulings erupted in some areas of the country,[53] both in the form of out-and-out defiance and in the form of end-run actions such as placing vehicles—in some communities called "prayer wagons"—on or near school grounds and releasing children during the school day to pray there together. The Court responded by upholding policies that allowed release time for religious students to visit these places for worship, but not if they were located on school premises. School-sponsored prayer during school hours on school property remained unconstitutional.[54]

Prayer that takes place in schools after school hours, if initiated by the students themselves, is a different matter. In 1990, the Court upheld a federal statute under which schools were required to permit extracurricular student prayer groups to convene on school property during noninstructional time.[55] Applying an earlier decision that required a state university to make its facilities available to a student prayer group on terms similar to those offered other student groups,[56] the Court held that "secondary school students are mature enough and are likely to understand that a school does not endorse or support student speech that it merely permits on a nondiscriminatory basis."[57] The Court thus allows some religious activity in public schools, provided that the schools do not place their official imprimatur on it. That is, school-sponsored prayer is unconstitutional, but student-initiated prayer is not.

This tolerance of student-initiated prayer marks the Court's movement away from strict separation of church and state toward a more accommodationist approach to religion in the public sphere. This recent shift has been precipitated by several forces, including a change in Court personnel and the insistence of some religious people and constitutional lawyers that the strict separation approach resulted in case law that wrongly permits the schools to inculcate any values *except* religious ones. These observers claim that the Court discriminates against Christian fundamentalist students in a manner that is just as arbitrary and destructive of subcultural autonomy and cultural pluralism as are race and gender discrimination.

They note that the only public school curriculum content decisions that the Court ever has overturned have been ones that reflect Christian viewpoints. As evidence, they cite both the prayer cases and the creationism decisions, in which courts overturned laws that prevented science teachers from teaching Darwin's theory of evolution and that required "equal time" for the Genesis account of man's evolution whenever Darwinism was discussed.[58] The Supreme Court believed that the sole justification for the bans on the teaching of Darwinism was that Darwinism conflicted with "a particular interpretation of the Book of Genesis by a particular religious group."[59] When a curricular decision was based solely on a particular sect's conviction, the Court determined that it cannot stand.

Some religious parents, of course, deny that laws that require "equal time" for creationism whenever Darwinism is taught are an improper exercise of curricular power[60] and strongly object to the refusal to allow the Genesis account to be discussed as one of many theories. Instead, they side with dissenting Justice Antonin Scalia, who argues that such "voluntary governmental accommodation of religion is not only permissible but desirable.[61] Indeed, they insist that the Court's decisions on religion in schools—with the exception of the cases that permit student prayer groups to meet on school property—contradict the original spirit of the Constitution, which they claim is tolerant of religion in the public sphere. Some of them have set out to correct this heresy through litigation and to prove that public schools have been proselytizing their own brand of religion—secular humanism. Their argument is that, if Christian concepts can be excised from the curriculum because they are inspired by a particular sectarian belief, then secular humanism concepts should be excised from the curriculum on the same ground.

The most significant of these recent attacks on public education are *Mozert v. Hawkins County Board of Education*[62] and *Smith v. Board of School Commissioners of Mobile County*.[63] Both cases reveal how far-reaching some religious objections to the public school curriculum can be and how irreconcilable the differences are between secularists and those who believe that religious themes should be incorporated into school curricula.

In *Mozert*, Vicki Frost requested that her children be excused from a reading program that involved exposure to the Holt, Rinehart, and Winston basic reading series.[64] Mrs. Frost's objections to the Holt reading series were that it contained passages that concerned secular humanism, futuristic supernaturalism, pacifism, magic, false views of death, and other themes inconsistent with her religious beliefs.[65] She testified that "many political issues have theological roots and that there would be 'no way' certain themes could be presented without violating her religious beliefs."[66] Themes she identified as satisfying this test included evolution, feminism, false supernaturalism, magic, and telepathy.[67] She therefore asked that the public schools eliminate all references to these subjects in order to avoid a conflict with her religion.

The federal appellate court refused her request on the ground that if the school were to accommodate her sweeping free exercise demand, it would violate the Establishment Clause principle, set in the creationism cases, that a public school cannot tailor its curriculum to satisfy a particular religion.[68] The court held that mere exposure to the themes contained in the Holt series was not an undue burden on the plaintiff's free exercise of religion, given that the students were not required to affirm any belief or to engage in a practice prohibited by their religion. Moreover, Tennessee would have permitted Mrs. Frost to send her children to a private sectarian school or to teach them at home. Having elected to send her children to public school, she could not excise all portions of the curriculum that she found offensive.

In *Smith v. Board of Commissioners of Mobile County*, Ishmael Jaffree sued the Mobile County School Board on the ground that certain prayer activity in the public schools violated the Establishment Clause.[69] Douglas Smith and others intervened in the case and argued that if Jaffree were to win his case then the court would be violating their Free Exercise rights. In the alternative, these religious parents argued that the Alabama public schools had established the religions of "secularism, humanism, evolution, materialism, agnosticism, atheism, and others."[70] As in *Mozert*, their objections to the public school curriculum included the value relativism built into the textbooks.[71] The intervenors also complained that the history and social studies textbooks downplayed the importance of religion in history and American society. The intentional omission of these facts, they argued, should be just as offensive to First Amendment values as was the mandated omission of discussion of evolution in earlier Court decisions.[72]

The appellate court disagreed, noting that "[s]electing a textbook that omits a particular topic for nonreligious reasons is significantly different from requiring the omission of material because it conflicts with a particular religious belief."[73] Although the curriculum may have contained ideas that were consistent with secular humanism, it also contained information consistent with theistic religion. The principal purpose in using the textbooks, despite the omissions and coincidences with secular humanism beliefs contained in their texts, was not to establish the religion of secular humanism but to advance the legitimate secular purpose of "attempt[ing] to instill in Alabama public school children such values as independent thought, tolerance of diverse views, self-respect, maturity, self-reliance, and logical decision-making."[74]

Had the courts in *Mozert* or *Smith* ruled otherwise, of course, virtually all curricular decisions would have become potential constitutional land mines. Much secular material has theological resonance, as Mrs. Frost herself noted. Thus, if the court were to characterize secularism as antireligious, and thus a violation of the Establishment Clause, it could "leave public education in shreds."[75] Yet the claim that the curriculum cannot be cleansed of all religion without establishing secular humanism or establishing an areligious environment that for religious students is alien, even hostile, is hardly frivolous. Rather, like the Catholics of the 1840s who objected to the strongly Protestant and overtly anti-Catholic bias of northeastern urban schools, Christian fundamentalists of the late 1900s as well as members of some other religious minorities have reason to feel that the modern public schools' emphasis on value relativism, tolerance of difference—including different religions, sexual practices and other differences—is hostile to their religious tenets. Like similar efforts of the nineteenth century Catholics, however, their attempts to tailor the public school curriculum to their parochial religious preferences is likely to fail, given American religious heterogeneity and the express First Amendment proscription against establishment of religion.

Neither religious parents like Vicki Frost or Douglas Smith nor secularist parents like Ishmael Jaffree are likely to be satisfied fully by the Court's balance of assimilation and religious pluralism concerns. All want a constitutional right to their version of religious freedom. Frost and Smith believe that the public schools must acknowledge religious principles and give greater curricular space to religious doctrine. At the least, they request the unchecked right to opt out—to be let alone by the secular world, unmolested, for free religious inquiry and practice. At the most, they request transformation of public culture to match their religious values. Neither request is likely to become a constitutional right.

Strong secularists, in contrast, believe that public schools should give no curricular space to teaching religious values—though they can teach about religions, as relevant to secular courses. They, too, seek to be left alone, but in a different sense. They demand that, in the public sphere, religion must be absent or must, at most, assume a muted, nonaspirational, and, above all, noninculcative role. In the future, this request likewise is unlikely to receive constitutional protection, at least not in its strongest form. The current Court has evinced an increased willingness to allow greater government accommodation of sectarian beliefs through tax credits,[76] exemptions from federal discrimination laws,[77] policies that permit prayer groups to meet on public school property,[78] federal grants awarded to organizations tied to religious denominations that promote abstinence and adoption as alternatives to abortion,[79] and rules that bar health care providers who are recipients of federal funds from discussing abortion as an option with patients.[80] That is, religion need not be cleansed from the public sphere and now may even receive some support through public funds.

Yet American society, like the Court, remains conflicted over this compromise and over the extent to which religion should play a role in public discourse, public values, or public policy. Some believe that the strict separation of church and public education remains the best approach to preserving freedom of, and freedom from, religion. Others disagree and prefer an approach that would grant greater freedom to the government to accommodate religion and that would even permit government to promote religion by granting religious parents and institutions government benefits and financial support on terms equal to those of nonsectarian institutions.

The Court in 1992 was asked to revamp its Establishment Clause doctrine and expressly to renounce the strict separation approach in a case involving a school-sponsored graduation prayer at a public junior high school.[81] It declined, on this occasion, to reject outright the test that it has applied to Establishment Clause challenges since 1971. But several justices indicated in their separate opinions that they now are far more willing to defer to government policy that touches on religion than the Court's past decisions allow. This may mean—as it did in *Smith*—deference to laws that burden some people's religious freedom. Or it may mean—as it did in the student-initiated prayer group cases—deference to laws that permit greater intermingling of religious and secular values in the public sector.

What, precisely, this evolving law of religious freedom and its greater tolerance of religion in public life actually will mean for public education remains to be seen. What is clear is that the hard wall between public education and religion is becoming a somewhat porous screen. Just how much religion, and what kind, will be permitted to seep into the public school curriculum increasingly will depend on the particular school officials' curricular choices, as the Court becomes more willing to defer to their decisions even when they touch on the sensitive matter of religious beliefs.

IMPLICATIONS FOR A NATIONAL CORE CURRICULUM

If, as seems probable, the modern Court stays its course of deference to most public school laws, then school officials will enjoy broad power to create, by themselves, a balance between giving religious parents control over their children's educational destinies (as the Court did in *Yoder*), and respect for the need for uniform obedience to democratic will (as the Court showed in *Smith*). Again, whether one views this as a positive development hinges on one's confidence in the ability of school officials to effect a proper balance.

The religion cases foreshadow more practical than legal obstacles to a national curriculum and national education standards. The national curriculum most likely to gain widespread support either would avoid explicitly religious themes altogether—as have the public schools in the past several decades—or would offer, at most, a neutral presentation of a range of religious viewpoints rather than the appearance of endorsing any one religious perspective. Yet both silence and neutrality are unacceptable alternatives to some devout parents, especially to some Christian fundamentalists. Although they have no constitutional right at present to object to either approach, they may bring considerable political pressure to bear on education policy makers, who should take seriously their pluralism and autonomy-based concerns.

Two responses to their concerns are conceivable. One is to make the national curriculum optional; that is, allow parents who so request to have their children excused from the general requirements, as their religious beliefs dictate. A second, nonexclusive option is to establish a national core curriculum that is silent on religion but that permits local private schools to supplement that curriculum with any religious instruction they believe should be added. Indeed, this latter option likely is required by the Court's decisions in *Pierce* and *Meyer*.

Any viable national curriculum proposal likely would include both options, though the first—to permit parents to opt out of the curriculum—clearly could undermine the objective of a common national culture. The most challenging issue is whether the opt-out requests would be freely granted or available only to religious families that match the stringent criteria imposed in *Yoder*. In other words, how many citizens should be allowed to grow up without the common knowledge that is Hirsch's objective? At what point does their secession doom the project?

This case law highlights the important constitutional implications of these questions. Permitting parents to opt out of the national curriculum on religious grounds would further the First Amendment value of freedom of religion. But denying them that option would promote the democratic value of granting the government power to enforce generally applicable laws that further public policy as democratically determined. Preserving the neutrality of the curriculum, rather than infusing it with a particular religious viewpoint, would respect the constitutional interest in avoiding establishment of religion and thereby better preserve religious freedom and the common interest in avoiding political hostility and disruption. Yet cleansing the curriculum of all religious themes might so alienate devout parents that they would withdraw their children from the public schools, thereby deepening divisions between these families and the larger community as well as forcing them to assume the significant financial burden of private school tuition or the time and expense of home schooling.

Despite the complexity of this dilemma and of the religion case law, one matter is clear: in the United States, the issue of whether, and to what extent, the common concern for uniform education trumps the individual interest in escape from uniform standards is widely recognized as a difficult issue that involves two cherished values in perpetual tension. In the bitter struggles over where to draw the line, we often lose sight of the striking consensus among us about what is at stake. Few Americans, upon reflection, would deny that the Amish, members of the Native American Church, and Mrs. Frost all raise colorable constitutional concerns when they resist common standards. Likewise, few thoughtful observers deny that at some point religion-based resistance becomes intolerable, given our common interest in at least minimal shared obligations and values. As such, we likely can agree that any American curriculum must consider both interests though not on how it should do so. The final chapter returns to this consensus and conflict and elaborates on their concrete curricular implications.

IDEOLOGICAL PLURALISM AND THE CALL FOR COHERENCE

Many argue that the chief danger of a national core curriculum is not that it might favor the secular over the religious but that it would discourage local curricular experimentation and could undermine ideological diversity. That is, it would undermine freedom of expression.

These people point out that whenever government is allowed to fund, regulate, and deliver formal schooling on state-designated topics, freedom of expression is imperiled. To allow the federal government or any national-level body to set uniform curricular standards for all American public schools would increase this risk because the power over school content would become even more centralized than it now is. Freedom of expression within the schools thus could be compromised by Hirsch-like reform.

Yet what does it mean to claim that schools should respect freedom of expression? Freedom of expression principles typically presuppose a rational, autonomous, adult right-bearer; but in the elementary and secondary school context the individual is a child, not a mature decision maker. This immaturity means that many adults—parents, teachers, the local community, and the state—must and do control the child's exposure to ideas and her freedom to speak and act. Yet the child's immaturity and impressionability also make the unbridled exercise of this adult influence and control highly problematic. This suggests a conundrum: freedom of expression is in some respects both incompatible with, yet indispensable to, formal schooling. We expect, in a liberal society, government neutrality toward various constructions of the good life. But education of children simply cannot be done in a wholly viewpoint-neutral fashion.[82]

In the religion context, the government can attempt to avoid endorsement of a particular viewpoint by divorcing religion from the public school curriculum. Only those who deem all secular instruction to be a form of religious favoritism can claim that religious viewpoint discrimination is occurring. Yet with the remaining school subjects—such as history, civics, and literature—viewpoint discrimination, even on political issues, is impossible to avoid. Indeed, American public education intentionally attempts to "predispose children to accept those ways of life that are consistent with sharing the rights and responsibilities of citizenship in a democratic society."[83] Public education is a form of "government speech"[84] that is funded by public money; government therefore necessarily must exercise viewpoint control over its content.[85] For example, most citizens would object strongly to publicly funded education that renounced the constitutional values of freedom of religion or expression, that taught racial inequality, or that denied due process.

A further complexity of First Amendment analysis in the public education context is that K through 12 schooling is compulsory and day-long. The constitutional right to opt out of these compulsory education requirements is severely circumscribed. That schooling is compulsory means that the potential threat to liberal values—of which freedom of expression is arguably most critical—is exceptional. That the student spends her entire day at school in multiple contexts means that her interest in free expression may change from setting to setting throughout the day: speech in the classroom may deserve treatment distinct from speech in the locker room, in the student newspaper, or during a school assembly.

For all of these reasons, public schooling raises especially difficult First Amendment dilemmas. At root, these reflect a classic, irresolvable conflict, which Mark Yudof describes as follows:

> The ideal education necessarily requires the location of an Archimedean point, a point positioned somewhere between critical reflection and grounding in the contingent circumstances of society. . . .
>
> How, then, is society to account for and to achieve the Archimedean point in education? . . . [T]here may be no optimal, theoretical balance between basic education and an all-pervasive indoctrination. Instead, there may only be an evolutionary process, worked at day by day, and guided by common sense, moderation, and an appreciation of conflicting values.[86]

Put another way, the ideal democratic education process must seek to achieve "conscious social reproduction in its most inclusive form",[87] yet also to avoid repression, indoctrination, or subordination—a complex task indeed.

The following cases show how the Court's view of this task has changed over time. During the 1960s and 1970s, the Court was critical of public school policies that chilled students' freedom of expression or demanded conformity, in the absence of a showing that the speech would disrupt school operations. During the 1980s, however, the Court swung toward broad acceptance of regulation of student expression, despite the potential compromise of free speech values. These incompatible constructions of school authority and individual dissent collided head-on in 1982, when a factionalized Court could not muster a consensus as to how public schools must reconcile the relevant concerns when making library book removal decisions.

The current Court's primary response to the complex challenge of reconciling freedom of expression interests with compulsory schooling requirements is to defer to local school officials. Once again, this means that public officials and the general citizenry—not the courts—are primarily responsible for protecting ideological minorities from unreasonable domination by the majority. Multiculturalists and other minority spokespeople thus must depend upon average Americans' appreciation of the value of dissent and ideological pluralism when making their appeals for a noisier, less fixed, multiperspective canon, or for the right to develop and teach their own curricula.

In the 1960s and 1970s, the Court established an important baseline assumption that, despite the public schools' undeniable interest in controlling school operations, student conduct, and curricular content, students did not "shed their constitutional rights to freedom of speech or expression at the schoolhouse gate."[88] On the contrary, the Court insisted that

> the vigilant protection of constitutional freedoms is nowhere more vital than in the community of American schools. . . . [T]he First Amendment "does not tolerate laws that cast a pall of orthodoxy over the classroom."[89]

Thus when, in 1965, Des Moines school officials adopted a policy that no student could wear an armband to school, the Court struck it down as a violation of students' expressive freedom.[90]

The school principals had learned of a plan hatched by parents and students to publicize their objections to the Vietnam War by wearing black armbands and fasting.[91] Three students—ages thirteen, fifteen, and sixteen—wore armbands and were disciplined.[92] The Supreme Court ruled in *Tinker v. Des Moines School District* that these armband protests were not disciplinable because they constituted protected speech, which could not be punished without "evidence of . . . interference, actual or nascent, with the school's work or of collision with the rights of other students to be secure and to be let alone."[93] Rather, the forbidden conduct had "materially and substantially [to] interfere with the requirements of appropriate discipline in the operation of the school."[94]

This was a generous standard from the students' perspective. It rejected the view that the controlled nature of the school environment requires that students have no freedom of expression on campus. It likewise rejected placing the burden on students to show that their speech poses no danger to the school operations. On the contrary, the test required the school to justify its disciplinary decision if speech rights were involved.

Many school lawyers read *Tinker* to impose significant limits on schools' disciplinary authority. The implication was that schools should strive to resemble, as much as possible, the familiar First Amendment marketplace of ideas, and students should be treated as near-adult trainees in democratic freedom. Students should be given broad speech rights subject only to weighty public concerns, such as the likelihood of disruption or harm to others—concerns that even libertarians believe can justify government restriction of individual autonomy. *Tinker* sent a strong signal that the assimilation ends of public schools must be tempered by individualism and plural-ism, even at the elementary and secondary school levels. Inculcating *American* values, in other words, meant permitting students to question dominant cultural practices, including government policy. Dissent was to be tolerated within the public school setting.

This celebration of autonomy and ideological pluralism was fairly short-lived, though. As was true of *Yoder*, the opinion contained adequate qualifica-tions such that the Court later could claim that it remained good law, even as the Court so bridled the impact of the case that it became more exception than rule. For example, *Tinker* involved student speech, not teacher speech or the curriculum. Moreover, the form of expression was passive and silent, not loud or vulgar. No evidence of actual disruption of classes was indicated in the record, and the school allowed the wearing of other symbols of political or controversial significance. Thus, the school was regulating non-disruptive political speech on a viewpoint-specific basis, with no evidence that the speech would disrupt school operations. To deny these students' free speech claims would have been the death knell for virtually all student free speech claims. In ruling for them the Court arguably offered little restraint on school officials' authority to regulate speech under other cir-cumstances.

But later cases did more than limit the case to its facts. In several decisions in the 1980s, the Court all but abandoned the emphasis on the school as the marketplace of ideas in favor of an emphasis on order, civility, and broad deference to educators' pedagogical choices. These cases reflect a quite different and far less pluralistic vision of the assimilation power of the public schools.

REPUBLICAN CIVILITY

The first of the 1980s cases involved the discipline of a high school student for giving an allegedly lewd speech at a school assembly.[95] Matthew Fraser spoke at the assembly on behalf of a classmate who was running for student office. In endorsing his friend, Fraser referred to the candidate in terms described by the Court as "an elaborate, graphic, and explicit sexual metaphor."[96] An illustrative excerpt from his speech is the following: "I know a man who is firm—he's firm in his pants, he's firm in his shirt, his character is firm—but most . . . of all, his belief in you, the students of Bethel, is firm."[97] Other parts of the speech described to the candidate's tendency to "drive hard," even to "climax," and "nail it to the wall."[98] Student reaction to the speech included hooting and yelling, some gestures simulating the sexual activities to which

Fraser alluded, and—among other students—bewilderment and embarrassment. One teacher stated that it was necessary to spend part of the following scheduled class to discuss the speech with her students, though the Court did not elaborate on the nature of this discussion.

The Court upheld the discipline against Fraser in terms that suggest that *Tinker* no longer was the controlling take on student expressive freedom. Of course, the facts were different enough from those of *Tinker* for people to argue that the cases' holdings are consistent. But the tone of *Fraser* and of post-*Fraser* cases confirms that the case has narrowed the scope of student free speech.

The Court began its analysis with the now-familiar incantation that public schools must prepare students for citizenship and inculcate appropriate civic values. Among these values, said the Court, are "the habits and manners of civility."[99] The school had the power to "determine that the essential lessons of civil, mature conduct [could not] be conveyed in a school that tolerates lewd, indecent, or offensive speech."[100] As such, the school had the power to discipline speech such as that used by "this confused boy."[101]

The audience of the speech included "boys and girls," some of whom were "only" fourteen years old. As the Court noted, the speech "glorifying male sexuality"[102] may have been especially offensive to the girls in the audience. Given the students' age, that the students were a "captive audience" at the assembly, and that the school had the power to remove materials that are vulgar, the school acted well within its disciplinary authority.

One possible interpretation of *Fraser* is that it simply is an extension of the government speech doctrine. The assembly was sponsored by the school, and attendance was mandatory. As such, for the school to permit language such as that used by Matthew Fraser arguably would lend official force to his crass delivery. Under this interpretation, Fraser could use the same language in other school settings—such as the locker room—but not in any official, school-sponsored document or activity.

But there is a second, more compelling account: *Fraser* grants schools wide power affirmatively to inculcate particular values—in this case, civility and, perhaps, respect for females—such that Fraser could have been disciplined even if he had used the same language on the practice field or in the cafeteria. Just as the school could punish physical assaults, cheating, stealing, and other wrong behavior regardless of the school function or "zone" within which it occurs, the school likewise could ban talk like Fraser's anywhere on school property.

Yet *Fraser* does not *unambiguously* embrace either account. Rather, the

Court's analysis is simplistic and ignores the implications of its far-flung rhetoric. For example, *Fraser* arguably means that the current Court would approve of aggressive efforts by schools to inculcate nonsexist, nonracist values by proscribing language in the curriculum and elsewhere on campus that were offensive to females or to members of racial minorities. Such language might too be deemed "lewd, indecent or offensive." Whether proscribing sexist and racist talk would be a defensible and worthwhile policy for a public school to adopt—of considerable contemporary, practical concern[103]—was unclear. The Court likely did not consider any application of its unqualified support for disciplinary action based upon school officials' estimations of vulgarity or civility.

More apparent is that the Court intended to establish a strong presumption in favor of broad school authority over student speech at official school functions. Unlike *Tinker*, in which the analytical touchstone was street-corner discourse, *Fraser* treated the public high school more like the site of a governmentally funded performance of a public morality play. Students are children, and the teachers' job is to protect them. Civility, not just civics, is part of the common lessons that public schools properly should convey. Adults need to demonstrate that civility and need to be able to enforce it without judicial interference.

Nothing in *Fraser* explains how this open-ended power should be reconciled with the Court's concern in the 1960s and 1970s that schools not be shrouded in a pall of orthodoxy and not let their inevitable desire for order chill dissent, even when the dissent is tasteless or evokes discomfort in some. As it did in *Smith*, the Court in *Fraser* simply deferred uncritically to school officials, based on apparent confidence in those officials' ability to balance correctly the interests of autonomy and assimilation. In doing so, the Court declared vulgar, if not obscene, a speech that many secondary school students of 1966, let alone 1986, would consider tame.

Fraser posed a tougher, subtler, and potentially more significant dilemma than the Court's opinion suggests. It could have been, but was not, the occasion of a nuanced discussion of the multiple constitutional values at stake. Instead, the Court offered a simple, slogan-filled indictment of a "confused boy's" lapse into trashy "vulgarity" and offered no meaningful check on local officials' power to inculcate "civility."

Two years later, the Court took only five pages to dispense with the argument that high school students have a strong right to freedom of expression in student newspapers that are financed by school funds and supervised by school employees. *Hazelwood School District v. Kuhlmeier*[104] established virtually unreviewable government power over any "school-sponsored expression." This power extends beyond formal classroom teaching to all "school-sponsored publications, theatrical productions, and other expressive activities that students, parents, and members of the public might reasonably perceive to bear the imprimatur of the school."[105] With respect to such expression, the school's censorship authority is subject only to the following limitation:

> [I]t is only when the decision to censor a school-sponsored publication, theatrical production, or other vehicle of student expression has no valid educational purpose that the First Amendment is so "directly and sharply implicate[d]," . . . as to require judicial intervention to protect students' educational rights.[106]

Hazelwood makes plain that the Court regards the school curriculum as government speech and that the government has vast power to control its own messages. It rejects the understanding, shared by many lower courts and school officials prior to *Hazelwood*, that student newspapers are public fora and thus not regulable in the manner of the formal, school-endorsed curriculum. In so ruling, the Court noted that the faculty advisor chose the student editors, assigned stories, and was in other ways the final authority of the content of the paper and that the principal reviewed each issue before it could be distributed. Given these facts and that school funds were used to produce the paper, the Court declared that the school had not created an open, public forum and thus could impose content restrictions on the newspaper as it could on the rest of its curriculum.

The conclusion that the formal curriculum is not an open forum surprised no one. Indeed, the curriculum, more than any other aspect of the public school, surely cannot be deemed an open forum in the sense that *all* dissenting voices of students and others may demand a chance to be heard as they might be on the street corner. In one way, therefore, this is a sensible reflection of the government's right and responsibility to control its messages. The school's interest in its lessons exceeds that of maintaining order, such that even nondisruptive challenges of the curriculum should not be allowed to compete with the school's message. *Tinker*, which speaks in terms of maintaining order rather than of inculcating values, offers too little power to the school officials in the arena of curricular control.

But this was not the Court's only option. The curriculum clearly is the school's most powerful potential influence on its students; so, to give the government, in the form of school officials, unreviewable power to craft its content is, or should be, a serious First Amendment concern. Indeed, it is arguably more serious than to permit the government vast disciplinary power over student extracurricular speech. Moreover, speech within a student newspaper is not as likely to be seen as school-sponsored expression as are teacher-delivered lessons. *Hazelwood* therefore stunned many commentators, as it dismissed so easily the powerful claim that a newspaper is distinguishable from the formal curriculum—that, at the least, it has a bivocal character (student and school-sponsored) that deserves recognition, particularly given the constitutional link between a free press and full freedom of expression. Students, many commentators believed, were being taught bad civics when school officials were allowed to impose prior content-based restraints on their student newspaper.

The most worrisome implication of *Hazelwood*, however, is that school officials now enjoy virtually unbounded power to control all "school-sponsored" expression and to assure that speech in school not be "vulgar" or uncivil, at least not when other students are present and may be upset. Only when school officials' decisions have no valid educational purpose—an exceedingly liberal standard—is the Court willing to intervene. Moreover, because *Fraser* and *Hazelwood* dealt with high school students, one can assume that the officials' power is even stronger at the elementary level. So, although *Tinker* may have offered these officials too little power over the curriculum, *Fraser* and *Hazelwood* offer them far too much, with little serious consideration of the potential First Amendment consequences.

Only once, in 1982, did the Court offer a more reflective analysis of the perils of granting to local officials unmonitored control over the public school curriculum and of how their provincialisms, prejudices, and desire to avoid political backlash can inspire censorship of worthy materials. Unfortunately, the Court was badly divided and offered little comfort to those who favor diversity in public school curricula or who fear that unmonitored local decision-making may result in exclusion of important texts and themes. This final freedom-of-expression decision is an especially good vehicle for exploring the tension between school inculcation power and the value of dissent, given the Court's multiple opinions and the politics that animated the school board's decision.

A "RIGHT TO RECEIVE IDEAS"?

In *Board of Education, Island Trees Union Free School District No. 26 v. Pico*, the Court addressed whether public school officials could remove several books from the school library on the ground that they were "anti-American, anti-Christian, anti-Semitic, and just plain filthy."[107] The removal decision was inspired by the activism of a conservative parents' organization, which had prepared a list of objectionable books. Two school board members received a copy of the list at a convention sponsored by the organization. After discovering that the high school and junior high school libraries contained some of these texts, the board retrieved them from the libraries to review them. The board then appointed a committee of four parents and four staff members to read the books and to recommend whether they should be retained. Although the committee recommended that most of the books remain on the shelves, the board ignored its advice and ordered that all but two be removed and that, of the remaining two, one be available only with parental approval.[108] The list of banned books included *Go Ask Alice, Soul on Ice, Slaughterhouse Five, The Naked Ape, Down These Mean Streets,* and *A Hero Ain't Nothin' But a Sandwich.*[109]

The case generated multiple opinions by the justices, though a plurality of the Court held that the decision to remove the books was unconstitutional. Even the justices who believed that the school acted improperly nevertheless went to elaborate lengths to make clear that their ruling applied *only* to book removal decisions, not acquisition decisions or curriculum decisions. By implication, these justices would not disrupt curricular decisions in the absence of facts more egregious than those before the Court in *Pico.*

The plurality opinion was written by Justice Brennan, who based his opinion on the students' alleged right to receive ideas.[110] He also based his result on the unique character of the school library, which he described as an environment that is "especially appropriate for the recognition of the First Amendment rights of students."[111] Use of the library is voluntary and optional, and students' book selections there are a matter of individual choice. Given the library's special characteristics, Justice Brennan concluded that school officials' discretion over book removals cannot be exercised "in a narrowly partisan or political manner."[112] None would deny, he said, that a Democratic school board could not remove all books written by Republicans. The constitutional test should be whether the motivation of the school board members was based on narrow political or partisan views, not whether it was based on the members' sense that a book is vulgar or educationally unsuitable. A school may protect itself from a First Amendment challenge, even under the Brennan approach, simply by adopting "established, regular, and facially unbiased procedures for the review of controversial materials."[113] Thus, the plurality invited districts to empanel committees to make removal decisions and hinted broadly that these decisions would be upheld if proper procedures were observed.

Justice Blackmun wrote a separate opinion in which he agreed with Justice Brennan's result but not with his more sweeping assertion that the outcome was based on a right to receive ideas or even on the unique nature of the library.[114] Rather, he concluded that school officials necessarily must choose among books without judicial interference, based on their assessment of suitability for students, the importance of the subject, and the amorphous public welfare; but they cannot act for the sole purpose of restricting access to political ideas or social perspectives. A constitutional problem therefore is not raised by the mere failure to provide an idea; the Constitution bars discrimination *between* ideas for partisan or political reasons.[115] Justice Blackmun then summarized the critical tension at issue in *Pico* as follows:

> Certainly, the unique environment of the school places substantial limits on the extent to which official decisions may be restrained by First Amendment values. But that environment also makes it particularly important that some limits be imposed.[116]

This entails, he said, a "delicate accommodation" of competing constitutional concerns.[117] Moreover, he observed that the accommodation must be made in curricular matters as well as in library book removal matters. Unfortunately, he offered no more specific instructions as to how officials should effect this balance or as to how courts might monitor them.

Given the weaknesses in both the Brennan and Blackmun analyses, Justice Rehnquist's acerbic dissent was the most powerful opinion and the most likely to influence the post-Brennan Court. Rehnquist began by "cheerfully conced[ing]" that Brennan's "extreme example" of a Democratic school board removing all texts by Republicans would constitute a constitutional violation.[118] But he then catalogued the many differences between government-as-educator and government-as-sovereign and noted that, as educator, government must inculcate values and engage in the selective conveyance of ideas, which is a role "fundamentally inconsistent with any constitutionally required eclecticism in public education."[119] He therefore deemed it entirely appropriate for school officials to act on their personal, social, moral, and political views and ridiculed Brennan's "right to receive ideas" proposition. At most, Rehnquist remarked, school children have a—limited—right to *express* ideas.[120]

Rehnquist recommended that students who wish to explore themes not included in the school library obtain books at the public library after school hours and denied that the school library is a place for free-wheeling inquiry. He also deemed senseless Brennan's distinction between book removal and book obtention, as both decisions affect what ideas are available to the students. Likewise, both bad motives and good motives can produce the same bad outcome: restricted access to ideas. Thus Brennan's analysis was incoherent and inconsistent. Instead, Rehnquist proposed that schools be permitted to remove whatever textbooks they wish, provided they do not preclude discussion about the books or their themes. That is, curricular and related school-content decisions lie beyond the First Amendment, except in the extreme cases cited by Brennan. In all other cases, the inculcative role of public schools makes traditional First Amendment analysis inappropriate.

THE EMERGING CONSENSUS

Despite their internal divergences, the justices all agree that public school officials' authority is greatest when it concerns school-sponsored expression, which includes but is not limited to the curriculum. Most of them believe that in this area the government has virtually free license, short of systematic and intentional deletion of one strand of mainstream political thought, such as Republican ideas, or presentation of sectarian religious ideas that have no secular justification. When the speech is not school-sponsored, however, such as student speech in the cafeteria or on the playing field, then school officials are more constrained. They can discipline the student only if the speech poses a threat to the orderly operation of the school or interferes with the rights of other students. Yet because schools also try to instill in students the value of civility, school officials may also be able to discipline vulgar, offensive speech even when no actual disruption occurs.

All of the justices likewise agree that part of the job that government performs in the public schools is to inculcate specific values—a nonneutral and often viewpoint-specific exercise. Though they deny that government may indoctrinate students, few educational practices short of a compulsory flag salute satisfy their definition of indoctrination. Curricular silences that do not reek of intentional and extreme political bias or that are an attempt to keep strictly religious values apart from public schooling are constitutional. Compulsory exposure to ideas, as opposed to forced affirmation of them, is constitutional. Censorship of offensive, age-inappropriate, vulgar, educationally unsuitable, or other incorrect or undesirable speech is permissible, even commendable. As a matter of doctrine, then, Rehnquist is correct: at most, public school students have only a modest constitutional right to express their ideas; they have no practical right to receive them.

The Court's justifications of school actions in *Tinker* and in *Fraser* and *Hazelwood*, however, represent two very different accounts of First Amendment values in public schools. In *Tinker*, the Court justified school disciplinary power in classic liberal terms: the school must preserve order and prevent harm to other students. Speech that poses neither threat cannot be suppressed, lest students' individual autonomy be unreasonably constrained. But in *Fraser* and *Hazelwood*, the Court justified school power in assimilationist terms: the school must fulfill its role as the guardian of the young students and inculcate in them the habits and manners of civility.

The *Tinker* justification is an embrace of neutrality, as liberals would define it. The intervention of school officials may not be based on the content of the student speech but on the harmful effects it produces. This harm may not, one might infer, include the harm of persuading the audience to agree with the content of the speech. The *Fraser / Hazelwood* justification, however, is an open embrace of nonneutral inculcation of values. Intervention can definitely be based on the content of the speech, especially if the speech might be construed as school-sponsored expression.

Like *Yoder* and *Smith* in the religion context, *Tinker* and *Fraser / Hazelwood* represent competing parts of the American personality: a liberal instinct to permit dissent and escape from common standards struggles with an assimilationist instinct to enforce common standards. Moreover, like *Yoder*, *Tinker* remains ostensibly good law despite subsequent case law that limits its impact.

The problem in both areas is that the Court evades the internal contradictions in its doctrine and imposes no requirement that state and local officials always consider *both* instincts when designing the curriculum or other school policies. Moreover, the current Court, led by the statism of Justice Scalia, seems profoundly unconcerned about protecting the liberal instinct from overweening assimilationist forces.

At least part of the problem is that defining the liberal limits could require the Court to pour content into its phrases habits and manners of civility, common values, good citizenship, the public welfare, or democracy American-style. The Court has excellent reasons for not wanting to do this, ranging from institutional incompetence to make such judgments to federalism. But it also—and less understandably—has abandoned even the more humble, supervisory role of demanding that the school officials justify the content that *they* pour into the phrases. That is, although the Court need not define the phrases itself, it clearly could do a more forceful and sophisticated job of defining the stakes, the relevant concerns, and the constitutional boundaries of the officials' decisions. Otherwise, nothing whatsoever prevents public schools from gutting the curriculum of all controversial themes, demanding that a student newspaper comport with school officials' tastes, or censoring any expression that the faculty or administration officials deem vulgar. If, as seems plainly right, American public schools are not exempt from the First Amendment despite their need for discretionary power over the curriculum, then the courts should not abandon their constitutional role of defining and enforcing schools' First Amendment duties.

Moreover, lest one think that aggressive censorship is a far-fetched possibility, it is worth noting that case law since *Fraser* and *Hazelwood* has upheld school curricular authority to excise such classical texts as *Lysistrata* and Chaucer's *The Miller's Tale* on the ground that they were sexually explicit and excessively vulgar.[121] If these classical texts are censorable, then one can only wonder what the fate of modern literature may be, particularly if it deals with human sexuality. Indeed, scholars who have examined the pattern of censorship in the United States offer discouraging evidence that the threat of a gutted curriculum is serious indeed, especially for ideas that threaten mainstream cultural values.[122]

IMPLICATIONS OF A NATIONAL CORE CURRICULUM

The people who object most to government's vast power to craft the curriculum are parents and students on the fringes of the dominant community's notions of civility, offensiveness, and educational suitability. One such group includes religious fundamentalists, who view the schools as godless, amoral, and corrupting centers of secular humanism. A second important group includes feminists, critical equality theorists, and some members of racial and ethnic minority groups, who likewise view the curriculum as skewed toward particular interests, though their objection centers on its white, male, Eurocentric, Protestant tilt. At the college level, still other groups claim that the tilt now is toward left-centered, gender, race, and ethnic particularism, with the unfortunate consequence of chilling diverse viewpoints and encouraging a regime of "political correctness."

Gay activists more recently have joined this clamor to charge that the curriculum is overtly hostile to gays, lesbians, and bisexuals, to the great psychological detriment of its students and staff members who are themselves gay or bisexual, have gay or bisexual parents, or who are dealing with emerging sexual identity issues.[123] Perhaps ironically, the gay activists' arguments resemble most those of the fundamentalists—their fiercest opponents—in that both groups urge that their ideas are systematically and intentionally purged from the lower school curriculum, and both groups complain that even open acknowledgment by school officials that they are suppressing these ideas jars few peoples' sense of the First Amendment. On the contrary, they note, many people believe that curricular suppression of both fundamentalism and homosexuality is the proper role of public school officials. Teachers who endorse either religion or homosexuality in the classroom risk discipline and even termination.

Yet to the extent that these groups demand curriculum access, more balanced treatment of their concerns, or even the deletion of unfavorable references to their groups or their issues, *Hazelwood* and *Fraser* suggest that they stand little chance of success in the courts. If they instead request that their children be excused from lessons they regard as inhospitable or overtly hostile to their beliefs, they likewise are unlikely to prevail. Those who seek to secede altogether have no constitutional right to do so unless they can match the very restricted criteria set forth in *Yoder*.

This leaves marginal groups with little constitutional recourse other than attending (and paying the tuition of) private schools that respond to their concerns, if any exist. The practical or actual unavailability of the private school option as well as a sense of outrage or injury at being excluded from the common curriculum have caused many of these groups to redirect their principal energies to the people and processes that determine curriculum content. Their lobbying has focused not only on the high-visibility decision makers—such as state and local school officials—but also on low-visibility decision makers, such as librarians, textbook companies, and other hidden influences on curricular content.

The question common to all of these strategies is—again—how broadly and pluralistically shall "we" define the "society" we wish to reproduce? Should the public school curriculum inculcate only the value of secular tolerance or should it include Christian "family values"? Should gender equality or female deference to male authority be the public school's emphasis? Should New York City schools teach students about AIDS and its transmission and about the particulars of "safe sex" practices between male partners? Should a public school library include materials aimed at gay and lesbian or bisexual teenagers that depict homosexuality or bisexuality in positive, accepting terms? That is, *which* voices should be heard in public school classrooms? Thus far, the Court's answer has been that the voices need be only those with the cultural authority or other influence necessary to be heard by those who draft the curriculum. Silences on some topics, and even intentional censorship, are not necessarily unconstitutional.

Yet, as *Tinker* and *Pico* show, judicial confidence in the likelihood that school authorities or their decision making process will preserve adequate room for dissenting voices is not unbounded. Here again, our constitutional hope, if not our enforceable right, is that the decision makers will respect the First Amendment value of vigorous, critical debate and will include a range of voices in the curriculum. One counterweight to a strongly assimilative, viewpoint-specific curriculum is the First Amendment tradition of expressive freedom within the marketplace of ideas. Indeed, and somewhat ironically, it represents a national public value that must be part of the schools' assimilation agenda yet that checks or qualifies other aspects of that agenda. Again, whether school officials and citizens generally appreciate this irony and this tradition is debatable. What is clear is that the current Court has left the matter almost entirely in the officials' and citizens' hands. What we do with this power may depend on whether we are aware that we possess it and on whether we apprehend the First Amendment values at stake.

EQUALITY AND THE CALL FOR COHERENCE

Whether a national curriculum must include a range of voices not only is a matter of individual expressive and religious freedom; it also is a matter of equality.

Indeed, the most commonly expressed objection against a Hirsch-like national curriculum is that it gives unequal treatment to African-American history, to women's history, and to other minority groups' history, literature, language, and cultural concerns. That is, this curriculum debate is, among other things, a debate about the meaning of equal treatment in a pluralistic society.

Americans clearly do not share one account of equality, however, and disagree violently about the proper remedy for inequality.[124] To some Americans, equality means simply that similarly situated persons should be treated the same, whereas to others it means that all persons are entitled to equal opportunity, with the ultimate goal being equal outcomes. Within each approach people diverge over who is similarly situated, what treatment is the same, and what an equal outcome looks like.

Determining which of these accounts should govern American educational policy is central to debates about education programs for children with disabilities, bilingual education, Afrocentric curricula, tracking, educational testing, sex education, vocational education, privatization of schooling, home schooling, vouchers, and—of course—the core curriculum.

The following pages outline the Supreme Court's attempts to define equality and place particular emphasis on its efforts to define racial equality. The decisions discussed here have shaped all other discussions of constitutional equality and are a critical backdrop to contemporary claims that the traditional curriculum is tainted by a national history of discrimination. This section also will address, though in less detail, the complicating equality issues of gender, socioeconomic, language, mental and physical abilities, and sexual identity differences.

EQUAL PROTECTION UNDER LAW

The meaning of constitutional equality lies in the competing constructions of the Equal Protection Clause of the Fourteenth Amendment. Adopted after the Civil War, that Amendment provides that no state shall "deny to any person within its jurisdiction the equal protection of the laws." This mandate does not mean, of course, that laws never can distinguish among citizens, as this would prevent states from providing welfare benefits only to its poorer citizens, providing tax incentives for businesses that promote certain state policies, or offering year-round schooling only to students with special educational needs. Rather, the mandate requires that government distinctions among citizens be reasonable—a very minimal requirement— or, in rarer circumstances, be based on compelling reasons—a very demanding requirement. The dilemma, of course, is to determine which distinctions among citizens are justifiable under either standard.

The classification that the Court deems most difficult to justify is a race-based one. The Fourteenth Amendment was adopted principally "to assure to the colored race the enjoyment of all the civil rights that under the law are enjoyed by white persons."[125] Because eliminating race-conscious laws is the amendment's principal task, any race classification must be based on a compelling and benign state purpose. More than any other form of government classification, race-conscious measures today trigger close judicial scrutiny and are rarely upheld.

Nevertheless, for many years after the Court first began to enforce the Fourteenth Amendment, it found no "unequal protection" even in state action that established separate facilities based on race. Indeed, in 1896 the Court in *Plessy v. Ferguson*[126] upheld enforced separation of whites and blacks on railroad cars. In the Court's view, if these separate facilities "stamp[ed] the colored race with a badge of inferiority," it was "solely because the colored race [chose] to put that construction upon it."[127]

The Court finally renounced *Plessy* over fifty years later in *Brown v. Board of Education of Topeka*,[128] a case involving racially segregated schools. Justice Warren, writing for a unanimous Court, stated unequivocally that "[s]eparate educational facilities are inherently unequal"[129] and thus unconstitutional. The following year, in *Brown II*, the Court sought to enforce *Brown I* by ordering that states desegregate public schools "with all deliberate speed."[130]

Brown has been the subject of endless critical commentary. Some writers have celebrated the case as a breakthrough in empathic understanding,[131] while others have argued that the case was an abuse of judicial power.[132] Still others, such as Professor Derrick Bell, argue that the decision "cannot be understood without some consideration of the decision's value to whites [able] to see the economic and political advantages at home and abroad that would follow the abandonment of segregation."[133] Critics also have condemned the Court for imposing a weak and virtually unenforceable standard for compliance with its desegregation mandate.[134]

The criticisms of *Brown* and its enforcement aside, the case clearly marked a turning point in American constitutional law, if not in American attitudes about racial equality.[135] The decision stressed the link between education and a successful adult life and illuminated education's role as "a principal instrument in awakening the child to cultural values, in preparing him for later professional training, and in helping him to adjust normally to his environment."[136] Moreover, the Court recognized that an equal educational opportunity goes beyond provision of equal physical facilities and extends to intangible factors that can affect the student's "ability to study, to engage in discussions and exchange views with other students."[137] Finally and significantly, the Court acknowledged the stigmatic harms of racism and of treatment that, though ostensibly equal, nevertheless may generate a feeling of inferiority in African-American schoolchildren.[138] The case spoke in terms of the harms of segregation on *all* African-American schoolchildren rather than on any particular student. For these reasons, some people have argued that *Brown* stood for at least limited judicial recognition of group, rather than only individual-based constitutional rights, and for an "equal outcome" construct of educational equality.

The decades after *Brown* were tumultuous and marked not only by massive resistance, foot-dragging, and even total noncompliance but also by the eventual dismantling of intentional, de jure segregation.[139] Although de facto segregation persisted, as did race-based disparities between students' educational achievement levels, the instances of express, intentional, government-sponsored racial classifications all but disappeared, except within remedial statutes designed to undo the impact of past discrimination.

As de jure overt discrimination became less common, judicial attention eventually turned to whether the Equal Protection Clause barred only such intentional discrimination by government or whether it also prohibited private intentional acts or official acts that had a disparate impact on racial minorities but that were not intentional. A majority of the justices took the position that only intentional governmental acts of discrimination violated the Equal Protection Clause.

Relying on this position, the Court in the early 1990s signaled its intention to begin the withdrawal of the federal courts' supervision over school districts on the ground that any remaining racial disparities or segregation patterns in the schools likely flow from private choices, not from intentional, government-sponsored discrimination.[140] The justices do not believe that the Constitution prevents private, societal discrimination that may cause people to cluster with members of their own race, lower members of some racial groups' self-esteem, or cause minority-race students to perform less well than their majority-race peers.

The leading proponent of the contraction of federal court supervision of school officials' policy making has been Justice Scalia, who in *Freeman v. Pitts*[141] made the following observation about modern patterns of racial disparities:

> At some time, we must acknowledge that it has become absurd to assume, without any further proof, that violations of the Constitution dating from the days when Lyndon Johnson was President, or earlier, continue to have an appreciable effect upon current operation of the schools. We are close to that time. . . . We must soon revert to the ordinary principles of our law, of our democratic heritage, and of our educational tradition: that plaintiffs alleging Equal Protection violations must prove intent and causation and not merely the existence of racial disparity, that public schooling, even in the South, should be controlled by locally elected authorities acting in conjunction with parents, and that it is "desirable" to permit pupils to attend "schools nearest their homes."[142]

The Equal Protection Clause today proscribes only intentional race discrimination; legislation that has a racially disparate impact but was not inspired by a purpose to discriminate is constitutional, provided it is otherwise valid and reasonable.[143] So, if a government agency uses an employment test that has a disparate impact on black applicants, this does not deny equal protection unless the plaintiff can prove that the agency selected this test for the purpose of eliminating black applicants. By itself, disparate impact is not enough proof of this purpose.

The Court now defines equal protection as, at most, a guarantee of equal treatment, rather than of equal outcomes or even equal opportunity. Even unequal treatment, however, is permissible as long as it is not intentional.[144] Yet, as many critics of this approach have observed, discriminatory purpose is extremely difficult to establish: few government actors today are likely to make overtly discriminatory remarks or write laws in expressly race-conscious terms. And, as Professor Charles Lawrence has explained, much harmful racism is unconscious and thus escapes scrutiny under the Court's test.[145] To require a showing of intentional discrimination ignores that unintentionally insensitive policies may inflict the same harms as purposeful discrimination. It also accepts as constitutional many private forms of discrimination and implicitly assumes that any public policy that appears neutral on its face is not the result of present and prior governmental choices.

Whether our present official and private policies perpetuate past race discrimination, even without evidence of intent to discriminate, is a fault line that divides many Americans. Justice Scalia believes that it is "absurd" to assume that any present racial disparities are the result of government policies of the 1960s, and many other observers share his skepticism about whether race today determines one's political, social, or economic standing and, if so, whether this is because of intentional racism. Other observers regard it as absurd to assume otherwise unless one takes the dubious position that racial disparities are more easily explained by race-based intellectual and social inferiority of racial minorities than by the existence of interdependent, persistent, public, and private racist practices.

By defining discrimination solely as intentional governmental acts, the Court narrowed possible equal protection claims dramatically. Insensitivity to the concerns of racial minorities, like the insensitivity to the concerns of religious and ideological minorities, becomes a cost of living in a democratic society. Any remedy for racially disparate outcomes that flow from racially neutral policies must come from the legislature not from the courts.

Of course, state and federal legislators responded to these concerns and drafted statutes designed to reverse the effects of past societal and government discrimination. Significant among the early measures were the Civil Rights Act of 1964 and the Voting Rights Act, which, along with other civil rights acts, prompted significant changes in government practices. Most controversial of these changes was the adoption of so-called affirmative action policies, as well as other expressly race-conscious measures designed to expand opportunities for historically underrepresented groups. These policies, more than any other civil rights legislation, have been deeply divisive both on and off the Court.

The constitutional dilemma posed by race-conscious policies is plain when one contrasts Justice Harlan's famous statement that "our Constitution is color-blind"[146] with Justice Blackmun's subsequent counter-adage that "[i]n order to get beyond racism, we must first take account of race."[147]

Perhaps the greatest constitutional challenge for the Court in the late twentieth century has been to reconcile these competing insights.

In education, these judicial aphorisms collided head-on in 1978, when Allan Bakke challenged a public California medical school's policy of setting aside a fixed number of places in the entering class for members of designated racial groups.[148] Bakke, a white applicant, was denied admission to the medical school and claimed that the set-aside policy constituted racial discrimination. His challenge eventually was heard by the United States Supreme Court, where the justices were as divided as other Americans about his claim.

Writing for a plurality of the Court, Justice Lewis Powell concluded that the policy was unconstitutional.[149] He first remarked that *all* race-based classifications, including those designed to benefit an historically underrepresented group, should be subject to the same strict standard of judicial review. He then rejected the arguments that the Equal Protection Clause extends to group-centered rather than individual rights and that programs designed to benefit racial minorities are costless. On the contrary, Powell noted, both the dispreferred candidates and those who benefit from a racial set-aside may be hurt. The former may lose out on a spot in the medical school; the latter may suffer the stigma of having been admitted primarily because of their race rather than for their academic qualifications. Powell therefore required Cal-Davis to offer compelling reasons for the set-aside.

Powell rejected all but one of the school's justifications for the program. First, he noted that any plan designed to assure a particular percentage or quota of minority race members in each class is invalid. Second, he concluded that, although an effort to ameliorate past discrimination may be constitutional, there had been no finding that this school had committed a statutory or constitutional violation. An unelected, low-visibility faculty committee should not be allowed to decide for itself who is a deserving victim of discrimination. Third, Powell rejected as unproven the school's claim that minority medical school graduates are more likely than white graduates to provide health care to an underserviced segment of the population. The school's fourth justification—to promote diversity—*was* legitimate but could not be advanced through the unnecessary and rigid means of establishing a fixed number of places for minority candidates.

The dissenting justices argued that race classifications adopted to benefit racial minorities should be reviewed under an intermediate standard rather than under the Court's more rigorous strict scrutiny test. In their view, the discrimination against whites that may flow from these race-conscious remedial plans is substantially different from the discrimination against blacks that inspired the Fourteenth Amendment. Thus, they should be subject to a different standard of judicial review. Justice Thurgood Marshall was the most forceful of the justices on this point, arguing that to be black in America is to be treated differently and that this different, less favorable treatment is directed at blacks as a *group*.[150] Group-based remedies, such as this one, are a justifiable response to group-based harms. As such, group-based measures that benefit racial minorities serve an important, legitimate governmental purpose, whereas similar measures that benefit whites do not.

Eventually, however, the Powell notion that "race is race is race," for purposes of equal protection analysis prevailed. Although in several interim cases the Court hinted that it might approve of race-conscious remedial measures in certain circumstances, in 1988 it retreated from these cases and required that state and local governments first prove that past, local discrimination by the government agency in question caused the racial disparities before they could adopt a voluntary race-conscious remedial plan. Only race-based classifications authorized by U.S. Congress can be justified by a less demanding standard of proof.[151] As a practical matter, this means that state or local government agencies, including schools, now cannot adopt race-conscious plans except in response to a specific finding of past, intentional discrimination by that government agency. The holding casts doubt on a host of measures designed to increase diversity in education, such as scholarships and hiring policies that give preferential treatment to minority applicants.

The reigning spirit of the current era of equal protection doctrine is best captured by Justice Scalia's remark that "where injustice is the game, . . . turn-about is not fair play."[152] In his view, as in the minds of many Americans, even racial preferences designed to improve the status of racial minorities are offensive because they perpetuate the division of society by race and constitute unlawful discrimination against nonminorities. He refuses to endorse a race "spoils system" that redistributes social and economic goods without regard to whether the specific beneficiaries in fact have suffered from race discrimination or to whether either the government agency in question or the dispreferred victims of such programs caused that discrimination.[153] Such programs, to Scalia and others, are not remedial in the usual legal sense of the word; instead, they are crude and often unfair measures that wrongly treat race as a determinative factor in redistributing wealth.

The countervailing sentiment—shared by fewer justices and by other Americans—is captured best by Justice Marshall's angry dissenting argument that the battle against racism or its effects is nowhere near won and that the harm to whites from remedial measures that benefit minorities, such as minority set-aside programs in some industries, is not equivalent to discrimination against racial minorities.[154] To claim otherwise or to argue that the past effects of discrimination no longer infect contemporary society is to constitutionalize wishful thinking.[155]

The current Court likely will continue to be skeptical of race-based classifications in both employment and education. Justice Marshall retired and has since died. Fellow liberal Justice William Brennan has retired. Most of the remaining justices seem to accept that Justice Harlan's interpretation of the Equal Protection Clause "—[o]ur Constitution is color-blind"—should be national policy and that "[w]e are close to that time" when no race-based measure should withstand judicial scrutiny, even if it is designed to promote diversity. Moreover, the Court now has for decades embraced the view that only purposeful, overt, and facially discriminatory acts violate the Constitution; acts that merely result in racial disparities do not. The Court is unlikely to retreat from this position. Thus, if government avoids acts of intentional discrimination, then the Court will not overturn its actions on constitutional grounds, despite any adverse impact on racial minorities. Moreover, if a state or local government voluntarily adopts a race-conscious measure, the measure will be struck down unless it is a remedy for the government's own documented, recent, and intentional discrimination. Nevertheless, as the split among the justices reveals, the Court's work in this area remains extremely controversial. Its approach to voluntary efforts by state and local officials to adopt race-conscious measures is unlikely to mollify those who, like Justice Marshall, still believe that this nation is nowhere close to eradicating racial discrimination or its vestiges.[156] These dissenters therefore are likely to direct some of their civil rights reform efforts to the nation's schools. If private conduct is beyond the reach of the Constitution, then much hinges on how private citizens are taught to think and act with respect to race.

THE COMPETING TAKES ON RACIAL JUSTICE

The differences between Justice Scalia's and Justice Marshall's takes on racial equality under the Constitution highlight a wider schism within American thinking about racial justice. Just as the justices disagree strongly about the meaning of equality and the continued need for government-sponsored, race-conscious remedies, so people beyond the Court disagree strongly about both. The opposing poles, described here as "conservative" and "activist" views, generally are as follows.

Conservatives argue that equality is symmetrical, in that one standard or process should apply equally to all similarly situated persons. Under this account, law should be based on neutral principles, and judges should obey these principles rather than resort to subjective or intuitive notions of the public good. Race, under this view, is not a legitimate basis for employing a different standard or procedure or for reaching a different outcome. Rather, conservatives favor what could be described as a fixed income-distribution curve with no arbitrary barriers to participation. Redistributive measures are unlawful and unwise policy.

Conservatives would analyze whether an arbitrary barrier to participation has occurred on a case-by-case, organization-by-organization basis, rather than by looking at societal patterns beyond the organization or person in question. They thus adhere to an individual rights account of civil liberties rather than to a group rights account. Indeed, they view racial grouping in law as a form of "racial balkanization" that "creates, and even celebrates, barriers . . . that in the end impoverish the human race."[157]

To conservatives, discrimination is an illogical, cost-ineffective, and low-frequency occurrence that has largely been eliminated. As such, the law's role in securing equal rights is nearly completed, and any remaining work should be a matter of private choice, not constitutional command. They disbelieve the claim that affirmative action plans are benign, pointing to the harms to innocent white males and the stigma placed on qualified minorities and women.[158] In general, they favor limited government and maintenance of a strong distinction between the public and private sectors. They deny that this constitutes preservation of a white-dominated status quo or that the current system is in need of dramatic change in order to secure equal rights for racial minorities. They also deny that discriminatory practices of thirty years ago, let alone of the pre–Civil War period, are the principal cause of any current racial disparities. Members of some minority racial groups, they point out, have prospered within the American system without set-asides or affirmative action in other forms. American blacks thus do not need these programs to succeed and are demeaned by a system that assumes that they do need this assistance.

Activists counter that equality is often asymmetrical, meaning that, if the goal is to meet the same set of basic needs for all, then different standards and procedures may have to be used from case to case in order to take into account relevant human differences.[159] Proponents do not believe in a fixed income-distribution curve but in refashioning the curve to permit greater and more equal participation in wealth. Redistributive measures, to them, are essential to equality. In defining discrimination, they look beyond a particular job site or educational institution to consider wider societal patterns—past and present—that contribute to racial disparities and that are reflected in the ostensibly neutral practices of employers, educators, and other public and private actors. Activists argue that the proper goals are liberty and freedom, not neutrality. Procedural equality, while a valuable goal, should not supplant the pursuit of substantive, or outcome, justice. They often embrace group rights discourse because they believe that race discrimination is a group-centered harm that must be fought with group-centered remedies. Moreover, they stress that human personality is shaped by group (including race group) membership in a way that individual rights discourse ignores. Recognition of communal ties, they argue, is critical to political and personal life. Indeed, they view failure to recognize these ties as a principal shortcoming of the brand of individualism that the conservatives endorse.

Activists see discrimination as logical, intentional, and cost-effective for the discriminator and believe that racism continues to be a high-frequency occurrence rather than a low-frequency relic of the past. Government action still is necessary to rearrange private discriminatory choices. Failure to do so is not a neutral act or a justifiable preservation of the public / private distinction; rather, government inaction implicates government in the racial disparities that a biased and unfair private sphere continues to produce wherever no laws prevent it. In response to the claim that affirmative action plans harm innocent whites, activists argue that there are no "innocent" whites insofar as they continue to enjoy significant, often unnoticed, and unearned social and economic windfalls simply because they are white. Turn-about thus is fair play, because anything less will freeze past inequities and block any hope of future racial equality. To the claim that affirmative action stigmatizes its beneficiaries, the activist responds that the alternative—no affirmative steps—stigmatizes them more.

Activists challenge the assumptions that limited government best secures human liberty and that the current political order is based on the consent of the governed to rules that are necessary for the good of all. They argue that limited government will tend to preserve the status quo and that the free market theory that undergirds much American law is illusory for subordinated groups that lack economic, social, or political power to bargain freely. They therefore believe that law—including constitutional law—must take aggressive steps to undo racial disparities and to secure civil liberty for all Americans. To believe otherwise, they agree, is to constitutionalize wishful thinking.

In recent years, this conservative / activist dialogue about racial equality has generated several off-shoot discussions, one of which is of increasing significance to the core curriculum debate. Specifically, some commentators urge that we should reconsider the *Brown*-based notion that integration is the ultimate goal of race reform because it ignores ways in which the mainstream culture is neither neutral nor objective and is inhospitable to the needs of members of nonmainstream cultures it seeks to integrate.[160] They insist that, like the "melting pot" ideal of the early 1900s, the integrationism ideal of the mid- to late 1900s underestimates cultural differences and exaggerates the benefits of shaping one cohesive, cultural norm. Awareness of, and respect for, cultural group distinctiveness—including racial group distinctiveness—thus is not always an arbitrary or irrational prejudice. Rather, race-consciousness is an acceptable, permanent part of the social order, not merely a time-bound aspect of remedial steps toward a color-blind, future ideal.[161] Like Horace Kallen and other strong multiculturalists of the early 1900s, modern race-consciousness advocates insist that all race and cultural differences are not inherently arbitrary or baseless. Social reform should seek, not to efface these differences or to integrate and assimilate all cultures, but to respect and accommodate these differences in ways that do not consistently favor white, Protestant, Western European cultural norms over all others. Under this view, *Brown* points us in the wrong direction and blocks positive reform efforts, such as the Detroit and Milwaukee African-American-centered academies.[162] That is, *Brown* rests on a mistaken assumption of universalism and neutrality and is a liberal pipe-dream.

Critics of the new race-consciousness—which include some long-time political liberals as well as many conservatives—respond that the argument of race-consciousness itself is based on a mistaken assumption of uniformity; to the extent it concentrates on the allegedly common traits of all members of a racial group, it ignores important intra-racial cultural differences. Moreover, whether or not permanent race-consciousness ever is a proper part of private social relations, it should not be a part of public legal principles. More bad than good, say these critics, will flow from making race a legitimate legal classification, except as necessary to remedy discrimination.

IMPLICATIONS FOR A NATIONAL CORE CURRICULUM

The issues of race-consciousness and, more generally, of racial equality are unlikely to disappear. Consciousness of race, of course, is the problem that led us to take account of race as necessary to readjust the equality balance. Few people, however, define similarly the point at which "benign" race consciousness—whether remedial or celebratory—becomes offensive racial particularism, determinism, essentialism, separatism, reverse racism, or other -isms that may defeat, more than advance, the goal of combating harmful discrimination. Perhaps the most that can be said with some assurance at this point in our history is that we agree that public recognition of race-consciousness is not always evil, though some would restrict it very narrowly to remedies available to specific individuals harmed by express, intentional government action. Thus, to insist that race-consciousness is never appropriate seems clearly mistaken. Rather, the more compelling modern questions are the following: "What kind of race-consciousness is legitimate?"; "Under what conditions?"; and the often overlooked issue of "What do we mean by 'race'?"

These competing takes on race, racial equality, and race consciousness show how distinct and contradictory "our" answers to these questions can be and how different our assumptions are about how things are, how they got that way, and how they might be improved. To understand American race relations and their volatility, one therefore must appreciate that a wide range of incompatible normative and descriptive claims currently dominate racial justice discourse.

This racial justice discourse plays a central role in the multiculturalist critiques of a national curriculum and in the heated resistance to some of their proposed alternatives. The competing views might be seen as lines drawn on a continuum where at one end is the most conservative, symmetrical account of equality and at the other is the most radical, asymmetrical account of equality. One's position on this continuum will influence strongly one's attitude toward a common curriculum composed primarily of traditional materials insofar as the curriculum becomes, in a sense, a form of fixed income-distribution curve. Those who believe in refashioning the curve in a manner that considers past unequal distributions of curricular and social influence or power tend to favor refiguring the curriculum—perhaps even developing race-conscious curricula designed to celebrate and preserve racial distinctiveness. Those who believe instead that arbitrary barriers to access should be eliminated, but who also insist that one standard—one curriculum—should apply equally to all citizens regardless of race, might favor greater participation in shaping a common curriculum for racial minorities rather than tailoring several curricula based on the race of the student participants or of the authors whose works appear within them. The goal of the national curriculum should correspond to the larger goal of a society in which race is *irrelevant* to one's ability to participate equally in all aspects of public life. Race-consciousness thus should be eliminated, not perpetuated.

One's equality ideal also inevitably will affect the education methods one prefers. Moreover, neutrality among these colliding approaches is not an option, as they make inconsistent, irreconcilable curricular demands. We cannot have it all ways on this issue, and much depends on which way we choose to have it.

Nevertheless, the Supreme Court will allow educators to make whatever curricular decisions they deem appropriate, short of ones that have no reasonable pedagogical purpose. This means, again, that the primary responsibility for choosing among the competing accounts of equality in making curriculum choices lies with the educators. If a national curriculum is adopted, and—as is likely—local or state participation in it is voluntary, then there is almost no chance that the Court would find a constitutional violation if the adopted curriculum slighted African-American history or other materials that multiculturalists deem to be essential to their social reform agenda. Likewise, however, the Court likely would not interfere with a local district's decision to supplement any national curriculum with these materials or even to teach the national curriculum in a way that emphasized a multicultural ideal. Diversity—including race diversity—remains a valid public purpose even under the Court's conservative account of equality. The Court would intervene only if the schools began to segregate students on the basis of race or refused to allow some individuals or groups any input into curriculum planning on the basis of an expressly race-conscious policy. As such, the meaning of race, racial pluralism, and racial equality actually conveyed within any national curriculum will depend on its drafters' constitutional vision, not on the Court's. Moreover, the deep divisions among Americans about these terms virtually guarantees that any outcome will be controversial and likely to anger at least some groups within the national community.

BEYOND RACIAL EQUALITY

Inequality-based objections to a national curriculum obviously go beyond potential racial inequality. Among the more important of these are ones based on gender, socioeconomic, linguistic, physical and mental capacity, and sexual identity differences. All complicate the task of creating equal educational opportunities, including equal curriculum opportunities, for all students and compete with other difference dilemmas for first-tier reform priority.

GENDER AND EQUALITY

Equality challenges to American schooling have been raised by American feminists, who complain that school texts, language, admissions, testing, athletics, hiring and promotion, and other aspects of the public school program often reinforce archaic and overbroad gender stereotypes[163] and tend to channel females to gender-bound roles in which they are subordinate to males, earn less money than their male counterparts, shoulder a disproportionate burden of domestic responsibilities, and are expected to forego the economic and personal benefits of working outside the home.[164] The proposed remedy is to reexamine all aspects of schooling, including the curriculum, with an eye toward eliminating gender inequality.

The feminist call for gender equality, however, has been expressed and heard in different ways by different people. There are conflicting views on the difference gender actually does, or should, make in the public and private sphere. Once again, United States Supreme Court opinions mirror some of these evolving, divergent views.

In the late 1800s, for example, the Court rejected outright the notion that men and women are equal and embraced the view that women are made for a distinct and separate sphere from men. Thus, in 1873 the Court refused to compel Illinois to grant a woman, Myra Bradwell, a license to practice law, because "[t]he paramount destiny and mission of woman are to fulfil the noble and benign offices of wife and mother."[165] This destiny was, the Court continued, "the law of the Creator," which law the state of Illinois was entitled to respect.

In the 1970s, however, the Supreme Court began to overturn gender-based classifications on the ground that they violated equal protection under the law. The Court finally confronted the confounding question of whether and where a gender-based classification was based on relevant and "real" differences between the sexes rather than on archaic or overbroad stereotypes.[166] It concluded that gender-based distinctions are sometimes valid and thus should receive less strict judicial scrutiny than race-based classifications.[167] For example, a female-only bathroom, health club, social organization, or even public school program may be justifiable, while a whites-only policy for all four would violate most people's sense of equality. That is, unlike race, gender more often still is seen as a "real" difference that public institutions properly can observe without judicial interference.

The problem, of course, is how to distinguish "real," reasonable, and benign gender-based distinctions from socially constructed, arbitrary, and harmful ones. This, in turn, involves the thorny question of whether socially constructed gender roles deserve judicial respect, inasmuch as judicial intervention might displace cultural practices in favor of the equally arbitrary and less widely shared intuitions of unelected judges. Given the extreme lack of consensus among most people, including feminists, about the proper role of gender in an ideal world, some people insist that the Court should not constitutionalize its construction of gender equality. Others insist with equal force that for the Court to defer to existing cultural practices is to ratify a status quo that undervalues women's contributions and perpetuates their social and economic subordination.

The Court's response has been to approve most, but not all, gender-based classifications. For example, in *Mississippi University for Women v. Hogan*,[168] the Court held that the Mississippi University for Women's School of Nursing could not deny a male applicant admission solely because of his gender, because the state did not offer a comparable coeducational nursing program near the applicant's home.[169] Moreover, the state policy of making more nursing school openings available to women than to men tended "to perpetuate the stereotyped view of nursing as an exclusively woman's job."[170] In an opinion written by Justice Sandra Day O'Connor, the first and only female member of the Court, the Court nevertheless made clear that it was not ruling on the admissibility of female-only admissions policies at other state institutions or programs and expressly left open the question of whether separate but equal education for men and women could ever survive equal protection scrutiny.[171] Post-*Hogan*, a gender-based classification that imposes additional burdens on persons solely because of their gender is constitutional only if the state can justify that burden on "real" differences between men and women, rather than on stereotypical assumptions about "women's work."

Although the Court has rejected its late nineteenth century casual assumption that a "natural order" makes women and men fit for separate jobs and separate spheres, it has not discarded the notion that material gender differences still remain, despite the dramatic changes in the social and professional status of women. Some nonremedial gender-consciousness, unlike nonremedial race-consciousness, remains constitutionally acceptable. For example, the Court approved a nonremedial, gender-conscious statute in *Michael M. v. Sonoma County Superior Court*,[172] under which only males were deemed criminally responsible for acts of "consensual" sexual intercourse with females under the age of eighteen.[173] The Court believed that the statute was based on the valid assumption that "virtually all of the significant harmful and inescapably identifiable consequences of teenage pregnancy fall on the young female."[174] A state reasonably could choose to punish only the partner who suffers few of the adverse consequences because only he needs the additional deterrence of criminal sanctions. The Court rejected the defendant's argument that the statute was based on an unwarranted and stereotypical gender-based assumption that the male is always the culpable aggressor in sex.[175] Rather, it interpreted the statute to be based on the valid state interest in deterring illegitimacy and teenage pregnancy.[176]

Cases like *Hogan* and *Michael M.*, as well as the extensive critical commentary about them,[177] illustrate the ambiguity of gender equality. In one sense, *Hogan* may appear to have been an easy case. If gender equality means, at the least, equal access regardless of gender, then Hogan had a right to be admitted to the nursing school. Unless a biological difference between men and women makes men unsuitable for nursing, the state cannot use gender as an admissions criterion for nursing programs. The Court, however, did not see the case as easy, even in this symmetrical, straightforward sense of equality. Rather, it preserved a wider zone for gender-based admissions policies than this strict, biological-difference approach would have allowed. This implies that the Court believes that even differences between men and women that are not biological may justify different treatment, even in access to education.

And although the Court in *Michael M.* relied in part on strict biological differences—the girl may become pregnant, and the boy cannot—it also was influenced by the sense that a pregnant, unwed teenage mother in our culture still faces social ostracism that the teenage father does not. That is, cultural, not merely biological, differences between the sexes led the Court here to conclude that exempting only the female from the California criminal statute made sense. Indeed, a gender-neutral rule, here and in some other arenas, actually may harm females; both socially constructed and biological gender differences may cause ostensibly neutral laws to have an adverse and disparate impact on females. Yet laws that account for socially constructed gender differences may help perpetuate the harmful stereotypes on which they are based.

The complexities of the difference gender does, or should, make are most fully developed within feminist literature.[178] Although all of these feminist writers ask what Kate Bartlett calls the "woman question"[179]—that is, all of them analyze social, legal, and economic structures with an eye toward their impact on women—they vary widely on what that impact ideally should be.

Some feminists, sometimes called liberal equality feminists, propose that law and social institutions should treat men and women the same, with the exception of strict biological differences such as those of reproduction. To permit the law to do otherwise, they insist, will doom the feminist project because it will give cultural stereotypes and socially constructed meanings of gender the force of law. Within this school are those who believe that women really are, or could be, essentially the same as men as well as others who believe that the law should adopt an androgynous mean between men and women and treat both sexes the same pursuant to that mean.

Other feminists, sometimes referred to as difference theorists or as cultural feminists, reject the notion that equality means sameness, simply because men and women are not the same. Moreover, they argue that the differences go beyond strict biological differences and include cultural differences. Although they disagree about the extent to which the cultural differences are innate rather than learned, they insist that true equality should mean treatment that considers women's special needs and cultural differences.[180] Many difference theorists argue that not only traditional measures of moral reasoning but also other social, economic, intellectual, and legal measures often are based on unstated and hidden male norms that undervalue women's different skills, values, and ways of approaching problems. The most radical of the difference theorists claim that women's cultural differences render them superior in dealing with conflict and that women's values would better promote social harmony than the patriarchal values that now dominate our culture.

Still other feminists, most notably Catharine MacKinnon of the University of Michigan, argue that the difference that gender makes in society is socially constructed to preserve male power.[181] These theorists are sometimes referred to as dominance theorists. Women's role, they argue, is not only different, it is inferior; it is not chosen, but enforced. The allegedly different voice of women is the voice of the victim and should not be celebrated.

Internal feminist critiques of these theories include critical commentary by African-American and other scholars of color, who attack feminist theory that ignores or obscures differences between white women and women of color.[182] Likewise, lesbian and bisexual feminists uncover and critique heterosexual assumptions that devalue or mask the differences among gay, bisexual, and heterosexual women.[183] Feminist literature thus remains divided over whether there is a "woman's culture" and whether women's experiences ever can be generalized.

At present, none of the competing accounts of gender equality clearly dominates the Court's interpretation of the Constitution. Instead, the justices appear to wander from a symmetrical, liberal equality account to an asymmetrical, difference account and on rare occasions even have acknowledged that gender differences are based on arbitrary assertions of male power, as MacKinnon claims. Moreover, the Court's test for gender-based classifications can accommodate any of these accounts of gender equality because the test requires only that gender-based classifications serve "important" governmental objectives and be "substantially related" to the achievement of those objectives.[184]

In general, however, the Court tolerates explicitly gender-based classifications far more often than it tolerates race-based ones. Whether this means that the current Court would permit states and local governments to adopt gender-conscious affirmative action plans but not race-conscious ones, though, is unclear. What is clear is that the meaning of gender equality remains contested within the Court and American society.

The full impact of these varying visions of gender equality on the national curriculum controversy, like that of competing accounts of racial equality, remains to be seen. The most radical dominance account is, of course, least likely to wend its way into any mainstream policy, including curricular policy. Nevertheless, complete curricular silence on gender equality issues is unlikely to satisfy many Americans, who now seem to accept at least a minimal version of liberal equality feminism. Moreover, nearly all observers, including many feminists, view gender-consciousness in some forms as acceptable, even essential, within society and thus within the curriculum. As such, like the race issue, the gender issue is unlikely to disappear. Rather, the cultural significance of race and gender likely will remain contested, and both issues will continue to be curricular lightning rods.

FUNDING AND EQUALITY

Some observers regard school finance as the greatest equality problem facing modern schools and argue that the schools most affected by the current weak economy are those that serve poorer children and that can least afford a loss of funds.[185] The purported link between family income and educational achievement[186] has led them to urge that more public money be directed to resource-poor districts so that children in these districts will have improved chances of obtaining the academic skills that are increasingly essential to economic survival. Funding equalization, they argue, is an essential first step toward making education the emancipatory vehicle that Horace Mann hoped it might become for the nation's poorer members. As such, they insist that all American schoolchildren should have a constitutional right to equal school resources.

Under current federal law, however, funding inequalities among school districts are not unconstitutional. Only when a state denies a child all access to public education does the federal Constitution stand in its way; the quality of that education need not be equal across students or districts.[187] The Court is unwilling to insinuate itself into the delicate process of measuring the relative quality of educational services or even into the arguably less subtle task of determining what constitutes "equal pupil expenditures." It thus does not require that all pupils receive equal educational resources, as this might prevent richer school districts from exceeding basic educational needs for their children if they so desired. To require equal outcomes of this sort, the Court fears, could lower the overall quality of schooling by compelling states to offer one standard, and arguably mediocre, education to all of its children. Deference to local decision-making power and to the strong liberty-based conviction that wealthier families and local communities should be able to purchase the best education that they can afford for their children explains the Court's refusal to remedy even gross disparities in educational funding.[188]

The national story, at least as expressed in federal constitutional case law, therefore is that children have no federal constitutional right to an equally funded education. Equality means, at most, that all children have a right to equal access to the minimum of whatever public education that the state happens to provide. Consequently, in 1987, East Aurora, Illinois, fourth graders each received an education that cost $2,900, whereas Niles, Illinois, fourth graders each received an education that cost $7,800,[189] and nothing in current federal constitutional law rendered this a denial of the East Auroran children's equal protection rights.

To the uncertain extent that funding influences the quality of education services, all American schoolchildren currently do not receive an equal education. Many Americans nevertheless continue to believe that economic disparity should be a matter of federal constitutional concern and that economic justice should be a national priority. Indeed, some state courts and legislatures have begun to act on this insight by interpreting state law to require funding equalization. Here again, the tension lies between those who believe that equality under law means merely a right to equal access and those who believe that equality under law should produce equal outcomes and thus should employ redistributive measures designed to achieve equal outcomes. But the tension surrounding the issue also betrays a larger rift between those who believe in a capitalist, free enterprise system and those who believe that laissez-faire economics guarantees a permanent economic underclass.

This rift is relevant to the national curriculum controversy in a subtle, yet important respect. Again, to the extent that the curriculum is a resource, some would argue both that it must be distributed equally and that a national priority should be to provide the funds necessary to assure this equal distribution. They would also point out, however, that until the gross disparities in educational resources are reduced, curriculum proposals of any sort are a mere band-aid on a gaping social wound. The curriculum thus cannot possibly produce the cultural cohesion that core curricularists seek or the subcultural dignity that some multiculturalists prefer because it cannot efface the more salient and divisive subcultural variable of relative wealth. In this view, as long as there is no insistence on equal outcomes, any national standards will at most set a common cultural baseline and will not prevent cultural stratification; some groups—often defined by their relatively greater wealth—will be able to exceed that baseline in ways that will render their children more mobile, more wealthy, and more powerful than children of others.

LANGUAGE, SPECIAL NEEDS, SEXUAL IDENTITY, AND EQUALITY

Remaining issues of equality that further complicate the task of forging any national curriculum include bilingualism, special needs education, and issues of sexuality.

Bilingual education and the more general issue of linguistic pluralism in American education are of the most direct relevance to the national curriculum debate. The controversy, of course, is whether the national curriculum should be premised on the assumption that English is the national language. Some education reformers believe quite strongly that the most important component of the "melting pot" ideal is a common language. Yet the ways in which language and culture are inextricably linked make this claim highly divisive, even within the linguistic communities that seek to be assimilated into the English-speaking mainstream.[190] The argument against English-only initiatives and in favor of bilingual, bicultural education is that meaningful access to public education and meaningful participation and representation within it require that children receive instruction in their first language.

Although federal statutory law now requires that schools receiving federal money accommodate students' language differences, the Court never has held that the Constitution requires bilingual education. Like its reluctance to demand equal school financing, the Court's reluctance to demand that all students be taught in their native language likely springs from its fear that it is ill-equipped to evaluate the financial and other implications of such a mandate. Again, this means that the legislatures and the schools bear the primary responsibility for accommodating minority linguistic communities within the school curriculum. As the American school population continues to grow more ethnically diverse, providing a truly bilingual, bicultural education for all students may become more difficult and consequently more controversial than it already is. Equal outcomes in this respect will be harder to secure and harder to deny.

Education of children with language, mental, and physical disabilities and education of gifted children are perhaps the most destabilizing equality issues, as they force educators to rethink baseline assumptions about academic achievement and aptitude and about common educational standards and goals. They also present agonizing choices about resource distribution, as per-student expenditures for special needs students may be far greater than for other students. These students now have an impressive array of federal and state statutory rights, including the right to be taught in the "least restrictive environment." Like bilingual education, however, special education services for handicapped students currently is a statutory, not a constitutional, mandate.

The final and currently most controversial equality issue is the growing insistence of some scholars and activists that the public school curriculum should include materials that depict homosexuality and bisexuality in positive terms, that speak frankly about AIDS and its transmission, and that provide support for students whose emerging sexual identity is gay, lesbian, or bisexual.[191] Relying on studies that show an increased risk of suicide among gay and lesbian teens,[192] as well as on the notion that sexuality may be biologically determined and thus a purely arbitrary basis for discriminating against gay people,[193] these commentators claim that the schools should take affirmative curricular and other steps to combat negative attitudes toward homosexuality and bisexuality. Resistance to official efforts to encourage acceptance of gays is profound, however, and has inspired local grass-roots initiatives and state constitutional amendments that seek to ban any public-sponsored attempts to promote tolerance of gay, lesbian, and bisexual "lifestyles."[194] The heart of this resistance is a conviction that public schools should not teach acceptance of homosexuality in particular or values tolerant of sexuality in general. Neither those who favor nor those who oppose inclusion of gay themes in the public school curriculum are likely to prevail in the courts, given the deference given to school officials' curriculum choices. At most, religious parents who object to inclusion of these materials on sexuality may be entitled to have their children excused from lessons that touch on these concerns. Again, this means that whether and to what extent a school includes gay themes in its curriculum will be a matter of local and regional choice.

IMPLICATIONS FOR A NATIONAL CORE CURRICULUM

The kaleidoscopic array of viewpoints within each cluster of equality-based concerns shows that the national story about equal protection under the law is hardly monolithic, static, or plain. Rather, it is a fractious debate about who belongs, on what terms, and according to whose definition of equality, community, biological and sociological determinism, sameness and difference, morality and blasphemy, individualism, and governmental responsibility for the unequal distribution of social and economic goods. That our debates about equality within education become high-pitched and tense thus should come as no surprise. So much about which we agree so little is so clearly at stake.

The Court's racial equality decisions, in particular, highlight the defining lines of the equality debates. They demonstrate that intentional exclusion of citizens from important public goods and opportunities simply because of their race is clearly unconstitutional but that, beyond this minimal conception of equality, the justices are deeply divided about what equal protection under law means.

These same divisions surface beyond the Court when educators, parents, and students consider the role of race in education, including in curriculum planning. Like the Court, they are divided over whether and in what way race-consciousness should be part of the curriculum. Like the Court, they disagree about whether current racial disparities are the product of past or present discrimination and, if so, whether *discrimination* means only the intentional acts of government. Also divisive, even explosive, is whether a person's race does in fact, or should ideally, matter to her cultural identity or otherwise, as people debate whether the race of an author should be relevant to decisions about which authors to include in a literary anthology, whether the race of an applicant should be relevant to her admission to an educational program, whether race-based slurs are disciplinable speech, or whether people of a particular race are essentially different from those of another.

When one adds to these race-based concerns the range of concerns raised by differences based on religion, economic class, gender, ethnicity, physical and mental abilities, and sexual identity, the prospect of forging "a" national curriculum dims. Stanley Fish's claim that it is "difference all the way down" grows more compelling, and the risk that any one curriculum will obscure these differences grows more considerable and worrisome. Even the United States Supreme Court—surely no radical organ of counter-cultural thought—cannot agree about this tension between our differences and our common identity. What becomes obvious is that, while a commitment to equal protection under law is central to the American aspirational *unum*, it often is rendered impossibly complex by our pluralism. Consequently, to talk meaningfully about equality—our political sameness—one must also be prepared to discuss the multiple aspects of human identity that may modify or qualify this political sameness and that constitute actual or imagined boundaries among citizens.

CONCLUSION

Taken together, these First Amendment and equal protection cases offer several messages for curriculum planners. First, they highlight central national concerns. Freedom of religion, freedom of expression, and equality undeniably constitute, in a broadly symbolic way, expressions and carriers of values that are thought to be widely shared in the United States. Talk about these constitutional issues—especially when conducted by the national-level Supreme Court—highlights who we think we are and who we wish to become. As such, these discussions should be important components of any national core curriculum.

Second, the conflicts within and beyond the Court illustrate that these constitutional values are contested, even within the ranks of ideological allies. The Supreme Court cases on these issues are all hard cases, even when the justices feign otherwise. To teach about these cases is to teach about conflict and about competing versions of fundamental questions. Indeed, even a thoroughgoing traditionalist must acknowledge that the central constitutional issues remain unresolved, fluid, and multisided.

Third, the case law reveals the current Court's steady movement toward delivering greater power to "the people" and less to the courts to monitor the performance of government officials—including school officials. Freedom of religion and expression, as well as equality, are more the citizens' job to define and enforce than that of the judiciary. How and whether our children are educated about the constitutional conflicts thus has become more critical, lest those who will inherit this power be unable to see, let alone effect, the complex balance that these constitutional conflicts demand.

Fourth, the case law teaches that within a liberal democracy calls for national solidarity must always be contingent, qualified, and sensitive to the dangers of the solidarity instinct. National history reveals that in significant moments, especially when most frightened of aggression from foreign powers, Americans have betrayed a tendency to engage in an "hysterical taking of stock" of the American personality. Moreover, the Court has not always responded with restraining reason but instead, in tragic cases that took decades to overrule, has supported senseless repression of difference. Those who rebel against strong appeals for a national, coherent core—whether in education or in other areas of domestic policy—have ample historical and constitutional reasons to sound an alarm. Awareness of this national judicial and human tendency therefore should be an abiding and critical part of any discussion of national values or lessons.

Our constitutional history also reveals that from our constitutional beginnings—not merely from the civil rights battles of the 1960s—we have been a nation in turmoil over our ideological, racial, cultural, ethnic, religious, and gender pluralism. Knowing the history of constitutional conflicts thus is an important part of knowing America and of understanding the deeper sociopolitical bases of the arguments for and against a national curriculum.

In sum, our national constitutional tradition is one of perpetual struggle to balance multiple competing concerns. Solidarity in respecting democratic processes and the outcomes they produce is important. But demanding that our general practices accommodate our ideological, religious, racial, gender, ethnic, and multiple other differences is equally important. Americans are joined most distinctively and paradoxically by a constitutional commitment to the right to dissent—though not by unanimity on the limits on that right. The challenge, then, of any national curriculum is to convey this struggle and paradox in terms that will enable all students to participate equally, meaningfully, and productively in it. The final chapter outlines the features of a curriculum directed toward this goal.

6   Toward Constitutional Literacy

Socialization has to come before individuation, and education for freedom cannot begin before some constraints have been imposed.—Richard Rorty

Teach the conflicts.—Gerald Graff

INTRODUCTION

Our commitment to the right to dissent and our sharp disagreements about the content and the borders of this right do not mean there are no common terms, texts, or themes that bind the nation. Likewise, that our common knowledge is provisional and thus may be fallible does not mean that we cannot or should not impart it to our children.

The disagreements and fallibilities among us do mean, however, that, to the extent that education seeks to pass on the current state of our national knowledge, it should "teach the conflicts"[1] along with the consensus. "Teaching the conflicts" means that reformers must take seriously both the force of E. D. Hirsch's lament that our students suffer from profound fact gaps in traditional subjects and the multiculturalists' arguments for an expanded American anthology.

But how, exactly, should curriculum planners implement this vague goal? What must a curriculum include to make practical sense of the claims that both stability and change, both commonality and pluralism, are crucial?

This final chapter responds to this practical aspect of the core curriculum debate by outlining several curricular implications of the preceding historical, philosophical, and especially constitutional materials. The focus in this chapter is on the social studies segment of the K through 12 curriculum and, in particular, on subjects relevant to what can be called *constitutional literacy*, because these subjects are illumined most clearly by the constitutional case law.[2]

The chapter describes several gaps in the common knowledge of American law students that are relevant to their constitutional literacy.[2] In particular, entering law students display weaknesses in language skills, knowledge of traditional aspects of United States government and history, and knowledge of the history of contemporary conflicts regarding race, gender, ethnicity, and religion. Even the nation's best students lack much of the knowledge that both the core curricularists and the multiculturalists deem "basic." For example, some do not know baseline civics—such as how a bill becomes law—and are unable to locate significant, culture-defining events—such as major wars—within an historical framework. Many more know little of the historical background of our civil rights—such as when the Nineteenth Amendment was passed.

Addressing these deficiencies in all students—indeed in all adults—is an appropriate national objective because the knowledge and skills at issue are essential both to constitutional literacy and, in turn, to meaningful participation in the constitutional conversation, especially to deliberations about our racial, religious, and other differences. Pervasive constitutional illiteracy compromises our collective ability to confront the dilemma of our differences with a common sense of the interests at stake and with a common commitment to effecting policies that take adequate and informed account of our different histories, beliefs, and interests. That is, constitutional literacy is important not only to intelligent self-governance but also to the mutual respect and toleration that is necessary for peaceful co-existence within a heterogeneous culture.

To argue that constitutional literacy should be a national goal, however, is not necessarily to endorse federal-government-imposed standards or even to assert that a national level body must determine the content of the constitutional curriculum. But, if state and local governments are not fulfilling this objective, then *as a nation* we have cause for alarm, and national-level officials should explore various means by which the objective might be achieved. If state and local governments can be inspired to act without federal intervention, then there is no reason to involve national institutions in this aspect of education. In short, whatever institutional responses are most likely to achieve the preferred curriculum results in the most efficient manner should be allowed to do so. The main ambition of this book is to identify one category of these preferred results rather than to analyze the many possible organizational, pedagogical, or other reasons why constitutional literacy is not being achieved under the current system.

OUR CONSTITUTIONAL ILLITERACY

Hirsch and other core curricularists claim that education is failing our students because they graduate with little common knowledge of history, geography, science, literature, and other baseline subjects. Their evidence of this is their own observations and the many national studies that test this information. Experience with law students lends further support to the core curricularists' claims that the knowledge gaps they identify are real and serious.

Law students' knowledge gaps are particularly relevant to debates about the curriculum at other levels because these students' gaps are very likely to be shared by most other Americans. Law students are drawn from all disciplines and from a range of American colleges and universities. There are no mandatory pre-law courses, and most come to law school directly from college. Nothing, other than superior undergraduate grades and solid LSAT scores binds this group together. As such, law schools have a bird's-eye view of some of the very best and most motivated recent graduates of the nation's post-secondary schools. Nevertheless, these students mirror several of the serious problems that educators at the undergraduate and secondary school level already have identified and thus offer especially compelling evidence of the pervasiveness of these knowledge gaps.

First and most significantly, law students betray weaknesses in writing skills. Poor grammar, spelling, syntax, and organization are common enough problems that some law schools have hired English teachers to assist their students. Moreover, teachers of legal writing often find that students' inability to draft logical, coherent legal memoranda stems more from basic writing problems than from difficulty in handling the subtleties of the law.

Although the causes of these writing problems likely are complex, one contributing factor seems to be the students' lack of monitored writing experience in their earlier education years. When asked, few students can recall a time in their post-secondary education when a teacher analyzed their writing or demanded a rewrite of an assigned paper. Some students managed, even at prestigious undergraduate schools, to escape with very little writing experience. Even those who did considerable writing throughout college sometimes report that they received little or no critical feedback on their writing other than a final grade. Writing problems, of course, can betray analytical problems, some of which can be explained by the inaccessibility of legal doctrine and its often arcane vocabulary. But even when asked to write on nonlegal subjects, some students have difficulty communicating grammatically, persuasively, and logically. Whatever the cause of these problems, they have become so noticeable that few professors would deny that they compromise the students' ability to communicate ideas effectively.

Moreover, if—as much writing theory suggests—a writing problem betrays an underlying thinking problem, then there is reason to believe that law students' critical analytical abilities are not as developed as one might hope. A disorganized or poorly reasoned essay often may reflect a student's inability to read others' arguments accurately, synthesize them, and to interpret them critically. Yet analyzing arguments obviously is essential to a wide range of other tasks, including voting, that are critical parts of productive public and private life. Some entering law students complain that they have little prior training in this type of rigorous analysis and thus are unable, at first, to subject arguments to critical inquiry. Therefore, to the extent that some core curricularists believe that American students' language and critical thinking skills are weak, law schools lend support to their thesis.

A second, central claim of the core curricularists is that American students lack basic knowledge of United States history and government. Many national studies conducted during the 1970s and 1980s indicate that current students know less history and civics than did the generations before or after them, because they were educated during the period in which American students' performance in most subjects—including history and civics—declined.[3] Even as late as 1988, however, national studies of fourth, eighth, and twelfth grade students indicated that most American students had a limited grasp of United States history.[4] Moreover, national assessments of trends in achievement in civics indicated that the average proficiency of seventeen-year-olds in 1988 was significantly less than that of their counterparts in 1976 and 1982.[5] Although a majority of seventeen-year-olds in 1988 could write what the study report deemed an acceptable definition of democracy,[6] only one-half showed a detailed knowledge of major government structures and their functions, and only six percent betrayed a more developed understanding of a wide range of political institutions and processes.[7] This was so, even though ninety-three percent of these students had taken at least one course in this area during high school.[8]

Here again, this general claim of knowledge deficiencies is corroborated by experience with law students. Few law students today likely left secondary schooling without learning such historical facts as when the Civil War and World Wars I and II were fought. Nonetheless, law classroom discussions of court decisions rendered during these time periods often must be prefaced with reminders that they are war-era cases. That is, even our highly motivated, bright, and accomplished law students do not all possess a rudi-

mentary—let alone an elaborate—internalized and readily accessible historical time frame into which they can fit the new material.

The students recognize this and are quite eloquent in expressing their
deep frustration with an education that left them unable to locate themselves in an historical time frame. They feel, correctly, that they have been
betrayed by American education and now are lost, in an important intellectual sense. As Hirsch puts it, they lack a *schema*, a way of organizing and
making sense of facts, and thus are unable to remember and apply them. Put
another way, they have considerable data, but no program.

The depth of these history and government fact gaps is illustrated by a
remark made by one first-year law student several years ago. In an introduc-
tory lecture about the court system in the United States, I mentioned that
there were two systems of courts—federal and state—with different, though
at times overlapping, jurisdiction. One student said, audibly and sincerely,
"Well, I'll be damned." Basic principles of federalism are not, it seems,
common knowledge among entering law students.

One teacher's anecdotes do not, of course, a theory make. Those who
condemn Hirsch and others on the ground that they rely too heavily on such
anecdotes have a valid concern, in that the narratives can be overdramatic
and can obscure other data that highlight the students' strengths rather than
their weaknesses. Moreover, claims that modern students have weaker academic skills than their predecessors often ignore that the student population
of post-secondary professional schools has changed as higher education has
opened the door to students who before were denied access. And those who
declare that we face a literacy crisis can exploit the American tendency
quickly to embrace *any* negative assessment of our national academic proficiency. As the earlier chapters in this book have shown, this tendency is a
long-standing American tradition.

Nevertheless, these front-line anecdotes also are data that, in this case,
reinforce and animate numerous national test scores. That is, both the
anecdotal and the systematic empirical evidence support our sense of our
own weakness when it comes to our knowledge of national history and
government. Moreover, even if this common knowledge is no worse than it
was in decades past, it remains surprisingly and depressingly thin.

Not all students, of course, are as uninformed as the lowest test scores or
the most depressing anecdotes suggest. Instead, law teachers confront different "reading groups," which range from a few blue-ribbon students to
some who would score quite low on the national measures of knowledge in
history and government. Professional schools now face the same problem
that first plagued undergraduate schools in the early 1900s, when they began

to admit highly intelligent but untutored immigrant students along with the well-tutored students. No longer could the faculty assume that all under-graduates shared a common set of literary, historical, or other facts or skills. Similarly, law school faculties today cannot assume that entering students share a common base of sophisticated knowledge of United States history or government.[9] And, when law professors cannot assume that their entering students possess this knowledge, then it is fair to say that one cannot assume this knowledge is possessed by many other groups of Americans.[10]

If our students are weak on traditional history and government knowl-edge, however, then they are weaker still on the historical and other knowl-edge that multiculturalists wish the tests and curriculum would emphasize. There are not yet national studies that measure the average twelfth grader's mastery of women's history, African-American history, Native American history, or histories of other nondominant groups. At present, therefore, our best window into the average American student's familiarity with these subjects is an analysis of the contents of history and civics textbooks to which most of them have been exposed.

The influence of textbook contents on actual curriculum content is im-mense, as many commentators have observed.[11] The constraints of teacher time and imagination, local school board and state board of education directives, and the desire for uniformity in instruction all give elementary, secondary, and even post-secondary textbooks a powerful role in shaping curricular content. Their contents thus are an important gauge of what most students actually are taught, which of course has some bearing on what they learn about a particular subject.

As Frances FitzGerald has reported in her eye-opening book, *America Revised*,[12] the textbook choices are limited and often are determined by the textbook selection decisions of a handful of populous states. For example, California, with its large population and centralized textbook selection pro-cedure, wields massive influence over the textbooks available throughout the United States because textbook companies develop books that match the demands of their biggest customers. Although the availability of paperback books and other alternative materials enables creative teachers, especially in wealthier districts, to supplement the basic texts, research suggests that most teachers rely on basic textbooks.

Much nonetheless has been made in the popular media and in some recent academic works about the alleged skewing of historical texts to accommodate feminists, people of color, and other groups that seek to modify the standard histories taught in American schools. The claim is that political compromises made with such groups, rather than intellectual integrity and a commitment to balanced and accurate presentation of facts, have governed textbook and curricular content decisions of late. In particular, the New York State School Commission was publicly condemned by Arthur Schlesinger, Jr.,[13] and others for bowing to pressure to teach a more Afrocentric social studies curriculum in the New York public schools.

The older texts and supporting materials certainly lacked the balance and nuance essential to an accurate sense of American history.[14] And, although textbook inroads have been made by racial minorities, feminists, and other groups seeking to complement the traditional texts, they often are limited to slender sidebar discussions of the contributions of racial minorities, women, and other groups to American history, merely tacked on to the main text, rather than integrated into it.[15] What little multiculturalism has made its way into the texts tends to be a thin and marginalized version of it, which often means only a handful of selections about women and African-Americans, rather than an extensive and pervasive presentation of a wide range of subcultural groups. For example, a text might mention Booker T. Washington and Elizabeth Cady Stanton, but not Carter Woodson, Marcus Garvey, W. E. B. DuBois, Sojourner Truth, or Mary Wollstonecraft and may omit altogether central figures from other subcultural groups.

Indeed, despite the politically loaded nature of the issue, most observers likely would concede that the popular textbooks fall far short of the multiculturalists' demands. As Frances FitzGerald has reported, interest-group pressures more often cause textbook companies to delete materials than to add them.[16] These companies seek to produce books that are noncontroversial and inoffensive to the widest possible range of consumers. The predictable result often is bland presentation, silences, and at times, a grossly simplified and superficial discussion of complex, controversial, and serious social issues.

The evidence about what our elementary and secondary school students do not know again is corroborated by experience with graduate students. Law classroom discussions of gender and race equality, of economic justice, of ideological and religious freedom, and of sexual identity all indicate that students have little common knowledge about these subjects. For example, few can name even the approximate year in which women were given the right to vote or are aware of the varied and competing strands of feminist thought or of the rich debate about the social implications of gender. Common knowledge of racial politics in American history often is restricted to a general impression that things once were very bad—"we had slavery"—then progressed to an era of "separate but equal," followed by the civil rights era, which resulted in legislation that some think "went too far" with "quotas and affirmative action" and that others think is still necessary because "discrimination is still happening," given continued racism and disparities in the opportunities available to African-Americans and whites. Many do not know about pre–Civil War abolition efforts, about the range of arguments for and against civil rights legislation, or the names or contributions of significant African-Americans other than Dr. Martin Luther King, Jr., and, perhaps, Booker T. Washington.

Little evidence, moreover, supports the claim that most college graduates have been so overpowered by feminist, leftist, or multicultural-leaning undergraduate professors that they have emerged from college like-minded, cowed, or even especially familiar in these issues. Those who accept the sensationalist claims that college campuses now are indoctrinating students into multicultural radicalism underestimate the resilience of the traditional curriculum, the domesticating power of promotion and tenure processes, the glacial pace of fundamental changes in pedagogy, and students' natural resistance to ideas or methods that threaten their existing beliefs and values. Even students who were required to take some courses with what might be termed a multicultural or feminist theme show no signs that the exposure effected their political transformation or that it even made them more conversant in feminist, African-American, or other nontraditional history or literature than peers who did not have such courses. Those few who took several elective courses in these areas or who majored in women's studies or African-American studies often were drawn to the subject because of intellectual and political tastes that were formed before they enrolled in the classes.

There is, however, a critical difference between students' lack of knowledge about the nontraditional literature and their lack of knowledge about traditional national history and civics. Few students regard ignorance of nonmainstream history as worrisome. They thus are far less motivated to pursue such studies on their own. Indeed, students often resist any discussion of race, gender or ethnicity either because they view these as "political" themes irrelevant to their coursework (even when the course topic is as politically and socially charged as, for instance, constitutional law) or because they have preconceived notions about how these themes should be introduced and what position one should take with respect to each. The main point here, however, is not that students should adopt a particular stance toward multicultural approaches to American history or government; it is that they possess little of the knowledge on which these approaches are based and that their attitude toward the approaches often makes this knowledge deficiency hard to cure, particularly without mandatory distribution requirements.

Other areas of concern—which hardly exhaust all that are relevant to either the Hirsch or the multiculturalist thesis—include knowledge of current events, world history and geography, political theory, philosophy, economics, world literature, and intellectual history. In all of these areas, even a teacher of graduate students can assume very little shared knowledge. Not all of our students read a daily newspaper. Not all comprehend the meaning of the sentence, "The procedure was Kafkaesque," or of the words "normative" or "utilitarian." Many do not know how a federal bill becomes law or that the Bill of Rights constrains only governmental, not private, power. Very few know that the original Constitution protected slavery. Some do not know these things even after graduate school.

TOWARD CONSTITUTIONAL LITERACY

To name gaps in our students' readily accessible store of knowledge obviously is not to prove that they are cause for alarm. After all, law teachers and teachers in other disciplines still are able to communicate with students well enough to transmit the knowledge and skills necessary for them to become competent professionals. The heart of the core curriculum debate is whether these gaps *should* distress us and, if so, whether the answer is to require that all students be taught a common set of facts, allusions, or values. This in turn involves the question of whether we already have, or need to forge, a robust, common, national, and public vocabulary, identity, or value structure.

As was discussed in Chapter 3, those who argue for a national core curriculum insist that all nations, all cultures, need a common cultural literacy to survive and that the United States, in particular, is in desperate need of a unifying, rooting center. We have lost, some critics charge, even the minimal communal consensus and connection essential to a common morality, meaningful participation in public life, and civic consciousness. The dire consequences of this void, they believe, include the violent crime, racial and ethnic factionalism, and acute anomie and alienation that have become American commonplaces. Without some sense of the whole, and of our connection to others, people collapse into self-consciousness, a "culture of narcissism," and special-interest-group politics.

The critics of the call for coherence, whose views were considered in Chapter 4, reply that an institutionalized or government-forged communal consciousness is an oxymoron. Such consciousness would be contrived and jingoistic and likely to privilege some subnational communities' interests and traditions over others. Any drive to a unifying cultural center inevitably becomes, in the hands of its missionaries, a means of erecting boundaries to fence out non-Caucasians, non-Christians, non-Conservatives, and any people whose family values or personal practices depart from those of a conventional Judeo-Christian, Anglo-Saxon, middle class norm. That is, a national civic consciousness might be a fine theory, but it has proven to be, throughout American history, a repressive, discriminatory, and illiberal practice.

Moreover, continue these critics, no two groups of cultural coherence advocates agree on the analytical grounds of this coherence: there are disagreements on such fundamental points as whether there is a universal good, whether a political (as opposed to private) order based on communal principles is desirable, or to what extent community tends to shape or constitute personal identity.[17] As such, the phrase "foster common values" is impossibly vague—if not dangerous.

And finally, some say, it is fatuous to assume that the ability to recite discrete facts, chase down literary allusions, or recognize even half of the items on Hirsch's well-intentioned list is the type of shared national knowledge we should foster. Teaching students "national facts" does not mean they will learn to use these facts. Over ninety percent of all high schoolers take at least one course in United States history or civics. Most *are* given the basic facts but by testing time, or soon thereafter, lose them.

We thus begin to appreciate why calls to curricular action often go nowhere. Even those who think they agree on the need to foster the ideal of a national community often have very different aims and assumptions. Many people feel, quite deeply, the need for a core curriculum and some cultural centering. But some believe that the core community value is, among other things, individualism, whereas others believe it is, or should be, strong communitarianism. Some believe that a core curriculum should be based on conventional family values, whereas others believe that it should be based on tolerance of widely divergent family and other values.

Indeed, even if we set aside the enormous complexities of defining an aspirational core curriculum and sought only to teach about our *existing* commonalities, we still would face the complexities of describing this existing center, if it exists. That is, if we agreed that school should acculturate children into the world as it is, rather than forge a new world, we still would need to agree on what that world is. Thereafter, we might proceed to the ambitious task of defining the world as it should be and then crafting educational programs to help our children create that world. Serious discussions of either point, however, tend to bog down quickly into irresolvable differences, in part because both the descriptive and aspirational visions hinge on assumptions for which we lack sufficient empirical data to muster consensus. The debate inevitably lapses into hunches, anecdotes, myths, stereotypes, and polemics.

We might simply abandon the search for an existing set of core values and instead seek consensus only about " 'the conditions for political discussion of enduring moral disagreement.' "[18] That is, we could establish a curriculum that inculcated only the procedural value of according all arguments and all speakers an equal opportunity to be heard, in an effort to forge a society of "mutual respecters."[19] Yet this might skew the community toward compromise positions and thus might create a bias toward centrism as the core cultural value. It could, in turn, undervalue nonconformism and dissent and foster a depoliticization of our political arrangements.[20] Clearly, even a modest procedural request that everyone be given his or her conversational turn, during which all others are to listen and to take seriously the speaker's claims, is nonneutral and potentially divisive.

Does all of this mean that the quest for national literacy is doomed and that *no* meaningful word can be said on the matter? Will any national curriculum proposal reflect only a political power-grab, not reason or any common, public good? Is any common curriculum proposal vulnerable to such effective analytical, empirical, and normative criticism that none should be adopted?

To pose these questions is to suggest an answer. Many of us are not, when pressed, as alienated or ironic as we seem, especially when it comes to our children. Many of us do not want to relinquish the resilient progressivist dream of common national goals, and many of us still fear the negative consequences of the "centrifugal forces" that led Harvard educators in the 1940s to recommend common distribution requirements for all college students and a more uniform curriculum for all secondary and elementary students. And, in more basic and practical terms,

> [e]ven ardent radicals, for all their talk of "education for freedom" secretly hope that the elementary schools will teach kids to wait their turn in line; not to shoot up in the johns; to obey the cop on the corner; and to spell, punctuate, multiply, and divide.[21]

That is, despite our many serious and perhaps unbridgeable conflicts, there are convergences worth noting and bolstering. These convergences, as well as their limits, have several direct implications for the national core curriculum debate. Among them is that closing the history and other knowledge gaps described above should be a matter of national concern because the achievement of at least minimal knowledge and skills in these subjects is a worthwhile goal for all American schoolchildren. Indeed, some of us believe that access to these baseline lessons is so valuable that it should be every American child's birthright.

OUR CONSENSUS

Cynicism about education's benefits tends to melt when we confront the stark and terrible costs of illiteracy. We share a common concern that our children be literate in the most basic sense of that word. When schools produce students who cannot read, do basic math, or recognize the rough geographical and historical framework of traditionally important national and international events and ideas, then most people become deeply concerned, even outraged. Failure to assure that all able students be taught the basic elements of literacy is considered by many to be a denial of a fundamental human need, inasmuch as literacy is necessary to meaningful participation in modern economic, political, and social life. Much of the national curriculum doubtless should be devoted to assuring such literacy, a goal that likely is not hopelessly controversial.[22]

Convergences exist, however, not only with respect to these relatively objective academic subjects or skills—such as geography, reading, and math skills—but also in areas that involve the subjective matter of political knowledge and values. Specifically, a surprising number of American commentators argue that baseline constitutional commitments are one part of our national identity and should be included in all American schoolchildren's education.[23] Indeed, regardless of their political orientation, most writers who address themselves to citizenship education converge on several basic points. Virtually all favor instruction on the formation of the United States, the United States Constitution, and basic principles of government, as well as on the general history of the United States and of the world. Surprising, however, is that many liberal and conservative writers agree that teachers should expressly inculcate in their students respect for principles of due process, freedom of expression and religion, and equality. That is, despite disagreements over whether a national core curriculum, in theory, is possible, desirable, or dangerous, in practical application discussions common values emerge that bind many Americans together—values that most believe should be reinforced by the government, if necessary.

The common values that emerge repeatedly in these proposals are, roughly and generally, a restatement of the basic constitutional compact, described in Chapter 5. Just as the Court in *Pierce* concluded that a democratic education must seek both to mold students into respect for democratic principles and to free them from unreasonable dominant influences, most commentators likewise agree that a "democratic theory of education recognizes the importance of empowering citizens to make educational policy and also of constraining their choices among policies in accordance with those principles—nonrepression and nondiscrimination—that preserve the intellectual and social foundations of democratic deliberations."[24] Most favor an education that socializes students into respecting a decidedly nonneutral republican civility—the value expressed in *Fraser*—yet that also gives them the knowledge and analytical skills essential to critical liberal dissent—the value expressed in *Tinker*. Most commentators do not believe that our students need only the basics—that is, language and cognitive skills and bare, factual knowledge—as some strong individualists and others prefer. Rather, they urge that schools also engage in constitutionally grounded citizenship education: schools should teach students "widespread and enduring tolerance for different ways of life,"[25] to recoil at injustice and cruelty, to think critically about politics, to value self-determination as expressed in the right to vote and other forms of self-rule, to respect common laws that preserve the common interest in security and general public welfare, to value vigorous, informed dissent and the principle of equal justice under law, and to recognize that many of these interests are in perpetual tension with the collective interest in majoritarian democratic processes.

Simply and unfashionably put, many believe that students should be taught to respect the Constitution and the Bill of Rights. These people regard constitutional literacy as a proper curriculum goal that includes not only a relatively objective traditional knowledge component—basic language skills and mastery of United States history and civics—but also a subjective component—respect for constitutional values.

Closing the current, serious gaps in this constitutional literacy should be a high priority of any national curriculum initiative, and a curriculum that includes extensive, in-depth coverage of traditional language skills and social studies is a proper national goal. But the curricular relevance of the disparities among us is indisputable, and the hostility of some core curricularists toward multiculturalist critiques of the traditional curriculum, including the social studies curriculum, seems very misplaced.

OUR CONFLICTS

Even the justices of the United States Supreme Court disagree—sometimes bitterly—about what, precisely, the abstract constitutional principles of freedom of expression, freedom of religion, and equality mean in practice, under what circumstances public interest should trump individual or group autonomy, and how best to inculcate respect for both the public and individual interest. The areas of fiercest debate concern the historical and contemporary role of race,[26] gender,[27] ethnicity,[28] socio-economic status,[29] religion,[30] and sexual and reproductive freedom[31] within our public or civic virtues.

These issues are, of course, the ones that most divide modern curriculum planners, including social studies curriculum planners. The greatest challenge for contemporary teachers is how to address these particular issues within the classroom, and any option—be it silence, viewpoint-specific discussion, or open-ended debate—will be controversial and may spark criticism from students, parents, colleagues, or administrators.

Where consensus ends and conflict overtakes us, educators should follow Gerald Graff's advice to teach the conflicts that are present in society—not attempt to resolve them for the students. That is, American educators should teach not only an overall historical framework, specific knowledge of United States government and history, and the basic tools of literacy— reading, critical thinking, and writing—but also the unresolved constitutional conflicts canvassed in Chapter 5, and the competing interests at stake within each cluster of constitutional concern.

A "teach the conflicts" approach to our constitutional principles is implied, if not required, by our historical and contemporary constitutional theories and practices, especially our First Amendment commitment to freedom of expression and the so-called marketplace of ideas. By teaching the conflicts, a common historical time frame and a commitment to constitutional values need not translate into stale, 1950s-style civics or into repression of the best arguments against our common commitments. Likewise, social studies need not be reduced to "a narrow patriotism [or] a policy of isolation."[32]

To teach the conflicts would mean that the multicultural critiques of the traditional materials would become more visible and audible within the curriculum, not less so, for several reasons. First, the American history of excluding people on the basis of race, religion, ethnicity, and gender makes plain that these particular aspects of human identity have both compromised and at times strengthened our democratic principles. They have played a fundamental role in shaping Americans' social and economic opportunities and remain important cultural lightning rods in ways that deserve our best intellectual energy. To cleanse the social studies curriculum of competing interpretations of racial or gender equality or of the most destabilizing arguments of the critical and multiculturalist theorists is to stifle awareness of some of our most fundamental and agonizing social problems.

Moreover, the difficulties we continue to have in dealing with our differences indicate that we all need better knowledge about race, ethnicity, and gender. At present, all sides of public and classroom debates of these issues too often betray inadequate reflection about them and unwittingly reinforce the divisiveness some seek to overcome. *Ethnicity* often is treated as interchangeable with *black*, as if " 'black' [were] the only ethnic group in the United States."[33] Toni Morrison may be introduced to students as a "black female author,"[34] while Virginia Woolf's race goes unmentioned. *Multicultural education* typically translates into *African-American studies*—usually as an elective only—with no other curricular offerings designed to introduce students into the vast range of other American cultures.

When the term *ethnicity* is extended beyond black Americans it soon becomes so broad as to become virtually meaningless, as, "in America, *all* [people] can view themselves romantically as members of some out-group, so that combining the strategy of outsiderism and self-exoticization can be quite contagious."[35] Indeed, the elusiveness and fluidity of the terms *ethnicity* and *race* rarely are explored at all, such that many Americans are inclined to treat each as a fixed category "that explains other phenomena . . . rather [than] as that which needs to be understood and explained."[36]

The unfortunate consequence of this superficial treatment of race and ethnicity is that we often wrongly see only two possible approaches to both: ethnic/race consciousness and separatism or ethnic/race blindness and assimilation. This leads *either* to the trivialization of ethnicity and its cultural significance—"we are all ethnic"—or the effacing of its modern complexities—"only African-Americans are." The vast range of intermediate and hybrid possibilities never is explored, and public dialogue about race and ethnicity becomes unnuanced and unduly polarized. This binary thinking likewise infects our approach to the curriculum such that proposals for multicultural education are met with conversation-closing statements such as the following: "If we start accommodating one group—blacks—then we'll have the Haitians and the Vietnamese and the Pakistanis; where will it end?" No middle-ground or third-ground alternative can emerge because our discussions stall at the threshold.

Common knowledge about gender, religion, sexuality, and reproductive issues too is thin, which again leads to public dialogue about each issue that takes on an either/or, sloganistic cast. Feminist theory, though read by very few, nevertheless is described (usually by the nonreaders) as radical and as though it were monolithic and absurdly irrelevant to nonradical citizens.

Matters of sex and sexuality likewise are, as Judge Richard Posner has recently stated, ill-understood even by many educated judges, let alone by the average voter, which leads to decisions in which people substitute intuition, fear, and myth for careful research or reason.[37] Religion often is reduced to a signifier that means only Christianity and religious conflict to one that means only struggles between Christians and Jews or atheists. Other religions are exoticized such that they do not appear in our public vocabulary, and debates about religion glide over the vast terrain between the Christian / Jewish simplification of religious conflicts and the "we are all religious people" trivialization of religious identity.

We are not, in short, doing our constitutional homework, and our classroom and public conversations reflect it. Anecdote often masquerades as theory. The political opposition—however defined—is sensationalized and reduced to a cartoon, which then is easily mocked and dismissed. Emotionalism trumps dispassionate discourse, and any middle or qualified ground is treated contemptuously as the path of weak-minded intellectual sell-outs rather than as a viable course for people who in good faith wish to consider the evidence and feelings on all sides. Often missing from our debates is an audience—someone listening to learn and, perhaps, to change.

The most striking omission from many of these conversations, though, are facts, including historical evidence. Many discussions of race, gender, and ethnicity could be ground to a halt, or redirected to a more productive exchange, simply by asking the question, "What books or other evidence have led you to your conclusions about [feminism, racism, etc.]?" Instead, we separate into blocs of adherents and opponents and chant slogans across a vast, seemingly unbridgeable cultural divide.

Including multiculturalism issues within the curriculum and demanding that discussions of race, gender, ethnicity, and sexuality become more informed by study and evidence, and less of an exchange of unqualified and unexamined attitude, might help us to elevate the quality of our public deliberations about these important, elusive, contextual, and culture-wrenching concerns.

Closely related to these justifications for giving voice to the multiculturalist critique is an anthropological one. Educational philosophers agree that one purpose of education is to acculturate the youth of the culture, to transmit to them cultural knowledge, beliefs, and practices. Unlike a local education, which properly may stress subcultural homogeneity, a national education must reflect the United States's full range of traditions, practices, and beliefs. To know who "we" are, educators must go beyond traditional presentations of American history that obscure or ignore these race, ethnicity, religion, gender, and other subcultural complexities. Likewise, the national history of this country can be understood only if one understands American cultural and ideological heterogeneity and the fierce conflicts, including a civil war, that it has sparked. Consequently, under even the most conservative definitions of cultural literacy, the multiculturalists have a powerful claim to inclusion of at least some of their proposed additions to the canon, for all of our children's sakes.

A third reason to give multicultural critics of traditional education voice in the shaping of the curriculum is that our constitutional principles require it. To a constitutional historian, the multiculturalists' critiques of the core curriculum sound like an outgrowth of the ongoing, painful struggle of African-American and other groups to attain full citizenship and equality. It is no surprise, then, that members of the groups last or not yet afforded full constitutional citizenship are wariest of the modern call for a traditional core curriculum—national or subnational, and most eager to make that core more cross-representative. Like a jury that excludes black jurors and then determines the fate of a black defendant, an American anthology that excludes or dilutes the voices of African-Americans, women of all colors, non-Christians, gays and lesbians, or other cultural groups and then demands that they learn and be measured by their mastery of this traditional anthology, will be perceived by many Americans as undemocratic—indeed, as un-American.

Curriculum outsiders also may experience exclusive use of this anthology as a cruel denial of every person's natural interest in stories that stress her own origins, her ancestral participation in the shaping of American traditions. Indeed, a canon that emphasizes the history of only one segment of American society in effect asks the remaining members to claim the history of a cousin as their own and to regard her family album as meaningful, even if their faces appear nowhere in the pages or are only blurred or distorted images in the background. This request obviously may alienate, anger and wound the dispreferred, slighted family members. That the traditional canon feels this way to some Americans is best expressed in the multicultural critiques of that canon. Those who dismiss this feeling as trivial deny what is a common, deeply felt human need for recognition and respect.

A fourth reason to integrate multicultural perspectives into the common curriculum is that they may inspire students. Allan Bloom complained in *The Closing of the American Mind* that students today have no heroes and argued that heroes are important to our virtue, individual and collective. Yet if heroes are important, then it is sensible to present students with impressive role models who match the students' race or gender. Just as a coach may seek to encourage an aspiring male athlete more often with male rather than female athlete role models, so a history teacher may seek to inspire his female students with stories about Elizabeth Cady Stanton and Sojourner Truth. Obviously, moreover, these stories likewise may benefit his male students in at least two ways. The stories may inspire male and female students alike to defy unjust practices. They also expand both males' and females' store of images about women in ways that might enable the students to better comprehend females who depart from traditional gender roles.

The root of many multiculturalists' demands that their histories, biographies, poetry, languages, and religions become part of any core curriculum is both a thoroughly American request for democratic participation and a human request for recognition. Indeed, even the radical request for excusal from part or all of the common curriculum rings traditional constitutional bells and often is inspired by a commitment to common values. As Werner Sollors has observed, "Ironically, the very popularity of defiant ethnic revivalism and exclusivism in the United States suggests a widespread backdrop of assimilation against which it takes place. The process works only in a context where values, assumptions, and rhetoric are shared."[38] Responding to multiculturalists' arguments thus often will not defeat our common values as much as it will further them.

Finally, there are two quite practical justifications for a more multicultural education: the globalization of economic, environmental, and political affairs and the increasing ethnic diversity of the United States. Both may require students to understand more about other cultures and to master more languages than most Americans now do.

Moreover, such an international perspective could elevate students' consciousness of human commonalities, rather than promote ethnic particularism, and thus could further the ends of those who resist multicultural education on the ground that it promotes tribalism and racism. Indeed, contrary to the complaint that multiculturalism threatens to undermine the contributions of Western civilization to liberal education, it is a thoroughly Western concept, consistent with the very best of the Western traditions that core curricularists defend. As some writers have so eloquently and passionately observed, curiosity about "the other" is a distinctively Western trait. Multicultural literature that modern critics propose be added to the canon offers a particularly vivid pathway to "the other" and can be a powerful vehicle for hurdling cultural barriers and uncovering common human ties, as well as for illuminating human differences. As such, knowledge of this literature may complement, not necessarily subvert, the Western canon and may promote the values on which it is based.

CONSTITUTIONAL LITERACY FOR A
MULTICULTURAL NATION

An American education should render its students constitutionally literate in both traditional and nontraditional respects. The graduate should be literate in the sense of being able to read and understand the arguments of others, to think logically and critically, and to express her own ideas in a logical grammatical, and organized fashion. She also should have an historical framework into which she can place events and ideas, including those relevant to constitutional principles, and must master specific "constitutional facts"—such as what separation of powers and federalism mean—defined according to traditional but demanding criteria. Finally, however, she should understand that a range of conflicts animates constitutional doctrine and that Americans have divided and still do divide over matters of equality, the freedoms of expression and of religion, and other signal aspects of democratic life. These conflicts, moreover, should be defined capaciously, critically, and provisionally, such that they remain subject to perpetual reformulation and reconsideration. Constitutional literacy, so defined, would welcome multicultural critiques of our conventions, as well as the wide range of other critical responses to our ongoing struggle to balance pluralism and unity within a heterogeneous nation.

One possible, concrete step toward this constitutional literacy would be to teach the specific controversies outlined in Chapter 5 within their historical contexts. These cases and the conflicts they present are not beyond the grasp of a high school student and could easily be adapted for a younger population. Law schools do not demand that entering students have any particular subject matter background, so we know that constitutional principles can be taught to people without a college-level background in a particular subject. We also know that the issues can be taught in a manner that illumines the conflicts without resolving them for the students.

OBJECTIONS TO A CONSTITUTIONAL
LITERACY AGENDA

Like any education proposal, a constitutional literacy proposal will encounter opposition. Some of the most compelling potential objections are as follows.

First, some readers may scoff at the proposal on the ground that it is so obvious that schools must already be teaching everything that is essential.

Surely we must now be teaching the conflicts, as well as basic history, the Constitution, and even the multicultural perspectives on these materials.

In fact, however, schools do not currently teach about constitutional history or practice in this way. Although students may encounter the Constitution at three points in their education—in junior high / middle school United States history, in high school United States history, and in high school United States government or civics—the discussion tends to be restricted.[39] Moreover, during the 1960s and 1970s, the curricular emphasis shifted toward more social history and less political history, especially constitutional history.[40] Although law-related, which includes constitutional, education has become more popular in recent years,[41] constitutional knowledge, as defined here, remains weak. Again, both empirical studies and my own encounters with law students suggest that students either are not receiving, or are not retaining, even very baseline constitutional knowledge within an historical framework, let alone more sophisticated knowledge about constitutional history and changing Court interpretations. The available evidence further suggests that the multicultural education that students now receive is thin, marginalized, and not pervasive.

Other readers will worry that the "teach the conflicts" aspect of the proposal will only bewilder students or render them morally rudderless and thus will only exacerbate our existing problems of centerlessness and moral relativism. Such people, however, likely would fear far more a public school teacher who took it upon herself to resolve these constitutional ambiguities for her students. They might, of course, prefer a teacher who took "their" side on all constitutional issues. But such a public school teacher would thereby be subordinating the strong First Amendment interest in dissent and critical inquiry, as well as neglecting considerable American history, in favor either of an amorphous and highly qualified parental right to control the upbringing of the child or of a vaguer still community right to promote a particular viewpoint. As for the federal constitutional issues addressed here, a subnational community's interest in suppressing these conflicts should not trump the national community's interest in teaching truthfully and expansively about them.

Moreover, the casual assumption that young students cannot tolerate ambiguity or that early introduction to constitutional conflicts would bewilder them is belied by experience. Even fourth graders can appreciate the difference, for example, between a classroom discussion of a presidential race in which they simply express a preference for a candidate and one in which they are asked to explain and justify their preferences, to analyze and respond to arguments of classmates who favor a different candidate, and to identify the areas of disagreement. The upshot of such a discussion is not necessarily befuddled fourth graders but students with a richer understanding of their own choices, of the issues, and of their classmates' choices. To teach the conflicts does not lead inevitably to relativism or moral rudderlessness; it may strengthen convictions as often as it destabilizes them.

Parents' constitutional right to choose private school teachers who are inclined to teach in their preferred way should still be preserved, but only in privately funded settings. *Pierce, Meyer,* and *Yoder* reflect a workable balance of the competing concerns by preserving parents' bounded right to pursue the private school option subject to reasonable, minimal government regulation to assure that their private choices do not result in a form of educational child abuse—such as home-schooled children who do not learn to read or write or do not learn basic history, math, or science. This compromise is hardly costless, for reasons already discussed in earlier chapters; but it takes practical account of the likely futility of seeking to inculcate democratic values that the students' parents abhor as well as the risk of psychological conflicts within a child whose home values collide so violently with those taught in school that the parent would opt for secession.

This proposal is not necessarily inconsistent with voucher plans, provided that receipt of any public funds by families for private education were contingent upon the private schools' compliance with curricular standards. Parents could opt out of even these standards, however, provided that they funded their preferred alternative lessons themselves. That is, all children in public schools and all children whose education is funded by public money should be taught the constitutional curriculum, including the conflicts within it and among us. Removal would still be allowed, but subject to the same constraints that now limit exit from common education standards.

Local school experimentation likewise is not necessarily inconsistent with a proposal for constitutional literacy. Even mandatory national curriculum standards would set only a floor for, not a ceiling on, curriculum possibilities. The national standards or goals would address only those areas that are matters of national concern—information to which all Americans should be exposed—and would leave open the possibility of local supplementation of the national curriculum. Moreover, local schools might realize the common curricular ends in different ways. For example, one district might organize its entire curriculum along an historical time chart, such that all the subjects would be taught chronologically as the students progressed through school. In the ninth grade, the students might be immersed in an eighteenth century perspective on history, science, social studies, philosophy, literature, music, art, drama, and mathematics; then in the tenth grade they might proceed to a nineteenth century perspective on all of these. Another school might choose to meet the same common curricular ends through an entirely different structure, depending on the talents and interests of its faculty and students. Common curricular goals need not inspire pedagogical conformity or a reversal of the trend toward greater local control over school organization and other aspects of the school program.

Some people nevertheless surely will object that this account of constitutional literacy is too directive, in that it will domesticate our conflicts and bleed them of their radical potential.[42] These people likewise will object to its strong nod in favor of mastery of traditional history and language skills.

These are important objections to anyone who fears the strong conformism inherent in so much of formal education. Again, however, the option of resolving the conflicts for students seems inconsistent with our First Amendment commitment to free inquiry as well as with the contingent and contested nature of so many aspects of our social and political history and present lives. Teaching the conflicts may risk domesticating them, but not teaching them risks denying that they exist, and in turn risks disabling our students from making informed choices later in life.

Moreover, it is doubtful that those who minimize the relevance of knowing traditional history would be willing to raise their own children in ignorance of it. If for no other reason than that informed criticism of conventions hinges on knowledge of them, this knowledge is important even to a radical agenda. But many students and other Americans who express frustration about their ignorance of history correctly sense that an historical dimension to life, as conventionally understood, is extremely useful, perhaps essential. Chronology and context—time and space—are the most basic means by which one locates events, things, and lives. Without them, students feel and are quite lost. While the precise historical coordinates we tend to stress arguably are arbitrary in some sense—why, for example, choose the Civil War as an especially critical juncture?—some coordinates are necessary. In any event, a thoughtful educator should be able to justify the choice of particular coordinates, including the Civil War, to her students and, where appropriate, discuss the conflicts among historians about which ones are most critical. Thus the proposed chronological approach to history can be dynamic and inquiry-generative, rather than static or close-ended.

Other readers may question other empirical and normative assumptions on which this proposal appears to rest. For example, isn't the claim that "we" share constitutional commitments belied by accounts of the disagreements? By reports that many Americans might not approve of the written Constitution if it were put to a vote today? Even by the differences between the Republican and the Democratic party platforms during the 1992 Presidential election? That is, who are the "we" who share these "values"? What is left of the commitments once they are stripped of our conflicts about them? And, should the constitutional principles still be taught even if there were *no* consensus about them?

A related question concerns basing *any* part of a curriculum on the Constitution and Supreme Court cases. How can we rely for curriculum planning on a document this vague and horoscope-like (in the sense that it means whatever a reader chooses to read into it)? Why should any interpretation of this document, even the Supreme Court's, be privileged over other, more radical accounts or critiques? Indeed, why should educators rely at all on a document that is not of universal application and that might be modified, even repudiated altogether? Shouldn't education proposals be grounded on something stabler, purer, and more fundamental than this eighteenth century, imperfect political compromise?

These inquiries are difficult to answer briefly, because they involve the meaning of language and texts, and constitutional and political theory. A preliminary response is as follows: If our disagreements over the Constitution were so pervasive that we had no consensus, we would not be this far into this text; all readers would have tossed it aside either in confusion or disgust. More obviously, however, courts could not identify a constitutional issue, lawyers could not argue meaningfully about these issues, and law students would be informed that there is no constitutional law that can be discussed in common terms, if it really were "difference *all* the way down." Yet each year, law schools not only teach constitutional law but teach it in a manner that enables a law school graduate from Tucson, Arizona, to communicate meaningfully with a law partner in Atlanta, Georgia, or with a federal judge in San Francisco, California, or a legislator in Washington, D.C., about constitutional principles. There is, in fact, a reasonably intelligible, commonly accepted constitutional framework, despite the debates that rage within it. Moreover, a conflicts approach to constitutional literacy anticipates that the radical critiques of this framework would be discussed, not suppressed, as relevant to the ongoing debate about the Constitution. While the Constitution is undeniably vague, and may well be more horoscope than blueprint, this does not make it insubstantial. Rather, it has the several meanings that courts, commentators, and other citizens ascribe to it, all of which can be discussed and debated in a meaningful fashion.

As to the claim that the Constitution is not the source of our beliefs about liberty and justice, only an imperfect reflection of them, and that it thus should not be the center of any curriculum proposal, the introduction to Chapter 5 provides a response. Constitutional language certainly is not the only language applicable to the conflict between collective and individual interests or about competing meanings of equality. Yet this vocabulary has special cultural resonance and a familiarity that renders it superior to other discipline-specific or sect-specific vocabularies. More Americans can be persuaded to join the important debate about our collective and individual interests when it is expressed in constitutional terms.

And finally, as to the question whether there ought to be instruction in constitutional values even if there were no consensus about their importance, the answer must be yes. Freedom of expression, freedom of religion, and equality are values worth preserving regardless of whether some Americans might vote against the Bill of Rights. And constitutional literacy is the best way to preserve those values.

Some readers will raise practical objections to this proposal. For example, if students today are being taught some constitutional history and civics but are not retaining it, why aren't they doing so? Is it that they simply do not care about these subjects or that they fail to perceive their significance to their lives? If they do not care, then what good will teaching more of this do for them—especially when weighed against the multiple other demands for curricular space, as schools increasingly are expected to teach students everything from computer skills to sex education? Real-world survivalist education should be the national curricular goal, some will insist, not education based on romanticized and abstract notions about a "constitutional conversation" that means little to most Americans' daily lives. In any event, if the goal is to inculcate particular political values—that is, to encourage respect for the Constitution and the Bill of Rights—it is bound to fail, given evidence that schools do not influence students' values. Rather, family and peers are the far more powerful determinants of students' attitudes and behavior. Exposure to constitutional issues, even in the richer and more complex form advocated in this book, therefore will not make people more tolerant, analytically rigorous, sensitive, or wise. Although the quality of our public debates might improve, our political outcomes would not necessarily do so.

Although this plea for survivalist education is sobering and sadly pertinent, constitutional literacy is hardly a hopeless, useless luxury, even in these educationally hard times. Rather, constitutional literacy is as basic as math or science literacy, for the reasons given in Chapter 5. Meaningful exercise of the right to vote, to take an important example, requires that the voter possess the knowledge and skills of such literacy. Moreover, constitutional literacy would be only one part of needed educational reform: the argument for greater emphasis on the elements of constitutional literacy neither precludes examination of other reform issues nor bars them from higher priority in the curriculum.

Nor is it true that there is not enough curricular time for multicultural additions to traditional social studies. The race, gender, or ethnic implications of history and civics need not be taught as time-consuming tags to the conventional material, but as integral parts of it.

The claim that exposure to constitutional materials will not necessarily alter students' respect for freedom of expression, freedom of religion, or equality is correct. Likewise, however, students' exposure to poetry and literature won't necessarily make them admirers of the beauty of words or the world of ideas. Teaching them history won't necessarily convince them not to repeat it, and teaching them about religion won't make them believe in a transcendental power. But not teaching them about these things almost certainly will doom them to ignorance of them and thereby improve the chances that the knowledge and values we hope to transmit through these materials will not be passed on. Thus, while constitutional literacy will not necessarily translate into a more tolerant, just, or decent society, constitutional illiteracy almost certainly will not improve our collective lives and may well compromise our constitutional aspirations.

A final, critical question about a constitutional literacy agenda is intensely practical: how will teachers test the conflicts? Once we move away from mastery of objective facts and toward arguments and counterarguments, how do we evaluate academic achievement reliably? Won't the fact that the standard tests do *not* assess this knowledge subordinate the apparent importance of constitutional literacy to teachers and students? Yet if tests *did* try to assess constitutional literacy, wouldn't that lead to a rigidified, conventional account of the conflicts and thereby defeat the purpose of a conflicts approach?

Again, the experience of law schools is evidence that these objections likely can be overcome. Law schools traditionally rely on essay examinations to test students' mastery of constitutional principles and arguments. Even multiple-choice or short answer questions, though, have been constructed to test complex legal issues and arguments. So, while mastery of objective facts—such as the number of inches in a foot—doubtless is easier to assess with efficient, multiple-choice testing measures, mastery of more complex matters, too, can be tested well enough that this objection, taken alone, should not defeat a constitutional literacy initiative. If anything, it might inspire a closer look at the many shortcomings of standardized tests and the perils of relying too heavily on these measures of academic achievement.

CONCLUSION

Any national curriculum should stress, among other things, the kind of national knowledge that will enable our children to assume the complex duties of American citizenship. This includes not only baseline literacy and historical knowledge but also a rich appreciation of our conflicts and pluralism. In this country, a national education cannot be taught otherwise without being what James Baldwin once called a "cruel lie."

E. D. Hirsch, Jr., and fellow core curricularists have made a persuasive case that our students lack a common knowledge framework and that democratic life depends, in part, on having this framework. This book argues that this framework should include constitutional literacy, which means not only recognition of constitutional terms, constitutional dilemmas, and historical assumptions on which the Constitution arguably rests but also recognition of the paradox on which the document is based, its dynamism, and its multiple contested interpretations. Social studies, including law-related studies, should not be taught as a static, discrete, or harmonious body of purely historical knowledge but as a sometimes chaotic set of conflicts throughout history that inform our contemporary practices and problems.

In short, any national curriculum must be true to our national experiences, but "our" must be defined pluralistically. Only such a curriculum is likely to improve the quality of our public discourse and to prepare our students adequately for the complex demands of American citizenship in the twenty-first century.

The debate over a national core curriculum concerns critical aspects of our public and private lives, in particular the meaning of American citizenship. As this debate continues—and history strongly suggests that it will continue—we should recognize its constitutional implications. As we advance our proposals and launch our objections to others' proposals, we likewise should consider that the quality of our public debates depends not only on the right of all to express their ideas freely but also on a community willing to listen to their views. That is, meaningful participation in the constitutional conversation involves both speech and reflective silence, as other speakers, especially those least like ourselves, take their turn. Good citizenship in this sense remains a commendable public value, one worth cultivating in the nation's children.

Notes

2 THE RISE OF FORMAL SCHOOLING AND THE
"AMERICAN "PAIDEIA"

1. Massachusetts School Law of 1647.
2. Thomas Jefferson, "Bill For the More General Diffusion of Knowledge (1779)," in 2 *The Works of Thomas Jefferson* (P. Leicaster ed., 1904).
3. Lawrence A. Cremin, *American Education: The National Experience, 1783–1876*, 486–99 (1980); Ira Katznelson & Margaret Weir, *Schooling for All: Class, Race, and the Decline of the Democratic Ideal* 74 (1985).
4. *See* "10th Annual Report to the Massachusetts Board of Education," published in *The Common School Journal* (1847) (edited by Horace Mann); *see also* "12th Annual Report to the Massachusetts Board of Education," published in *The Common School Journal, Journal* (1849).
5. *See* Lawrence A. Cremin, *supra* note 3, at 126.
6. *See* Joel Spring, *American Education* 6–7 (4th ed. 1989); Rush Welter, *Popular Education and Democratic Thought in America* 26–27 (1962).
7. Mortimer J. Adler, "This Pre-War Generation," in Mortimer J. Adler, *Reforming Education* 9 (1977).
8. For a more complete review of the rise of formal, compulsory education, in the United States, see Lawrence A. Cremin, *supra* note 3; Michael B. Katz, *A History of Compulsory Education Laws* (1976); David B. Tyack, *The One Best System* (1974); David B. Tyack, "Ways of Seeing: An Essay on the History of Compulsory Schooling," 46 *Harv. Educ. Rev.* 355 (1976).
9. *See* note 1, *supra*.
10. *See* Rush Welter, *supra* note 6, at 10.
11. *See* note 2, *supra*.
12. *Id*.
13. *See* note 1, *supra*.
14. *See* Lawrence A. Cremin, *supra* note 3, at 123 (describing two proposals submitted in response to a 1795 essay contest on education).

15. *See id.* at 163–64.

16. *See* Rush Welter, *supra* note 6, at 105.

17. An example of this sentiment is the observation of William Godwin that "[h]ad the scheme of a national education been adopted when despotism was most triumphant, it is not to be believed that it could have forever stifled the voice of truth. But it would have been the most formidable and profound contrivance for that purpose that imagination can suggest." William Godwin, *An Enquiry Concerning Political Justice* 238 (K. Codell Carter ed., 1971) (commenting on proposals for national education in England).

18. *See* John Stuart Mill, *On Liberty* 98 (Norton ed. 1975).

19. *Id.*

20. *Id.* at 99.

21. *Id.* at 99.

22. Lawrence A. Cremin, *The Metropolitan Experience 1876–1980* 644–45 (1988).

23. Public sentiment continued to swing between the poles of centralized and intensely local community control of education. *See, e.g.*, Diane Ravitch, *The Great School Wars: New York City, 1805–1973* (1974) (describing the movement toward and away from centralization of administrative authority over New York City public schools).

24. *See, e.g.*, Lawrence A. Cremin, *supra* note 3, at 142.

25. *See* 10th Annual Report, *supra* note 4.

26. Lawrence A. Cremin, *supra* note 3.

27. *See* 10th Annual Report, *supra* note 4.

28. *See* Lawrence A. Cremin, *supra* note 3; Ira Katznelson and Margaret Weir, *supra* note 3, at 74.

29. *See* 10th Annual Report, *supra* note 4. An important observation about these early stages of public schooling is that many people who favored government-funded education did not favor *compulsory* education. Even Horace Mann argued only that public education in Massachusetts should be available to all children, not required for all children. Other reform groups and some labor groups, however, did lobby for compulsory schooling. *See* Lawrence A. Cremin, *supra* note 3, at 156–57.

30. *See, e.g.*, David Hogan, "Capitalism, Liberalism and Schooling," in *Education and the State, vol. I: Schooling and the National Interest,* 31, 32 (R. Dale, G. Esland, R. Fergusson & M. MacDonald eds., 1981).

31. *See* Lawrence A. Cremin, *supra* note 22, at 149–50.

32. *Id.*

33. *See* Lawrence A. Cremin, *supra* note 3, at 507–11.

34. *See* Lawrence A. Cremin, *supra* note 22, at 172.

35. *See id.* at 644–45.

36. Lawrence A. Cremin, *Traditions of American Education* 87 (1977).

37. Lawrence A. Cremin, *supra* note 22, at 521.

38. Michael W. Apple, *Ideology and Curriculum* 78 (1979). Apple believes that the breakdown in the economic and of moral order stemmed from the following developments:
    > [It was] caused in part by rapid industrialization, the shift from the accumulation of agricultural to industrial capital, the growth of technology, immigration, "the perceived disintegration of community life, the increasing 'need' to divide and control labor to increase profits, and so on."

    Id.

39. *Id.* at 79. Professor Mark Kelman of Stanford Law School, in a telephone conversation

with the author, once described this reliance on testing as a means of sorting students as a product of "intelligence quotient fetishism."

40. *See* Tyler G. Anbinder, *Nativism and Slavery: The Northern Know Nothings and the Politics of the 1850s* (1992).

41. James M. McPherson, "Patterns of Prejudice," *The New Republic*, 43, 45 (Oct. 19, 1992) (quoting Archbishop Hughes).

42. Diane Ravitch, *supra* note 23, at 35.

43. *Id.* at 44.

44. *Id.* at 35.

45. *Id.* at 44.

46. *Id.* at 21.

47. *See* Stanley Fish, "Bad Company," 56 *Transition* 60, 60–61 (1992) (discussing texts of the late nineteenth century and early twentieth century that describe immigration as a peril to American unity).

48. *See* Lawrence A. Cremin, *supra* note 3, at 218–51.

49. *See* John A. Hostetler, *Amish Society* (3d ed. 1980).

50. Arthur M. Schlesinger, Jr., *The Disuniting of America* (1991) (discussing contemporary apprehensions about cultural disunity).

51. For discussions of modern concerns about these same issues see Robert Hughes, "The Fraying of America," *Time* 44 (Feb. 3, 1992); Mary Lefkowitz, "Not Out of Africa," *The New Republic* 29 (Feb. 10, 1992). *See also* chapter 3, *infra*.

52. *See, e.g.,* Lawrence A. Cremin, *The Transformation of the School: Progressivism in American Education, 1876–1957* 66 (1961).

53. *Id.* By 1909, 57.8 percent of children in the largest urban school centers were of foreign-born parentage. *Id.* at 72.

54. *Id.* at 66. *See also* Joel Spring, *supra* note 6, at 11.

55. Edward Hale Bierstadt, *Aspects of Americanization* 114–15 (1922), (quoted in Lawrence A. Cremin, *supra* note 52, at 68). For an instructive account of federal efforts to "civilize" Native American children by compelling them to leave their homes and attend boarding schools that would assimilate them into the dominant white culture, see Robert A. Trennert, Jr., *The Phoenix Indian School: Forced Assimilation in Arizona, 1891–1935* (1988).

56. Lawrence A. Cremin, *supra* note 52, at 74.

57. Horace M. Kallen, *Culture and Democracy in the United States: Studies in the Group Psychology of the American Peoples* 24 (1924).

58. *Id.*

59. *Id.*

60. *Id.* at 24–26.

61. *See* Michael W. Apple, *supra* note 38, at 65–68.

62. *Id.* at 67.

63. *See* A. Kopan, "Melting Pot: Myth or Reality?" in *Cultural Pluralism* 45 (E. Epps ed., 1974).

64. *Id.*

65. Horace M. Kallen, *supra* note 57, at 186–90.

66. *Id.* at 41–42.

67. *Id.* at 42.

68. *Id.* at 58.

69. *Id.* at 62.

70. *See* Ira Katznelson & Margaret Weir, *supra* note 3, at 54–55.

71. *Id.*

72. *See* Meyer v. Nebraska, 262 U.S. 390 (1923).

73. *Id.* at 401: "It is said the purpose of the legislation was to promote civic development by inhibiting training and education of the immature in foreign tongues and ideals before they could learn English and acquire American ideals. . . . It is also affirmed that the foreign born population is very large, that certain communities commonly use foreign words, follow foreign leaders, move in a foreign atmosphere, and that the children are thereby hindered from becoming citizens of the most useful type and the public safety is imperiled."

74. *See* Ralph Henry Gabriel, *The Course of American Democratic Thought* (1986); F. O. Matthiessen, *American Renaissance* (1941); Merle Curti, *Growth of American Thought* (1943); Reinhold Niebuhr, *The Children of Light and the Children of Darkness: A Vindication of Democracy and a Critique of Its Traditional Defense* (1944).

75. *See* I. B. Berkson, *Preface to An Educational Philosophy* 173 (1940).

76. Michael W. Apple, *supra* note 38, at 80.

77. *Id.*

78. *See* Ira Katznelson & Margaret Weir, *supra* note 3, at 77.

79. Frederick Rudolph, *Curriculum: A History of the American Undergraduate Course of Study Since 1636* 90 (1977).

80. *Id.*

81. *Id.* at 159.

82. *Id.* (footnote omitted).

83. *Id.* at 165.

84. *Id.* at 196.

85. *Id.* at 256.

86. Historian Lawrence Cremin has summarized the central themes of the Progressive movement as follows:

   [F]irst, a broadening of the program and function of the school to include direct concern for health, vocation, and the quality of family and community life; second, the application in the classroom of more humane, more active, and more rational pedagogical techniques derived from research in philosophy, psychology, and the social sciences; third, the tailoring of instruction more directly to the different kinds and classes of children who were being brought within the purview of the school (for some, this meant teaching a common curriculum in very different ways; for others, it meant teaching differentiated curricula); and finally, the use of more systematically organized and rational approaches to the administration and management of the schools.

   Lawrence A. Cremin, *supra* note 22, at 229.

87. John Dewey, *Experience and Education* 35 (1938).

88. *Id.* at 36.

89. This "child-centered" orientation has roots in the ideas expressed by Quintillian, Comenius, Rousseau, and Testalozzi. *See Conflicting Conceptions of Curriculum* 3 (E. Eisner & E. Vallance eds., 1974).

90. John Dewey, *supra* note 87, at 34.

91. *Id.* at 30.

92. *Id.* at 60.

93. *Id.* at 46–47.

94. *Id.* at 49.

95. Lawrence A. Cremin, *supra* note 22, at 179.

96. Daniel Bell, *The Reforming of General Education: The Columbia College Experience in Its National Setting* (1966). For a general history of undergraduate education in the United States, see Frederick Rudolph, *supra* note 79.

97. *See* I. B. Berkson, *supra* note 75.

98. Daniel Bell, *supra* note 96, at 24.

99. *Id.*

100. *Id.*

101. Robert M. Hutchins, *The Higher Learning in America* 99 (1936).

102. Daniel Bell, *supra* note 96, at 33.

103. *Id.*

104. *Id.* at 15.

105. Robert M. Hutchins, *supra* note 101, at 66.

106. *Id.* at 15 (quoting *General Education in a Free Society: Report of the Harvard Committee* (1945) [the "Redbook"]). For a discussion of changes in curricular philosophy at Harvard since the 1945 Redbook appeared, see Seymour Martin Lipset & David Riesman, *Education and Politics at Harvard* 347–51 (1975).

107. Daniel Bell, *supra* note 96, at 39.

108. *Id.* at 40.

109. *Id.* at 41.

110. *Id.* at 173.

111. *Id.* at 172–73.

112. For an illustration of the depth of emotion that some educators experienced regarding these disagreements about "external verities," see Mortimer J. Adler, *supra* note 7, at 3. Adler argues that an exclusive trust in science and denial that philosophy or theology may have independent authority pave the way to fascism. *Id.* at 9.

113. Also, as early as 1940, some educators were decrying value relativism, American pragmatism, and the tendency of American education to reduce all morality to a cultural convention. *Id.* at 11. Indeed Adler's essay is strikingly similar to parts of Allan Bloom's 1987 book, *The Closing of the American Mind*. Other writers point out that Bloom's arguments are simply reformulations of the ideas of Bloom's teacher, Leo Strauss. *See, e.g.,* George Anastaplo, *In re Allan Bloom: A Respectful Dissent in Essays on the Closing of the American Mind* 267, 271–72 (R. Stone ed., 1989); Richard Rorty, "Straussianism, Democracy, and Allan Bloom I: That Old-Time Philosophy," *The New Republic* 28 (April 4, 1988); Harvey C. Mansfield, Jr., "Straussianism, Democracy, and Allan Bloom II: Democracy and the Great Books," in *Essays on the Closing of the American Mind* 106 (R. Stone ed., 1989).

114. *See* Frederick Rudolph, *supra* note 79, at 261.

115. Daniel Bell, *supra* note 96, at 39–40.

116. *See, e.g.,* National Endowment for the Humanities, *50 Hours: A Core Curriculum for College Students* (1989).

117. *See* Arthur E. Wise, *Legislated Learning: The Bureaucratization of the American Classroom* 2–3, 48–50 (1979).

118. *See* Frances FitzGerald, *America Revised* (1979). Indeed, the textbook industry, in concert with these few large states, exercises tremendous, low-visibility control over the content of public school curricula. A few companies always have tended to dominate the textbook market. For example, during the 1830s, the Samuel G. Goodrich series was the most

popular of all texts on American history. Lawrence A. Cremin, *supra* note 3, at 394. Like many of the textbooks of that era, the Goodrich series stressed the superiority of American institutions, American people, and Protestant values. *Id*. These early texts also depicted people of color as inferior, even though they described slavery as an evil institution. The latter position was typical of texts published in the Northeast, where most of the nineteenth century publishing companies were located. *Id*.

3 THE MODERN CALL FOR A NATIONAL CORE CURRICULUM

1. Some observers complain that school organization is too centralized and bureaucratized. *See, e.g.*, Arthur E. Wise, *Legislated Learning: The Bureaucratization of the American Classroom*, 2–3 (1979); Ivan Illich, *Deschooling Society* 19 (1971); Thomas T. Toch, *In the Name of Excellence* 264–271 (1991). In New Hampshire, arguments against centralized, state-level control of education recently prompted the State Board of Education to eliminate virtually all of its minimum education standards, which would permit local governments to set their own standards. This radical step has inspired opposition from some parents and school officials. *See* William Celis, "Furor in New Hampshire on Vote to Cut Standards," *N.Y. Times*, Aug. 26, 1992, at A20, col. 1. Others complain that it is too decentralized. *See, e.g.*, E. D. Hirsch, Jr., *Cultural Literacy* 19 (1988 ed.).

Others argue that students are factually impoverished. *See* notes 25–36 *infra*. Still others insist that schools are dreary inculcation centers in which facts are stressed instead of critical thinking and imagination. *See, e.g.*, Clarence J. Karier, "Business Values and the Educational States," in *Roots of Crisis: American Education in the Twentieth Century* 6, 24–25 (1973).

In recent years, the business sector has added its voice to the cry of school crisis and has expressed concern that schools are failing to produce an adequate number of qualified workers for a changing labor market. In some cases, businesses have applied private funds to encourage school innovations to correct for this problem. *See, e.g.*, William Celis, "Study Urges Preschool Role for Business," *N.Y. Times*, Mar. 1, 1991, at A14, col. 2 (describing study by New York group of business and educational leaders that urges business community to become more active in health and social programs for young children); Eurich Nell, *Corporate Classrooms: The Learning Business* (Study of the Carnegie Foundation for the Advancement of Teaching, 1985) (describing efforts of business to fill gaps in workers' education through corporate-sponsored schools); Ezra Bowen, "Schooling for Survival," *Time* 74 (Feb. 11, 1985); "Nabisco Awards $9.7 Million in Grants to 15 Schools," *N.Y. Times*, Apr. 17, 1991, at B7, col. 1 (describing award of grants by Nabisco to innovative schools). *See also* E. D. Hirsch, Jr., *supra*, at 1. These developments worry some commentators, who argue that business and education already are inextricably bound, such that educational policy often is directed toward capitalistic interests, with inadequate regard for social reform, and self-actualization of students. *See* Clarence Karier, *supra*.

Many reformers argue for deregulation of the public schools, and greater parental choice over the public school that a child can attend. The school choice advocates favor a restructuring of public schooling at the elementary and secondary level, under which parents could choose which school their child attends, rather than schools assigning children to particular locations on the basis of where the child lives. *See, e.g.*, John E. Chubb & Terry M. Moe, *Politics, Markets, and America's Schools* (1990); Don Fuhr, *Choices:*

Public Education for the 21st Century (1990). *Cf.* John J. Miller, "Opting Out," *The New Republic* 12 (Nov. 30, 1992) (noting that some conservatives have become skeptical of choice because it may lead to greater regulation of private schools). The more radical choice advocates believe that parents should receive public money for education—in the form of "vouchers"—which they then could apply to public or private, sectarian or secular, education of their children. *See* Susan Chira, "The Rules of the Marketplace Are Applied to the Classroom," *N.Y. Times*, June 12, 1991, at A1, col. 5 (describing two choice programs that have emerged in New York City and Milwaukee); Susan Chira, "Bush Presses Bill Allowing Parents to Choose Schools," *N.Y. Times*, April 19, 1991, at A1, col. 6 (describing Bush proposal whereby federal money devoted to needy children would follow the child to whatever schools their parents choose, public or private); "62 Percent of Americans Support School Choice, Poll Finds," *N.Y. Times*, Aug. 23, 1991, at A16, col. 1 (reporting on annual poll of public attitudes toward public schools); Amy Stuart Wells, "A Bold Plan for Choice in Delaware's Schools," *N.Y. Times*, Feb. 27, 1991, at B8, col. 1 (describing DuPont proposal for choice in Delaware public schools); Robert J. Samuelson, "Back-to-School Economics," *Newsweek* 53 (Sept. 23, 1985) (arguing for break-up of the public school "monopoly"); Dennis P. Doyle, Bruce S. Cooper & Roberta Trachtman, "Education: Ideas and Strategies for the 1990s," *The American Enterprise* 25 (Mar. / Apr. 1991) (arguing for vouchers for low-income students and for parental choice in selecting schools for all children); Christopher Jencks, "Is the Public School Obsolete?" 2 *The Public Interest* 18, 21–27 (Winter 1966) (arguing for alternatives to public school organization, including tuition grants or management contracts to private organizations); John E. Coons & Stephen D. Sugarman, *Scholarships for Children* (1992); John E. Coons & Stephen D. Sugarman, *Family Choice in Education: A Model State System for Vouchers* (1971); Milton Friedman, *Capitalism and Freedom* 85 (1962); Henry M. Levin, "The Failure of the Public Schools and the Free Market Remedy," 2 *The Urban Rev.* 32 (June 1968); Samuel L. Blumenfeld, *Is Public Education Necessary?* 249 (1981) (arguing that "[t]he failure of public education is the failure of statism as a political philosophy.").

A related movement, the "home school" movement, would further reduce governmental control over education by allowing parents to teach their children at home, subject to limited state regulation. *See generally*, John Holt, *Teach Your Own Children: A Hopeful Path for Education* (1981); Christopher Klicka, *The Right Choice* (1992); Michael Knight, Note, "Parental Liberties Versus the State's Interest in Education: The Case for Allowing Home Education," 18 *Tex. Tech. L. Rev.* 1261 (1987); James W. Tobak & Perry A. Zirkel, "Home Instruction: An Analysis of the Statutes and Case Law," 8 *U. Dayton L. Rev.* 1 (1982); Ira C. Lupu, "Home Education, Religious Liberty, and the Separation of Powers," 67 *B.U. L. Rev.* 97 (1987). The movement has gained considerable force in the past twenty years. *See* Mary Esch, "Home Schooling on Upswing," *Ariz. Daily Star*, July 13, 1991, at B4, col. 1. Indeed, it has a strong national network, which includes a nationally distributed newsletter published by the Home School Legal Defense Association, entitled *The Home School Court Report*. The Association is headquartered in Paeonian Springs, Virginia.

Criticism of the school choice movement centers on the potential violation of church and state, as well as on the movement's potential for resegregating schools along racial, ethnic, and socioeconomic lines. *See, e.g.*, James S. Liebman, "Voice, Not Choice," 101 *Yale L.J.* 259 (1991). More recently, the Carnegie Foundation for the Advancement of Teaching issued a report that criticized choice on the ground that choice primarily benefits children of better-educated parents, is expensive, and will not solve the underlying problems that influence poor school performance, such as poverty, family problems, and health issues. *See* Susan Chira, "Furor Over 'Choice'," *N.Y. Times*, Oct. 28, 1992, at A16, col. 5; Susan Chira, "Research Questions Effectiveness of Most School-Choice Programs," *N.Y. Times*, Oct. 26, 1992, at A1, col. 4; Carol L. Ziegler & Nancy M. Lederman, "School Vouchers: Are Urban Students Surrendering Rights for Choice?" 19 *Fordham Urb. L. J.* 813 (1992); *see also* James B. Egle, "The Constitutional Implications of School Choice," 1992 *Wis. L. Rev.* 459. Arguments against home schooling tend to focus on concern that home-educated children will be underprepared for the challenges of a plural society and may lack critical social skills. Moreover, they may be indoctrinated by their parents into an unduly narrow, even intolerant, view of alternative philosophies. The cost to the child, as well as to society, may outweigh the benefit of increased parental liberty to direct the child's upbringing. Both the choice movement and the home school movement have been criticized as risks to the objective of assimilation into a common culture through common, public education.

2. *See, e.g.*, A. G. Powell, E. Farrar & D. K. Cohen, *The Shopping Mall High School: Winners and Losers in the Educational Marketplace* 1–8 (1985); E. D. Hirsch, Jr., *supra* note 1, at 19–21; Marvin Cetron & Margaret Gayle, *Educational Renaissance: Our Schools at the Turn of the Century* 96 (1991); Karen De Witt, "College Board Announces Project to Alter High School Curriculum," *N.Y. Times*, May 4, 1992, at A12, col. 5; Chester E. Finn, "Fear of Standards Threatens Education Reform," *Wall Street Journal*, Mar. 23, 1992.

3. *See, e.g.*, "Campus Life: Study of Sex Roles and Diversity Required," *N.Y. Times*, Dec. 10, 1991, at B4, col. 1 (reporting on new requirements at Stanford University, effective in the fall of 1991, under which undergraduates must take courses that address issues of sex roles and cultural diversity); Dinesh D'Souza, *Illiberal Education* 59–93 (1991) (discussing controversy at Stanford regarding Western Civilization distribution requirement); *Stanford Observer* 4 (Apr / May 1990) (describing new distribution requirements).

4. *See, e.g.*, E. D. Hirsch, Jr., *supra* note 1.

5. *See*, Karen De Witt, "National Tests Urged for Public Schools," *N.Y. Times*, Jan. 17, 1991, at A12, col. 1. *See also* Laura D'Andrea Tyson, "Failing Our Youth" 7 *New Perspectives Quarterly* 26, 29 (Fall 1990) (discussing the recommendation of the Commission on Skills in the American Workforce that the United States adopt national educational performance examinations). *See also* Karen De Witt, *supra* note 2 (describing "Pacesetter" project of the College Board, which would include development of a standard curriculum and test for high school students); Susan Chira, "Rivals Agree on Need for National School Standards but Differ on U.S. Role," *N.Y. Times*, Oct. 23, 1992, at A14, col. 1 (discussing education philosophies of 1992 presidential candidates George Bush, Bill Clinton, and H. Ross Perot, and noting that all three endorse the idea of formal national curriculum standards that outline what American students should know and a national testing system to gauge their mastery of this curriculum).

6. Amy Gutmann, "Educating for [Multiple] Choice" 7 *New Perspectives Quarterly* 48 (Fall 1990).

7. E. D. Hirsch, Jr., *supra* note 1, at 4.

8. *Id.* at 5–7.

9. *Id.* at 7.

10. *Id.* at 7–8.

11. *Id.* at 11.

12. *Id.* at 1.

13. *Id.* at 12.

14. *Id.* at 112.

15. *Id.* at 113.

16. *Id.* at 122–125.

17. *Id.* at 126.

18. *Id.* at 25. *See also* Marvin Cetron & Margaret Gayle, *supra* note 2, at 96–98.

19. E. D. Hirsch, Jr., *supra* note 1, at 26.

20. *Id.* at 92.

21. *Id.* at 94–95.

22. *Id.* at 100–101.

23. *Id.* at 101.

24. *Id.* at 18.

25. *See, e.g.,* National Commission on Excellence in Education, *A Nation At Risk* 8–9 (1983) (citing statistic that thirteen percent of all twelve-year-olds in the United States are functionally illiterate and that SAT scores declined steadily from 1963–1980); Ezra Bowen, "Are Student Heads Full of Emptiness?" *Time* 56 (Aug. 17, 1987); Alvin P. Sanoff, "What Americans Should Know," *U.S. News & World Report* 86 (Sept. 28, 1987); Karen De Witt, "Math Survey in Public Schools Shows No State Is 'Cutting It'," *N.Y. Times,* June 7, 1991, at A1, col. 1 (reporting on data released by federal government that show only one out of seven eighth graders nationally reaches the level of mathematics proficiency expected at that grade level); Karen De Witt, "Verbal Scores Hit New Low in Scholastic Aptitude Tests," *N.Y. Times,* Aug. 27, 1991, at A1, col. 4 (reporting that college-bound seniors scored all-time low on verbal part of SATs); Timothy Egan, "Oregon Literacy Test Shows Many Lag in Basics," *N.Y. Times,* Apr. 24, 1991, at B7, col. 1 (reporting on adult illiteracy in Oregon); Lawrence A. Cremin, *American Education: The Metropolitan Experience, 1876–1980* 662 (noting decline in American teens' performance on academic achievement test during the 1970s and 1980s).

26. *See 50 Hours: A Core Curriculum for College Students* (National Endowment for the Humanities, 1989) (reciting findings of 1989 survey funded by the National Endowment for the Humanities and conducted by the Gallup Organization). *See also* Julie Johnson, "Core Curriculum Urged for College Students," *N.Y. Times,* Oct. 9, 1989, at B1, col. 5.

27. *See, 50 Hours, supra* note 26, at 11. *See also* Nat'l Assessment of Educational Progress, *Changes in Political Knowledge and Attitudes 1969–76: Selected Results from the Second National Assessments of Citizenship and Social Studies* (1978) (noting decline in knowledge of American civics between 1969 and 1976).

28. *See* Amy Gutmann "Introduction" in Charles Taylor, *Multiculturalism and "The Politics of Recognition",* 3–9 (1992).

29. *See* "Forum: Who Needs the Great Works?" *Harper's* 43, 52 (Sept. 1989) (conversation in which Hirsch remarks that "[e]ssentially" he would approve of any consensus-drafted list, provided there is "a certain amount of common sense to get to consensus.").

30. In this respect, the education conservatives echo Thomas Jefferson, who argued in the late eighteenth century that education in baseline skills for all free whites in Virginia was a necessary component of a democracy. Thomas Jefferson, *Notes on Virginia.*

31. E. D. Hirsch, Jr., *supra* note 1, at 12.

32. Lawrence A. Cremin, *supra* note 25, at 673. As Cremin observed, to the extent that we have an American *paideia,* it is derived from Protestant Christianity, the British legal tradition, the Enlightenment, and American constitutionalism. *Id.*

33. *Id.* at 672.

34. The popularized version of the philosophical objectivist argument appears in the 1987 best-seller, *The Closing of the American Mind*, by Professor Allan Bloom.

According to Bloom, the central permanent concern of mankind is "What is man?" The purpose of a liberal education, consequently, is to provide access to alternative answers to this central question. More particularly, liberal education exists for the handful of students who will spend their lifetimes attempting to be autonomous and to resist the "deforming forces of convention and prejudice." *Id.* at 20–21. These individuals, the future scholars and intellectuals, will shape the destiny of our culture, insofar as they will become part of the handful of elite educational centers that have tremendous influence over how all Americans are taught. Thus, says Bloom, if the universities that train these people are ill, then the society is ill.

Bloom maintains that the United States is ill in that the universities are failing in their mission of cultivating the minds that will lead future generations. In particular, the universities are teaching the future intellectuals the wrong lessons, the wrong attitudes, and the wrong habits. The modern student, says Bloom, suffers from an overlearned and unreflective appreciation for the "anthropological insight" that all values are culturally relative and that truth, God, justice, and beauty are mere historical myths. In its most powerful form, which objectivists like Bloom find repulsive, the anthropological insight could lead a student to approve of genocide or sacrificing virgins to volcanoes, on the ground that the practices have cultural relevance and thus are justified within that culture's system of beliefs. A relativist believes that no independent anchor exists with which to ground criticisms of cultural practices other than the equally subjective attitudes and beliefs of one's original culture. Without an ahistorical, acultural means of distinguishing between good and bad cultural beliefs and practices, some relativists refuse to impose their own belief system on the "other" and decline to judge cultural practices. Bloom abhors this refusal to judge and believes that university educators who embrace relativism have perverted education, such that it no longer assumes its traditional role of teaching students what they need to make them both virtuous and competent. The consequences, he says, will be the demise of democracy and a withering of the ethics and morality of political life.

In support of his argument that relativism is undermining our virtue, Bloom offers the following profile of the modern student, which many readers have found compelling. The modern student, Bloom claims, is a person who believes that all truth is relative, not as a theoretical insight, but as a moral postulate and as a condition of a free society. The belief typically is conjoined with the student's principle of equality. That is, the principle of equality depends upon the belief that one person's truth is as weighty as another's. This attitude, argues Bloom, has replaced the historical framework of inalienable, natural rights. He contrasts the historical education of the "democratic man," with the modern education of the "democratic personality." Under the traditional framework, the student was taught the model of a rational and industrious man who was honest, respected laws, and was dedicated to his family. He knew the rights doctrine and was familiar with the Constitution and the Declaration of Independence. Moreover, he believed that the fundamental basis of mankind's unity and sameness springs from acceptance of the natural rights of all people.

Modern education, in contrast, has jettisoned the natural rights origins of the American regime. It has replaced natural rights with "openness," which has led to a neglect of civic culture. *Id.* at 29. Moreover, the modern student's genial acceptance of cultural relativism is, in essence, a rejection of the grounding principle of reason. This embrace of relativism ultimately turns people inward, not outward. As he puts it, "The Greeks believed in openness as a virtue that permitted us to seek the good by using reason. It now means accepting everything and denying reason's power." *Id.* at 31. The denial of reason atrophies the student's critical thinking and discriminatory reasoning abilities. It also makes the student vulnerable to despots and zealots. Believing that "all is relative," the student has no investment in any particular set of beliefs, including her own. She thus is unable to muster the conviction and intellectual force necessary to defend her beliefs against forceful challenges by others who *are* confident about the correctness of their cultural practices, however cruel, repressive, or illiberal those practices may be. The "opening" thus becomes instead a *closing* of the mind. More particularly, it also denies a central assumption on which the nation was founded and on which the organizing political documents depend—that the use of rational principles of natural rights offers a meaningful basis for the political order and for our public lives.

Bloom acknowledges that reason often is infected by prejudice, but he argues that we cannot prevent this by denying reason's claim to authority. Our alleged retreat from reason, to what Bloom describes as the deceptive comfort of historicism and anthropological wisdom, is a confused sort of nineteenth century romanticism, in which we believe that knowledge does not lead to greater happiness, are "melancholy about science," and wistfully reflect on the advantages of "primitive" cultures over our arguably more sophisticated one. *Id.* at 40.

Bloom offers several rejoinders to these tendencies. First, he notes that if historicism is taken seriously, then it undermines itself. Historicism, like all philosophies, must be a peculiarity of contemporary history, and so cannot transcend its own time or claim intellectual priority any more than natural rights theory can. Second, Bloom regards the relativists' ostensible humility about our culture as a disguised form of arrogance. In assuming that "primitive" cultures were less advanced, historicists betray their belief that modern culture is more sophisticated than earlier or primitive ones. Instead, argues Bloom, the historicists should be willing to test against nature the beliefs of other cultures, to assess whether they in fact knew, or know, something that we do not.

Bloom is especially critical of the tendency of modern relativists in education to stress that all ethnocentrism is evil and that the rise of minorities is a good thing, rather than a selfish, bad thing as (he claims) the Founders believed. Bloom argues that ethnocentrism with respect to our constitutional values is desirable, not bad. He contrasts the arguments of black separatists from those of Dr. Martin Luther King, Jr., and insists that the separatists mistakenly seized on black identity as the basis of their movement rather than on their identity as Americans and as human beings, as did Dr. King. Glossing over the practices that cause separatists to believe that they cannot achieve their goals without affirming their cultural or racial distinctiveness, Bloom criticizes the separatist instinct as counterproductive, countercultural, and, in essence, anti-American.

As such, Bloom apparently defines good ethnocentrism as one that embraces his version of original American values and is rooted in the Constitution and in Western philosophy. Bad ethnocentrism is that which denies reason, the central tenets of the Constitution, the principles of natural rights, and the goodness of liberal democratic government. Bloom's good life, and thus his good education, is one devoted to rigorous investigation of the question, "What is man?," with reason as the compass to this investigation. For Bloom, philosophy therefore is the most important discipline, and the health of the nation depends upon the ability of great universities to inspire the best students to become great philosophers.

Given these philosophical assumptions, Bloom likely would applaud Hirsch's proposal that all American schoolchildren be exposed to the national cultural canon. He surely would disagree, however, with the implication that the content of this list matters less than that it be shared by all; indeed, much of *The Closing of the American Mind* is dedicated to exactly this lack of concern over the specific moral and ethical content of the American personality. As such, Bloom would be dissatisfied with exposure to the Constitution through instructional methods that, for example, presented the Constitution as an artifact of a racist and sexist culture.

This dissent reveals the considerable philosophical gap between Hirsch and Bloom. Hirsch makes no claim of moral or epistemological absolutism; Bloom grounds his theory on reason and his affection for Greek philosophy. Hirsch attempts to reconcile the better parts of Deweyan pragmatism with insights from educational psychology and cultural anthropology. Bloom deplores pragmatism and shows little interest in psychological or anthropological spins on education theory. Hirsch concentrates on primary and secondary education. Bloom cares most, if not exclusively, about the state of education in the nation's elite colleges and universities as it is delivered to the finest students within those institutions. Hirsch's justifications for his core curriculum sound like those advanced in the Harvard Redbook in the 1940s for a similar core curriculum: cultural reproduction and survival depends on it. Bloom's arguments betray his Chicago roots, with their strong Aristotelian, aristocratic flavor. Bloom also would be dissatisfied with a "trivial pursuit" approach to mastery of the Hirsch list, whereby the student could identify a term but be unable to defend or critique it. Despite these differences, however, Bloom would applaud the Hirsch proposal of an American *paideia*, because the Hirsch list happens to reflect many of the philosophical premises on which Bloom's thesis rests.

35. *See* note 1, *supra*.

36. For a particularly thoughtful expression of this point of view, but one that is sensitive to the risk of exclusion and hurt to cultural outsiders, *see* Arnold Eisen, *"Jews, Jewish Studies, and the American Humanities,"* 4 TIKKUN 25 (Sept. / Oct. 1989).

37. Of course, belief in the need for a core curriculum does not necessarily translate into a particular substantive list. Many people regret the alleged erosion of a sense of community, but some would choose quite distinct cultural canons. The issue of an eroding sense of community has surfaced recently on college campuses and sparked a special report of the Carnegie Foundation for the Advancement of Teaching entitled *Campus Life: In Search of Community* (1990). The report focuses on principles of interaction on a college campus, however, not curricular standards. These principles are intended to provide a more relevant and appropriate substitute for the discredited *in loco parentis* doctrine.

In a different, and explicitly substantive effort to regain common ground on college campuses, The National Endowment for the Humanities issued a report in 1989 entitled *50 Hours, supra* note 26.

38. *See, e.g.,* "Campus Life: "White Male Writers" Is the Title of English 112," *N.Y. Times*, Mar. 4, 1991, at B4, col. 1 (reporting that at Georgetown, a course that discusses the works of Melville, Twain, and Hawthorne now is titled, "White Male Writers," which the department chair explained is an acknowledgement that white male writers are as defined by their race and gender as are black women writers). *See also* "Campus Life: Should a

Writing Class Teach Social Diversity?" *N.Y. Times*, Feb. 4, 1991, at B4, col. 1 (discussing U. Mass-Amherst freshman writing program that includes assignments that involve racial and social diversity and that requires all teachers and assistants in the program to participate in a three-day sensitivity training workshop); Kay Sunstein Hymowitz, "Babar the Racist," *The New Republic* 12 (Aug. 19 & 26, 1991) (describing efforts by some states and educational associations to promote multiculturalism at the primary school level as "some sensible, some plain crazy," and as putting the "pc into abc").

39. Arthur M. Schlesinger, Jr., *The Disuniting of America* (1991).

40. Arthur M. Schlesinger, Jr., "Toward a Divisive Diversity," *Wall Street Journal*, June 25, 1991, at A18, col. 3 (commenting on a report of the New York State's Social Studies Review Committee, which recommended that the curriculum be revised to emphasize multicultural education.). *See also* Arthur M. Schlesinger, Jr., *supra* note 39; Isaacs, "The One and the Many," in *Race and Schooling in the City* 107, 121 (A. Yarmolinsky, L. Liebman & C. Shelling eds., 1981) (arguing that "[A]ll political systems based on race / tribe / nationality are in total contradiction with the fundamental concept on which the American society is trying to base itself, namely popular sovereignty resting not on 'groups' but on the franchise of individual citizens. . . .").

41. *See, e.g.,* Anthony DePalma, "Separate Ethnic Worlds Grow on Campus," *N.Y. Times*, May 18, 1991, at A1, col. 1; Jacob Weisberg, "Thin Skins," *The New Republic* 22 (Feb. 18, 1991) (complaining that at Oberlin students increasingly "think, act, study, and live apart"); Shelby Steele, "Being Black and Feeling Blue," 58 *American Scholar* 497 (Autumn 1989) (arguing that racial separatism reflects self-doubt and is self-defeating).

42. *See* M. A. Farber, "An 'African Centered' School: How the Idea Developed and Why It Might Fail," *N.Y. Times*, Feb. 8, 1991, at A13, col. 1. *Cf.* "Judge Halts Plan for Male Schools," *N.Y. Times*, Aug. 16, 1991, at A6, col. 3 (reporting that federal judge struck down as unconstitutional Detroit public school plan for three all-male academies aimed at black male students).

43. Suzanne Daley, "Inspirational Black History Draws Academic Fire," *N.Y. Times*, Oct. 10, 1990, at A1, col. 2. *See also* Paul Gray, "Whose America?" *Time* 13–17 (July 8, 1991); Gary Putka, "Course Work Stressing Blacks' Role Has Critics But Appears Effective," *Wall Street Journal*, July 1, 1991, at A1, col. 1. *Cf.* Lance Morrow, "The Provocative Professor," *Time* 19 (Aug. 26, 1991) (discussing opposition to Leonard Jeffries, chair of African-American Studies at City College of New York, who attacks Jews, Italians, and whites in general in his charges of racism in America and who maintains that people of African descent are intellectually and physically superior to people of European descent). *See also* Joseph Berger, "Professors' Theories on Race Stir Turmoil at City College," *N.Y. Times*, Apr. 20, 1990, at B1, col. 2; Alan Finder, "No Action Asked on Racial Speech," *N.Y. Times*, Aug. 24, 1991, at A13, col. 1 (noting that faculty committee recommended that no action be taken against Jeffries for his racially charged speech).

44. William A. Henry, III, "Upside Down In the Groves of Academe," *Time* 66 (Apr. 1, 1991). *See also* Louis Menand, "Illiberalisms," *The New Yorker* 101 (May 20, 1991) (reviewing Dinesh D'Souza, *Illiberal Education*) (expressing concern that the effort to correct for the past of trivializing the significance of race and sex ends up now as treating them as though they were the most important aspects of a person).

45. Dinesh D'Souza, *supra* note 3, at 15–19 (1991). *See also* Roger Kimball, *Tenured Radicals: How Politics Has Corrupted Our Higher Education* (1990); Charles J. Sykes, *ProfScam*, 158–68 (1988) (blaming powerful faculty, specialization, the preference for research over instruc-

tion, and a compliant administration); C. Vann Woodward, "Freedom and the Universities," *The New York Review of Books* 32, 36–37 (July 18, 1991); William A. Henry, III, *supra* note 44, at 66 (Apr. 1, 1991) (describing courses that are "frequently . . . wedded to a combative political agenda or outlandish view of this nation's culture and values").

46. *See, e.g.*, Dinesh D'Souza, *supra* note 3, at 17–18.

47. For a collection of essays that discuss the "political correctness" phenomenon *see*, *Debating P.C.* (P. Berman ed., 1992). The countermovement to so-called political correctness has even launched its own publication, titled *Heterodoxy*, subtitled *Articles and Animadversions on Political Correctness and Other Follies*, which is published by the Center for the Study of Popular Culture, in Studio City, California. Defenders of many of the trends that this correctness countermovement denounces have formed their own group, the Teachers for a Democratic Culture, which in the fall of 1992 launched its own publication, entitled *Democratic Culture*.

48. Dinesh D'Souza, *supra* note 3, at 19 (describing the students as "like twigs carried by a fast current").

49. *Id.* at 1.

50. *See, e.g.*, "The Derisory Tower," *The New Republic* 5 (Feb. 18, 1991); Ken Emerson, "Only Correct," *The New Republic* 18 (Feb. 18, 1991) (criticizing emerging codes of conduct directed at offensive hate speech on campus).

51. *See, e.g.*, Irving Howe, "The Value of the Canon," *The New Republic* 42 (Feb. 18, 1991); *Forum, supra* note 29. "The Idea of the University," *Partisan Review*, 339 (Spring 1991) (remarks of Brigitte Berger). *See generally*, "The Changing Culture of The University," *Partisan Review* (Spring 1991).

52. *See, e.g.*, E. D. Hirsch, Jr., *supra* note 1, at 22 (pointing out that radicals have been most effective using the traditional forms of literate culture to effect social change); Arthur M. Schlesinger, Jr., *supra* note 40 (remarking that, although our democratic ideals are imperfectly realized, this European inheritance yields more good than bad in that Europe, unlike most cultures, "has also generated ideals that have opposed and exposed [Europe's own] crimes"); Arthur M. Schlesinger, Jr., *supra* note 39, at 76–78 (arguing the same point). *Cf.* William Phillips, "The Crisis in Our Culture," *Partisan Review* 192 (Spring 1991) (condemning postmodernist critique as an "intellectual fashion" that should be replaced by a return to "traditional values and distinctions").

53. Appendix, "What Literate Americans Know" in E. D. Hirsch, Jr., *supra* note 1, at 186–88. *See also* Joseph F. Kett & James Trefil, *The Dictionary of Cultural Literacy* (1988).

54. *See* Arnold Eisen, *supra* note 36, at 24.

55. *See, e.g.*, George Reisman, "Education and the Racist Road to Barbarism," 40 *The Freeman* 364, 369–370 (1990). One writer who is particularly dismayed by these tendencies has defined multiculturalism as "a twisted version of Western teachings, flourishing in the hothouse of a democracy that renders all distinctions suspect and all learning elitist." Edward Rothstein, "Roll Over Beethoven," *The New Republic*, 29, 34 (Feb. 4, 1991). In his view, the multiculturalists exploit liberalism's openness to serve their parochial, non-neutral, and explicitly illiberal ends. An open embrace of overtly political education, warns this defender of liberal neutrality, may lead to an education agenda that promotes political objectives that would horrify the multiculturalists. Without a collective commitment to toleration and free inquiry as guiding principles, only force can resolve intergroup hostilities. If those who deny the right of dissent are the most powerful, then the multiculturalists lose any chance of achieving their goal of cultural diversity. Liberalism,

despite its costs and limitations, thus is superior to the alternatives suggested by the multiculturalists because it tolerates difference and countertraditional thought. This means that a core curriculum centered on Western Civilization, like Hirsch's, is preferable to other possibilities because it respects liberal values and would tend to perpetuate this liberal heritage. Rothstein's apprehension is that "The multiculturalist is a Western liberal with so large a power of empathy that liberalism itself is dissolved, a rationalist with so transcendental a perspective that reason itself is discarded. The multiculturalist is a universalist without universalism, an artist without a vision of art, a monster child of Western culture; a baleful, unwitting tribute to the tradition he hungers to dispose."

56. *See,* Gary Putka, *supra* note 43; "African Dreams," *Newsweek,* 42 (Sept. 23, 1991).

57. Martin Bernal, *Black Athena: The AfroAsiatic Roots of Classical Civilization, volume I: The Fabrication of Ancient Greece 1785–1985* (1987). *See* Mary Lefkowitz, "Not Out of Africa," *The New Republic* 19 (Feb. 10, 1992).

58. *See, e.g.,* Dinesh D'Souza, *supra* note 3, at 2–5, 24–58.

59. *See* Marvin Cetron & Margaret Gayle, *supra* note 2, at 96–102 (1991) (describing the reform movement).

60. Chester E. Finn, Jr., "A Seismic Shock for Education," *N.Y. Times,* Sept. 3, 1989, at op ed page.

61. *Id.*

62. E. D. Hirsch, Jr., *supra* note 1, at 125.

63. *See* Susan Chira, *supra* note 1. *See also* Karen De Witt, *supra* note 5. For a recent report on the progress of the Bush *America 2000* plan, see Karen De Witt, "Education Panel Sees Modest Gains," *N.Y. Times,* Oct. 1, 1992, at A10, col. 1.

4   CRITIQUES OF THE CALL FOR COHERENCE

1. For an excellent introduction into several of the strands of this opposition, see *The Politics of Liberal Education* (D. J. Gless & B. Herrnstein Smith eds., 1992). *See also* Henry Louis Gates, Jr., *Loose Canons: Notes on the Culture Wars* (1992); David Bromwich, *Politics By Other Means: Higher Education and Group Thinking* (1992); *Debating P.C.* (P. Berman ed., 1992); *Beyond P.C.: Toward a Politics of Understanding* (P. Aufderhide ed., 1992).

2. *See* Marcus L. Hansen, *The Problem of the Third Generation Immigrant* (1938).

3. *See generally* Christine Sleeter & Carl Grant, "An Analysis of Multicultural Education in the United States," 57 *Harv. Educ. Rev.* 421 (1987). *See also* Peter Erickson, "What Multicultural-ism Means," 55 *Transition* 105 (1992).

4. *See* Horace Kallen, *Culture and Democracy in the United States* (1924); I. B. Berkson, *Theories of Americanization* (1920).

5. *See, e.g.,* Seymour W. Itzkoff, *Cultural Pluralism and American Education* 57 (1969).

6. *Id.* at 63. *See also* Gary Peller, "Race Consciousness" 1990 *Duke L.J.* 758, 791–802 (discussing black nationalists' resistance to integration on grounds that it was based on a mistaken assumption of universalism, ignored the way in which historical structures and group identity may create social meaning, typically preceded on the basis of unstated white cultural norms, and entailed the abolition of one of very few organized institutions of the black community); Derrick A. Bell, Jr., *And We Are Not Saved: The Elusive Quest for Racial Justice* 110 (1987) (noting that integration often implied assimilation into white cultural norms); *Malcolm X—By Any Means Necessary: Speeches, Interviews and a Letter* 16–17 (G. Breitman ed., 1970) (rejecting arguments against all-black schools as hypocritical

insofar as the critics of such schools do not condemn equally all-white schools in all-white neighborhoods).

7. Seymour W. Itzkoff, *supra* note 5, at 108–09.

8. *Id.* at 59.

9. *See id.* at 109. In other words, a strong sense of cultural community is what makes meaningful an admonition not to do X. The obligation not to do X is tied to being a member of Y community. *Because* one is a Y, one cannot do X. *Id. See also* Paul Selznick, "The Idea of a Communitarian Morality," 75 *Calif. L. Rev.* 445 (1987) (linking morality and political community).

10. Seymour W. Itzkoff, *supra*, note 5, at 109.

11. *Id.* at 142.

12. *Id.* at 140–42.

13. For a description of such curricula, see Suzanne Daley, "Inspirational Black History Draws Academic Fire," *N.Y. Times*, Oct. 10, 1990, at A1, col. 2; Mary Lefkowitz, "Not Out of Africa," *The New Republic* 29 (Feb. 10, 1992); M. A. Farber, "An 'African-Centered' School: How the Idea Developed, and Why It Might Fail," *N.Y. Times*, Feb. 8, 1991, at A13 col. 1; Gary Putka, "Curricula of Color: Course Work Stressing Black's Role Has Critics But Appears Effective," *Wall Street Journal*, July 1, 1991, at A1, col. 1. *See also* Note, "Creating Space for Racial Difference: The Case for African-American Schools," 27 *Harv. C.R.-C.L. L. Rev.* 187 (1992); Helaine Greenfeld, "Some Constitutional Problems With the Resegregation of Public Schools," 80 *Geo. L.J.* 363 (1991). *But see* Garrett v. Board of Education, 775 F. Supp. 1004 (E.D. Mich. 1991) (ruling that all-male public school with Afrocentric curriculum was unconstitutional violation of equality rights of female students).

14. *See, e.g.*, Diana Slaughter, "Alienation of Afro-American Children," in *Cultural Pluralism* 144, 165 (E. Epps ed., 1974).

15. *See* Richard Rodriquez, *Hunger of Memory* (1982) (describing the personal struggle of the author's attempt to reconcile a Mexican home culture and an Anglo school culture). *See also* Lawrence A. Cremin, *American Education: The Metropolitan Experience, 1876–1980* 122 (1988) (describing the arguments of Carter Woodson against both Booker T. Washington and W. E. B. DuBois regarding ideal education for African-Americans, in which he maintains that teaching blacks to admire only Greek, Hebrew, Latin, and Teutonic works would rob them of their African-American heritage and alienate them from their own community).

16. *See, e.g.*, A. Castenada, "Persisting Ideological Issues of Assimilation in America," in *Cultural Pluralism* 56, 60–61 (E. Epps ed., 1974).

17. They therefore would reject the view expressed by former University of Chicago President Robert M. Hutchins, in 1953, that, "Now, if ever, we need an education that is designed to bring out our common humanity rather than to indulge our individuality." (quoted in *Conflicting Conceptions of the Curriculum* 13 (E. Eisner & E. Vallance eds., 1974)).

18. *See, e.g.*, *id.* at 15–16 (describing the "fallacy of universalism" in some curricular theories, which "removes curriculum decision making from the arena of the empirical study of its context, placing it, instead, in the arena of rhetoric"); Stanley Fish, "The Common Touch, Or One Size Fits All," in *The Politics of Liberal Education* 241 (D. J. Gless & B. Herrnstein Smith eds., 1992).

19. *See, e.g.*, Renato Rosaldo, *Culture and Truth* 26 (1989) (arguing that authentic translation of cultures by cultural anthropologists requires that the cultures be evaluated in their own terms, not by imposing outsider's categories on the cultures).

20. They thus would reject a transcultural hierarchy of moral reasoning, such as that proposed by Lawrence Kohlberg in *The Philosophy of Moral Development: Moral Stages and the Ideology of Justice* (1981). *See, e.g.*, Carol Gilligan, *In a Different Voice* (1982) (challenging Kohlberg's work as biased toward hierarchies of abstract rules and as undervaluing responsibilities that arise from concrete relationships).

21. Thus the strong multiculturalist would reject neorepublican theories advanced in legal scholarship, such as those of Professors Frank Michelman and Cass Sunstein, to the extent that the neorepublicans' utopia is one in which group difference "are transcended in favor of a single, universal public-regarding point of view." Kathleen Sullivan, "Rainbow Republicanism," 97 *Yale L.J.* 1717 (1988). *See* Frank Michelman, "Foreword: Traces of Self-Government," 100 *Harv. L. Rev.* 4, 74 (1986); Cass Sunstein, "Beyond the Republican Revival," 97 *Yale L.J.* 1539 (1988).

22. *See, e.g.*, A. Castenada, *supra* note 16, at 57 (rejecting assimilation when the Anglo-Saxon cultural pattern is treated as the ideal).

23. *Id.* at 53.

24. *See* Lawrence A. Cremin, *supra* note 15, at 116.

25. *See id.* at 115–50. Walter Feinberg, "Fixing the Schools: The Ideological Turn," in *Critical Pedagogy: The State and Cultural Struggle* 69, 70 (H. A. Giroux & P. L. McLaren eds., 1989).

26. Ira Katznelson & Margaret Weir, *Schooling for All: Class, Race, and the Decline of the Democratic Ideal* 57 (1985). *See also* Harold Kolb, *Defining the Canon*, in *Redefining American Literary History* 35, 37 (A. L. Brown Ruoff & J. W. Ward, Jr., eds., 1990).

27. Brown v. Board of Education of Topeka ("Brown I"), 347 U.S. 483 (1954).

28. *See* Gary Orfield, "Why It Worked in Dixie: Southern School Desegregation and Its Implications for the North," in *Race and Schooling in the City* 24, 25 (A. Yarmolinsky, L. Liebman & C. Schelling eds., 1981).

29. Susan Chira, "Bias Against Girls Is Found Rife in Schools, With Lasting Damage," *N.Y. Times*, Feb. 12 1992, at A1, col. 3; *Gender in the Classroom: Power and Pedagogy* (S. Gabriel & I. Smithson eds., 1990). Roberta Hall & Bernice Sandler, *The Classroom Climate: A Chilly One for Women* (1982); Katherine Connor & Ellen J. Vargyas, "The Legal Implications of Gender Bias in Standardized Testing," 7 *Berkeley Women's L. J.* 13 (1992).

30. *See* San Antonio Ind. School Dist. v. Rodriquez, 411 U.S. 1 (1973).

31. *See* Note, Jonathan Banks, "State Constitutional Analysis of Public School Finance Reform Cases: Myth or Methodology?" 45 *Vand. L. Rev.* 129 (1991); Mark Yudof, "School Finance Reform: Don't Worry, Be Happy," 10 *Rev. of Litigation* 585 (1991); Note, "Unfulfilled Promises: School Finance Remedies and State Courts," 104 *Harv. L. Rev.* 1072 (1991).

32. *See, e.g.*, Gary Peller, *supra* note 6, at 806 (noting that "[i]n the historicizing perspective of black nationalists, knowledge was necessarily a social contrast. . . . Culture precedes epistemology").

33. *See, e.g.*, Mark Kelman, "Concepts of Discrimination in 'General Ability' Job Testing," 104 *Harv. L. Rev.* 1157 (1991) (discussing different theories of discrimination and pointing out how, even under the most conventional theories, general ability tests are biased). There is a rich legal literature that addresses the issue of cultural, gender, and racial bias in education testing and in other measures of academic, social, and economic achievement. Feminism, critical race theory, critical legal studies, and radical cultural anthropology are among the many important disciplines that have advanced this critique. For introductions to some of these issues within law scholarship see, Deborah Rhode, *Justice and Gender*

(1989); Catharine MacKinnon, *Feminism Unmodified* (1987); Catharine MacKinnon, *Toward a Feminist Theory of the State* (1989); Susan Moller Okin, "Defining Feminism: A Comparative Historical Account," 14 *Signs* 119 (1988); Mark Kelman, *A Guide to Critical Legal Studies* (1987); Roberto Unger, "The Critical Legal Studies Movement," 96 *Harv. L. Rev.* 561 (1983); Gary Peller, *supra* note 6; Mari Matsuda, "Looking to the Bottom: Critical Legal Studies and Reparations," 22 *Harv. C.R.-C.L. L. Rev.* 323 (1987); Kimberlé Crenshaw, "Race, Reform, and Retrenchment: Transformation and Legitimation in Antidiscrimination Law," 101 *Harv. L. Rev.* 1331 (1988); Kimberlé Crenshaw, "Foreword: Toward a Race-Conscious Pedagogy in Legal Education," 11 *Nat'l Black L.J.* 1 (1989); Derrick A. Bell, Jr., *And We Are Not Saved: The Elusive Quest for Racial Justice* (1987); Angela P. Harris, "Race and Essentialism in Feminist Legal Theory," 42 *Stan. L. Rev.* 581 (1990); Patricia Williams, "Alchemical Notes: Reconstructing Ideals from Reconstructed Rights," 22 *Harv. C.R.-C.L. L. Rev.* 401 (1987); Robert A. Williams, "Taking Rights Aggressively: The Perils and Promise of Critical Legal Theory for Peoples of Color," 5 *Law & Inequality* 103 (1987); Charles R. Lawrence, III, "The Id, the Ego, and Equal Protection: Reckoning With Unconscious Racism," 39 *Stan. L. Rev.* 317 (1987); Janet Halley, "The Politics of the Closet: Towards Equal Protection for Gay, Lesbian, and Bisexual Identity," 36 *UCLA L. Rev.* 915 (1989); Marc Fajer, "Can Two Real Men Eat Quiche Together? Storytelling, Gender-Role Stereotypes, and Legal Protection for Lesbians and Gay Men," 46 *U. Miami L. Rev.* 511 (1992).

34. *See, e.g.*, Lauro Cavazos, "More Parenting, Not More Money," 7 *New Perspectives Quarterly* 6, 7 (Fall 1990). *See also* Paul Gray, "Whose America?" *Time* 12, 15 (July 8, 1991) (citing statistics regarding changing demographics in United States).

35. *See* Harold Kolb, Jr., *Defining the Canon*, in *Redefining American Literary History* 35, 37 (A. L. Brown Ruoff & J. W. Ward, Jr., eds., 1990).

36. *See* Margaret Mead, *Culture and Commitment: A Study of the Generation Gap* 56–57 (1970).

37. *See, e.g.*, James Banks, "Multicultural Education: Characteristics and Goals," in *Multicultural Education: Issues and Perspectives* 2, 2–3 (J. Banks & C. McGee Banks eds., 1989).

38. *See* A. Castenada, *supra* note 16, at 65.

39. *Id.*

40. *See, e.g.*, Nancy St. John, "The Effects of School Desegregation on Children: A New Look at the Research Evidence," in *Race and Schooling in the City*, 84, 91 (A. Yarmolinsky, L. Liebman & C. Schelling eds., 1981) (describing evidence on the psychological impact of desegregation on black children, which suggests academic self-esteem is higher for black children in segregated schools than for those in desegregated schools). *See also* Diana Slaughter, *supra* note 14.

41. *See, e.g.*, Paul Gray, *supra* note 34 (describing the revisions of texts to accommodate the multiculturalists' appeals and the backlash by those who object to the revisionist moves).

42. James Baldwin, "A Talk To Teachers," in *Multicultural Literacy* 3, 8 (R. Simonson & S. Walker eds., 1988).

43. *Id.* at 9.

44. Consciousness-raising is a technique most strongly associated with contemporary feminism. In the 1970s, some women participated in sessions in which a small group of women gathered to share their experiences as women. These discussions often led the participants to realize—sometimes for the first time in their lives—ways in which being female translated into particular, often subordinate or personally stultifying role expectations, social and economic opportunities, and other socially constructed identities. The sharing of mutual experiences enabled consciousness-raising participants to see patterns within

society rather than merely perceiving their experiences as unique, individual occurrences. It also caused some participants to recognize that the patterns were not freely chosen, not empowering, and not neutral or natural. On the contrary, they concluded that the meaning of gender within a particular society is, to a considerable degree, contrived. Where, as in the United States, gender is used as a method of assigning social and economic privileges, the patterns of gender-based treatment can become oppressive for the disfavored sex. Consciousness-raising is the process by which many women became conscious of the specific ways in which American culture made being female the occasion of harm.

45. *See* "Legal Storytelling Symposium," 87:8 *Mich. L. Rev.* (1989); David Mura, "Strangers in the Village," in *Multicultural Literacy, supra* note 42, at 135; Michelle Wallace, "Invisibility Blues," in *id.* at 161.

46. *See* W. E. B. DuBois, *The Souls of Black Folk: Essays and Sketches* 180 (Vintage ed. 1990).

47. David Mura, *supra* note 45, at 135, 152.

48. *See, e.g.,* Gary Putka, *supra* note 13, (describing criticisms of African-centered curriculum); A. M. Rosenthal, "Suicide on the Fourth," *N.Y. Times,* July 5, 1991, at A11, col. 1 (describing multiculturalists as "the new segregationists," whose "excuse" for urging multicultural agendas is that youth are not taught enough about outgroups' contributions and who are "racial and ethnic propagandists on the campus").

49. *See, e.g.,* William A. Henry, "Upside Down in the Groves of Academe," *Time* 66 (Apr. 1, 1991).

50. *See, e.g.,* "Race on Campus," *The New Republic* (Feb. 18, 1991) (devoting several articles to the alleged rise of political correctness on campus but no articles in which the author discusses the statistics regarding racial, ethnic, sexual, and other forms of discrimination on campus).

51. *See, e.g.,* Katherine Bartlett, "Some Factual Correctness About Political Correctness," *Wall Street Journal,* June 6, 1991, at A17, col. 1.

52. *See* Gary Putka, *supra* note 13. *See also* Mary Lefkowitz, *supra* note 13, at 29; Robert Hughes, "The Fraying of America," *Time* 44 (Feb. 3, 1992); Frank Kermode, "Whose History Is Bunk?" *New York Times Book Review,* Feb. 23, 1992, at 3.

53. *See Choosing Equality: The Case For Democratic Schooling* 45–49 (A. Bastian, N. Fruchter, M. Gittell, C. Greer & K. Haskins eds., 1986).

54. Moreover, this focus on substantive outcomes, versus procedural formalities leads some multiculturalists to embrace a theory of equality in education that measures equality by education *results,* rather than by equal treatment. *See, e.g., Choosing Equality, supra* note 53, at 30–31.

55. *See, e.g.,* J. Hixson, "Community Control: The Values Behind a Call for Change," in *Cultural Pluralism,* 106, 116–17 (E. Epps ed., 1974).

56. *See, e.g.,* Mari Matsuda, "Public Response to Racist Speech: Considering the Victim's Story," 87 *Mich. L. Rev.* 2320 (1989).

57. The full range of their views, and the sub-divisions among the equality theorists, are beyond the scope of this book. For an introduction into the educational equality literature, *see* Christopher Jencks, "Whom Must We Treat Equally for Educational Opportunity to be Equal?" 98 *Ethics* 518 (1988); *Choosing Equality, supra* note 53; Henry Cisneros, "Four-Tiered Education," 7 *New Perspectives Quarterly* 15 (Fall 1990); *Multicultural Education: Issues and Perspectives* (J. Banks & C. McGee Banks eds., 1989); *Cultural Pluralism* (E. Epps ed., 2974); Seymour W. Itzkoff, *Cultural Pluralism and American Education* (1969).

58. The equality theorists diverge, however, on other strategies to combat these inequalities. Some adopt a symmetrical equality approach to combating discrimination, under which the aim is to assure equal treatment of all individuals, regardless of sex, race, ethnicity, or color. "Same treatment," under this model, is "equality." Others believe in an asymmetrical approach, which anticipates that for some groups equality may mean different and preferential treatment to account for past discrimination or to otherwise assure that group-status does not constitute a liability. *See, e.g.*, Kenneth Karst, *Belonging to America* 158–72 (1989). Thus, "same treatment" may not constitute equality, rather equal outcomes or alternative standards of equality may better satisfy "true equality". *See* Michael Rebell & Arthur Block, *Equality and Education* 19–26 (1985) (discussing differences between theories of equality of opportunity and equality of result). For discussions of the differing approaches to equality in feminist literature, *see* Deborah Rhode, *supra* note 33, at 12–14, 32–38, 306–15 (1989) (discussing differences among feminists regarding theories of gender equality).

59. Some equality theorists are individualists, who place the individual ahead of communitarian concerns. Others are more communitarian in defining the ideal relationship between the individual and society. *See, e.g.*, Frank Michelman, "Foreword: Traces of Self-Government," 100 *Harv. L. Rev.* 4 (1986); Cass Sunstein, "Beyond the Republican Revival," 97 *Yale L.J.* 1539 (1988); Suzanna Sherry, "Civic Virtue and the Feminine Voice in Constitutional Adjudication," 72 *Va. L. Rev.* 543 (1986). For a discussion of the differences between a multicultural and an anti-racism approach to educational reform *see* Peter Erickson, "What Multiculturalism Means," 55 *Transition* 105, 106–07 (1992).

60. *See, e.g.*, Kenneth Karst, *supra* note 58, at 187 (noting that "American history strongly indicates that the impulse toward racist domination [or its religious or ethnic counterparts] will be more powerful in a local community than it will be in the national as a whole").

61. *See* Henry Giroux & Peter McLaren, "Schooling, Cultural Politics, and the Struggle for Democracy," in *Critical Pedagogy, the State, and Cultural Struggle*, xi, xiv–xxi (H. J. Giroux & P. McLaren eds., 1989). *See also* Joel Feinberg, "Fixing the Schools: The Ideological Turn," in *id.* at 69–70.

62. Henry Giroux & Peter McLaren, *supra* note 61, at xvi.

63. *Id.*

64. *Id. See also* Clarence Karier, "Business Values and the Educational State," in *Roots of Crisis* 6– 26 (C. Karier, P. Violas & J. Spring eds., 1973).

65. Henry Giroux & Peter McLaren, *supra* note 61, at xvii.

66. *Id.* at xvii–xviii.

67. *Id.* at xx.

68. *See, e.g.*, Clarence Karier, *supra* note 64; Herbert Gintis & Samuel Bowles, *Schooling in Capitalist America* (1976); Herbert Gintis & Samuel Bowles, "Contradiction and Reproduction in Educational Theory," in *Education and the State, vol. I: Schooling and the National Interest* 45 (R. Dale, G. Esland, R. Fergusson & M. MacDonald eds., 1981).

69. Clarence Karier, *supra* note 64.

70. *See* Martin Carnoy & Henry M. Levin, *Schooling and Work in the Democratic State* 47 (1985).

71. *Id.*

72. *See* Henry Giroux & Peter McLaren, *supra* note 61, at xxi.

73. *See, e.g.*, Richard Rorty, "That Old-Time Philosophy," *The New Republic* 29 (Apr. 4, 1988).

74. *Id.* at 30.

75. *Id. See also* Richard Rorty, *Contingency, Irony, and Solidarity* (1989). *Cf.* Henry Giroux and Peter McLaren, *supra* note 61, at xi–xii (noting that "the spirit of hope and historicity which informs the contributions to this volume does not see the mechanisms of injustice as indelibly inscribed in the social order but rather as open to change and reconstruction through a critical rethinking of and commitment to the meaning and purpose of schooling in our society.").

76. Richard Rorty, *supra* note 73, at 32.

77. *Id. See also* Richard Rorty, "Two Cheers for the Cultural Left," 89 *South Atlantic Quarterly* 227 (1990); Richard Rorty, "Education, Socialization & Individuation," 75 *Liberal Educ.* 2 (Sept. / Oct. 1989). Indeed, one writer argues that critical surveys of multiculturalism from the left "demonstrate the ease with which a left intellectual perspective collapses and converts into a traditionalist approach when the canon question is called." Peter Erickson, *supra* note 59, at 112 (1992).

78. *See* Richard Rorty, *supra* note 73, at 32.

79. *Id. See also* Bruce Ackerman, *Social Justice in the Liberal State* (1980) (arguing for a similar, two-stage education).

80. Even liberal philosopher John Rawls concedes the need for education that prepares students for participation in society and that encourages political virtues. *See* John Rawls, "The Priority of Right and Ideas of the Good," 17 *Phil. & Pub. Affairs* 251, 267 (1988).

81. *See, e.g.,* Richard Rorty, "Education, Socialization & Individuation," *supra* note 77, at 5. Why these writers believe that the products of a traditional, acculturative primary and secondary education will be able, at age eighteen, to roam intelligently and confidently in the bazaar of ideas is unclear. Also unclear is the justification for assigning to colleges alone the role of introducing students to contingency and uncertainty, and thus excluding from these insights all students who do not go on to four-year colleges. The relativists' likely answer to these concerns is that they do not favor a primary or secondary education that is strongly assimilationist or dogmatic. Rather, they probably share the notion of Hirsch and others that the Great Books raise more questions than they answer and contain within them the tools of cultural self-criticism and self-doubt. Nevertheless, they have not, as yet, proposed concrete programs that would assure that the list is taught in an epistemologically and morally open-ended way.

82. Richard Rorty, *supra* note 75, at 82.

83. *Id.* at 84.

84. *Id.* at 87.

85. *See* John Stuart Mill, *On Liberty* 97–101 (Norton ed. 1975).

86. *Id.* at 98–100.

87. *Id.* at 98.

88. *See, e.g.,* John Rawls, *supra* note 80.

89. *See, e.g.,* Stephen Arons, *Compelling Belief: The Culture of American Schooling* 87–103 (1983).

90. *See,* Thomas Toch, *In the Name of Excellence: The Struggle to Reform the Nation's Schools, Why It's Failing, and What Should Be Done* (1991) (discussing reform proposals); John Chubb & Terry M. Moe, *Politics, Markets, and America's Schools* (1990) (advocating decentralization and choice); David Kearns & Dennis Doyle, *Winning the Brain Race: A Bold Plan to Make Our Schools Competitive* (1991 ed.) (describing current system as a failed monopoly).

91. In this respect, the strong individualists resemble the moderate multiculturalists and equality theorists, who likewise favor a constrained freedom from majoritarian will in order to assure that freedom does not become oppression. The equality theorists regard

equality as the constraining principle. The strong individualists regard respect for autonomy as the constraining principle. Some liberal philosophers argue that the principle of autonomy and concern for others' freedom are inextricably bound. *See, e.g.*, Joseph Raz, "Liberalism, Skepticism, and Democracy," 74 *Iowa L. Rev.* 761, 784 (1989) (arguing that "peoples' preferences should be freely pursued only within certain bounds"); Ronald Dworkin, "Liberal Community," 77 *Calif. L. Rev.* 479 (1989).

92. *See, e.g.*, James Hoetker, "Re-Hirsching Some Questions About Curriculum," 62 *The Clearing House* 319 (Mar. 1989) (noting that a representative high school social studies textbook contains more historical terms than does Hirsch's list); "Student Reading Lists Still Favor the Classics," *Ariz. Daily Star*, May 31, 1989, at A–12, col. 4 (reporting on study done by Center for the Learning and Teaching of Literature at State University of New York, Albany).

93. *See, e.g.*, April Brayfield, Marina Adler & Diane Zablotsky, "Gender, Race, and Cultural Literacy: Consequences for Academic Performance," 18 *Teaching Sociology* 362, 363 (July 1990).

94. Indeed, Hirsch himself concedes this, insofar as he describes a counterreform movement already underway in the 1980s that is "bent upon a return to a more traditional curriculum." E. D. Hirsch, Jr., *Cultural Literacy* 125 (1988 ed.). *See also* Marvin Cetron & Margaret Gayle, *Educational Renaissance: Our Schools at the Turn of the Century* 175–76 (1991), (describing the spate of reform efforts launched in the 1980s). For other evidence of a pre-Hirsch core curriculum reform movement, see, e.g., Nat'l Center for Education Statistics, *Digest of Education Statistics 1990* (1991) (indicating that SAT scores did not decline during the 1980s); Educational Testing Service, *What Americans Study* 1 (1989) (noting that "[i]ncreasing course requirements in key academic subjects has been a central theme of educational reform in [the 1980s].");" Nat'l Commission on Education, *Meeting the Challenge: Recent Efforts to Improve Education Across the Nation*, (1983). Daniel Cheever & Gus Sayer, "How We Defined Our Core Curriculum," *Education Leadership* 599 (May 1982); Ernest Boyer, *High School: A Report on Secondary Education in America* (1983); Mortimer J. Adler, *The Paideia Proposal: An Education Manifesto* (1982); Gerald Graff, "Curricular Imperatives for Renewing General Education," 34 *J. Gen. Educ.* 189–97 (1982).

95. Arthur E. Wise, *Legislated Learning: The Bureaucratization of the American Classroom* 27 (1979).

96. *Id.* at xv. *See also* Robert Perrin, "Can Cultural Literacy Be Tested?" 62 *The Clearing House* 284 (Mar. 1989); Susan Chira, "Study Finds Standardized Tests May Hurt Education Efforts," *N.Y. Times*, Oct. 16, 1992, at A13, col. 1 (reporting on a three-year, $1 million study funded by the National Science Foundation and conducted by Boston College's Center for the Study of Testing, Evaluation and Educational Policy).

97. Arthur Wise, *supra* note 95, at 60.

98. *See, e.g.*, Karen Spear, "The Paideia Proposal: The Problem of Means and Ends in General Education," 36 *J. Gen Educ.* 79, 82 (1984).

99. *See* Lauro Cavazos, "More Parenting, Not More Money," *National Perspectives Quarterly*, 6, 7 (Fall 1990).

100. *Id. See also* Jonathan Kozol, *Illiterate America* (1985). For a sharp critique of Hirsch on the ground that his proposal oversimplifies our social and economic problems, and offers the illusory promise of a quick fix, see Barbara Herrnstein Smith, "Cult-Lit: Hirsch, Literacy, and the 'National Culture'," in *The Politics of Liberal Education* 75 (D. J. Gless & B. Herrnstein Smith eds., 1992).

101. *See* Lawrence A. Cremin, *supra* note 15, at 233–34.
102. *Id.*
103. *Id.* at 234.
104. *See* Arthur E. Wise, *supra* note 95, at 50.
105. *See, e.g.,* Julie Johnson, "Teacher Union Faults History Books," *N.Y. Times*, Sept. 14, 1989, at A20, col. 4 (noting that five textbooks, which are read by two-thirds of the five million students in American high schools, relegate materials about women and minorities in history to special side boxes and features, rather than integrating them into the text as a whole). *See also* "Student Reading Lists," *supra* note 92 (noting that the classic list taught most often in public and private schools has changed very little over time).
106. *See, e.g.,* Mortimer J. Adler, "This Pre-War Generation," in *Reforming Education* 3 (G. Van Doren ed., 1977).
107. *See, e.g.,* Katherine Bartlett, "Some Factual Correctness About Political Correctness," *Wall Street Journal*, June 6, 1991, at A17, col. 1 (challenging the claim of some critics that certain colleges and universities have been captured by feminists or any other "leftist" groups).
108. *See, e.g.,* Julie Johnson, *supra* note 105 (noting that report on history texts indicates that material on women and minorities is relegated to special boxes and features, rather than integrated into the texts as a whole); Diane Ravitch, "Pluralism v. Particularism in American Education," *The Responsive Community* 32, 34 (Spring 1991) (noting that in too many cases, the histories of women, blacks, and ethnic minorities appear as sidebars to the main story in textbooks).
109. *See, e.g.,* Katherine Bartlett, *supra* note 107; Fox Butterfield, "The Right Breeds a College Press Network," *N.Y. Times*, Oct. 24, 1990, at A1, col. 2.
110. *See* Randall Kennedy, "The Political Correctness Scare," 37 *Loy. L. Rev.* 231 (1991).

5 CONSTITUTIONAL COMMITMENTS AND CONFLICTS

1. Professor Mary Ann Glendon has described this tendency as "both cause and consequence of our increasing tendency to look at law as an expression and carrier of the few values that are widely shared in our society: liberty, equality, and the ideal of justice under law." Mary Ann Glendon, *Rights Talk* 3 (1991). Thus, when we seek to persuade or justify ideas in the public arena, we often resort to these common values. As Glendon notes, "Certain areas of law, especially criminal and family law, have become the terrain on which Americans are struggling to define what kind of people they are and what kind of society they wish to bring into being." *Id.*
2. Education policy historically has been determined at the state or local level. Under the Constitution, education is a power reserved to the states, not the federal government. Thus, the norms that historically have received constitutional deference are those of the applicable state or local decision makers, not the federal government. Since the civil rights movement of the 1960s and 1970s, however, the United States Congress has adopted several statutes that have a direct bearing on local educational policy. Through its "purse-string" power, the Congress in particular has influenced the delivery of educational services to females, to children with disabilities, to members of racial minorities, and to children for whom English is a second language. No longer, therefore, are educational policies *exclusively* state or local community-driven. In fact, had national standards not already evolved over parts of education, the national core curriculum proposal would be an even more radical move than it now appears to be.

Despite these nationalizing trends, however, the school curriculum continues to be governed principally by state and local regulations and policies. These policies may vary among states and local communities. As such, when the Court defers to state and local education rules, it defers to a potential range of substantive outcomes. The outcome may be highly standardized, assimilative lesson plans or experimental, kaleidoscopic curricula. Only when the standard is unduly oppressive, according to the Court's estimation, will it be struck down as unconstitutional. Likewise, only when the education outcomes become too disparate, such that students receive vastly different educations, will state policy be overturned. In between these poles, the Court tolerates a wide range of education policies.

3. Sanford Levinson, "Constitutional Meta-Theory," 63 *U. Colo. L. Rev.* 389, 406 (1992). *See also* Sanford Levinson, *Constitutional Faith* (1988).

4. *See* Robert C. Post, "Cultural Heterogeneity and Law: Pornography, Blasphemy, and the First Amendment," 76 *Cal. L. Rev.* 297 (1988).

5. Minersville School District v. Gobitis, 310 U.S. 586, 596 (1940), overruled by West Virginia State Bd. of Educ. v. Barnette, 319 U.S. 624 (1943).

6. Robert C. Post, *supra* note 4, at 299.

7. *Id.*

8. 268 U.S. 510 (1925).

9. *Id.* at 530.

10. *Id.* at 531–33.

11. *Id.*

12. *Id.* at 534–35.

13. *Id.* at 536.

14. *Id.* at 534.

15. *See* Amy Gutmann, *Democratic Education* 42 (1987).

16. *Cf.* Allen Buchanan, "Toward a Theory of Secession," *Ethics* 101, 322–42 (January 1991) (discussing the surprising gap in political philosophy regarding any normative theory of secession and speculating that the impasse between modern communitarians and liberals may be their mutual failure "to take seriously the possibility of secession as a way of preserving a general commitment to the liberal framework while accommodating the fact that there are some forms of community that may not be able to flourish within it but which it would be wrong to force to conform").

17. The backdrop of the Oregon statute may help explain why the Court in 1925 was willing to overlook this potential danger of private education to the public interest. The legislation was an anomaly, in that most states did not require that all children attend *public* schools. Moreover, it was inspired by efforts of radical groups, including the Ku Klux Klan, that were caught up in the Americanization frenzy of the early twentieth century. *See* David B. Tyack, "The Perils of Pluralism: The Background of the *Pierce* Case," 74 *Amer. Hist. Rev.* 74 (1968).

18. For a thoughtful argument that *Pierce* merits reconsideration and that the Oregon statute should have been upheld *see* James S. Liebman, "Voice, Not Choice," 101 *Yale L.J.* 259 (1991).

19. Meyer v. Nebraska, 262 U.S. 390 (1923). Similar statutes in Iowa and Ohio were struck down at the same time by the Court.

20. *Id.* at 402.

21. Dissenting Justices Holmes and Sutherland would have given the state's interest in

requiring that all citizens learn English greater weight. Although he regarded the English-only rule as unwise, Justice Holmes concluded that it was not an unreasonable exercise of state education authority. *Id*. at 412.

22. *Barnette*, 319 U.S. 624. This case reversed the Court's 1940 decision upholding school power to require a flag salute. Minersville School Dist. v. Gobitis, 310 U.S. 586 (1940). *See generally* D. Manwaring, *Render Unto Caesar: The Flag-Salute Controversy* (1962); Peter Irons, *Courage of Their Convictions* (1988). *See also* Sherman v. Community Consol. School Dist. 21 of Wheeling Township, 714 F. Supp. 932 (N.D. Ill. 1989) *aff'd*, 61 U.S.L.W. 2340 (7th Cir. 1992) (holding that a public school can perform daily flag salute provided unwilling students are allowed to opt out).

23. *Barnette*, 319 U.S. at 641 (emphasis added).

24. *Id*. at 625.

25. *Id*. at 640.

26. Brown v. Board of Educ., 347 U.S. 483, 493 (1954).

27. Ambach v. Norwick, 441 U.S. 68 at 77 (1979). *See also* McCollum v. Board of Education, 333 U.S. 203, 216–17 (1948) (stating that America's public schools were "[d]esigned to serve as perhaps the most powerful agency for promoting cohesion among heterogeneous democratic people" and that "[t]his development of the public school as a symbol of our secular unity was not a sudden achievement nor attained without violent conflict").

28. *See, e.g.*, Bethel School Dist. No. 403 v. Fraser, 478 U.S. 675 (1986); Hazelwood School Dist. v. Kuhlmeier, 484 U.S. 260 (1988).

29. *Hazelwood*, 484 U.S. 260 at 273.

30. *Id*. at 273 (quoting Epperson v. Arkansas, 393 U.S. 97 (1968)).

31. *Wisconsin v. Yoder*, 406 U.S. 205, 211 (1972).

32. *Id*. at 213–15.

33. *Id*. at 229.

34. *Id*. at 222.

35. *Id*. at 226.

36. Employment Division v. Smith, 494 U.S. 872, 877 (1990).

37. *Id*. at 881.

38. *Id*. at 882.

39. *See, e.g.*, Michael W. McConnell, "Free Exercise Revisionism and the *Smith* Decision," 57 *U. Chi. L. Rev.* 1109 (1990). The Court in 1992 accepted certiorari in a free exercise case that some observers believe may be used to limit *Smith. See* Church of Lukumi v. City of Hialeah, 723 F. Supp. 1467 (S.D. Fla. 1989) *aff'd* 936 F. 2d 586 (11th Cir. 1991) *cert. granted* 112 S. Ct. 1472 (1992).

40. *Smith*, 494 U.S. at 885.

41. *Id*. at 890.

42. *Id*.

43. *See, e.g.*, Bender v. Williamsport Area School Dist., 741 F.2d 538 (3d Cir. 1984); Roberts v. Madigan, 702 F. Supp. 1505 (D.Colo. 1989) *aff'd* 921 F.2d 1047 (10th Cir. 1990); Smith v. Board of School Commissioners, 827 F.2d 684 (11th Cir. 1987); Grove v. Mead School District, 753 F.2d 1528 (9th Cir.), *cert. denied*, 474 U.S. 826 (1985); Mozert v. Hawkins, 827 F.2d 1058 (6th Cir. 1987), *cert. denied*, 484 U.S. 1066 (1988); Rhode Island Federation of Teachers, AFL-CIO v. Norberg, 630 F.2d 850 (1st Cir. 1980); Doe v. Human, 725 F. Supp. 1503 (W.D.Ark. 1989); Jackson v. California, 460 F.2d 282 (9th Cir. 1972); Cornwell v. State Board of Education, 428 F.2d 471 (4th Cir. 1970), *cert. denied*, 400 U.S. 942 (1970); McLean v. Arkansas Board of

Education, 529 F. Supp. 1255 (D. Ark. 1982); Roman v. Appleby, 558 F. Supp. 449 (E.D. Pa. 1983).

44. Nomi Maya Stolzenberg, " 'He Drew a Circle That Shut Me Out . . . ': Assimilation, Indoctrination and the Paradox of a Liberal Education," 106 *Harv. L. Rev.* 581, 621–22 (1993).

The charge that public education is driven by secular humanism, and thus is an impermissible form of values indoctrination, is more subtle and sophisticated than it may first appear. As Professor Michael McConnell, a leading theorist on freedom of religion, has stated, the scholarship of the left in the past half-century has done a convincing job of uncovering how nonneutral our seemingly neutral laws and other cultural practices truly are. *See* Michael W. McConnell, "Religious Freedom at a Crossroads," 59 *U. Chi. L. Rev.* 115, 134–35 (1992). For example, feminist scholarship demonstrates that gender roles often find no basis in nature but are culturally constructed. Moreover, standards of achievement have been shown to be based on unstated, nonneutral norms. Using the tools of this critical scholarship of the left, some Christian fundamentalists have argued that the brand of moral and cultural relativism that the dominant culture, or at least the public education culture, embraces is hardly neutral. Rather, it is a "politically correct" perversion of traditional values, which has no greater claim to truth than any other, rejected standards.

Although there is a response to the fundamentalists' philosophical argument, it is unlikely to weaken their resolve. The reason is that fundamentalists' argument that public education is nonneutral is a strategic argument only; it is not based on an underlying sincere belief that no dogma has a superior claim to truth. On the contrary, fundamentalists feel quite strongly that their own dogma is superior and that it is based on an ahistorical, transcendental truth. Their real objection is not that the schools are inculcating values or that they have abandoned neutrality as a guiding pedagogical principle; it is that the values schools do inculcate are antithetical to biblical authority. As such, the subtle epistemological argument raised by the secular humanism debate actually is a red herring. The real conflict here is whether the nonneutral values endorsed by public education and other areas of our public culture should be secular and not religious ones. This in turn involves the sometimes complex task of distinguishing religious from secular values.

45. *See* text accompanying notes 50–54, *infra*.
46. Amy Gutmann, *supra* note 15, at 103.
47. *Id*. (emphasis added).
48. *See, e.g.*, Abington School Dist. v. Schempp, 374 U.S. 203 (1963); Engel v. Vitale, 370 U.S. 421 (1962).
49. *See* text accompanying notes 58–60, *infra*.
50. *See Schempp, supra* note 48.
51. *See Engel, supra* note 48.
52. Indeed, even when a state mandated a moment of silence, rather than prayer per se, the Court struck down the measure because the legislative history revealed that the act was intended as a means of evading the Court's school prayer rulings. *See* Wallace v. Jaffree, 472 U.S. 38 (1985). *See also* Stone v. Graham, 449 U.S. 39 (1980) (per curiam) (holding unconstitutional public school posting of Ten Commandments in classrooms).
53. *See* Stephen L. Wasby, *The Impact of the Supreme Court* 129–33 (1970).
54. In the most recent of the Court's prayer cases, *Lee v. Weisman*, the Court was asked to consider whether a nonsectarian prayer at a junior high school graduation ceremony violated the First Amendment. The invocation, which was delivered by a rabbi, read as follows:

God of the Free, Hope of the Brave: For the legacy of America where diversity is celebrated and the rights of minorities are protected, we thank you. May these young men and women grow up to enrich it. For the liberty of America, we thank you. May these new graduates grow up to guard it. For the political process of America in which all its citizens may participate, for its court system where all can seek justice we thank you. May those we honor this morning always turn to it in trust. For the destiny of America we thank you. May the graduates of Nathan Bishop Middle School so live that they help to share it. May our aspirations for our country and for these young people, who are our hope for the future, be richly fulfilled. AMEN
112 S.Ct. 2649, 2652–53 (1992).

Here again, the Court held that the school-sponsored prayer violated the Establishment Clause, even though attendance at the graduation ceremony was not mandatory.

At issue in *Lee*, however, was more than the question of the role of prayer in public schools; government lawyers in the case asked the Court to use *Lee* as a vehicle for refashioning its approach to all Establishment Clause cases. By 1992 the case law had become a disaster area of internal contradiction, ambiguity, and uncertain direction, and many hoped that *Lee* would eliminate some of this confusion. Moreover, the argument that older case law forced a senseless wedge between religion and public life was gathering support beyond fundamentalist circles, including among some of the Supreme Court justices.

The focus of the justices' dissatisfaction with the older case law was the Court's 1971 decision, Lemon v. Kurtzman, 403 U.S. 602 (1971). *Lemon* forbids government action that (1) has no secular purpose; (2) has a primary effect of advancing or inhibiting religion; or (3) fosters an excessive entanglement with religion. *Id.* at 612. In its earlier applications, the test was construed to require a fairly sharp demarcation between religion and government.

Some commentators object that this strong version of *Lemon* mistakenly views religion "as an unreasoned, aggressive, exclusionary, and divisive force that must be confined to the private sphere." Michael W. McConnell, *supra* note 44, at 120. Others, however, argue that this version of *Lemon* was a worthy attempt to establish "a civil order—the culture of liberal democracy—for resolving public moral disputes." *See, e.g.,* Kathleen Sullivan, *Religion and Liberal Democracy,* 59 U. Chi. L. Rev. 195, 198 (1992). They believe that the exclusion of religion from public affairs is not a form of discrimination, but "the settlement by the Establishment Clause of the war of all sects against all." *Id.* at 199.

The current Court, however, has drifted away from the strict separationist position and has gravitated toward a more accommodationist account of church and state relations. It has begun to apply a *"Lemon*-lite" test, under which *any* secular purpose is adequate to survive the first prong, and government may assist religion without violating the remaining prongs.

Mounting dissatisfaction with *Lemon* even has prompted some of the justices to offer new tests. Justice O'Connor has suggested that the Establishment Clause should allow all accommodation of religion short of "endorsement." *See* Lynch v. Donnelly, 465 U.S. 668, 688, 691–93 (1984) (O'Connor, J., concurring); County of Allegheny v. ACLU, 492 U.S. 573, 621 (1989) (O'Connor, J., concurring). Endorsement occurs when government conveys religious messages that are meant to, or appear to, create the impression that a person's political fortune hinges on religious affiliations—that is, that the government divides the community up between insiders and outsiders based on their religion.

Other justices have suggested a weaker version of the Establishment Clause, which has been called a "coercion" test. *See Allegheny*, 492 U.S. at 668–74 (Kennedy, J., joined by Rehnquist, White, and Scalia, dissenting). Under this construction, the government can support and acknowledge religion, provided it does not "coerce anyone to support or participate in any religion or its exercise; [or] give direct benefits to religion in such a degree that it in fact establishes a [state]religion or religious faith or tends to do so." *Allegheny, id.* at 659. (Kennedy, J., concurring in part and dissenting in part) (quoting *Lynch*, 465 U.S. at 678).

This internal resistance to *Lemon*, coupled with the growing external resistance to the strict separation of church and state, led some observers to believe that the Court in *Lee* would officially reject *Lemon* and adopt a new, more accommodationist standard for Establishment Clause cases.

Although the Court in *Lee* declined the invitation to rewrite its Establishment Clause standards, the Court split five to four on what should have been an easy question, given the past prayer decisions. The split revealed how controversial the Establishment Clause doctrine had become within the Court and indicated that the doctrine likely will be revised in the near future.

55. Board of Educ. of Westside Community Schools v. Mergens, 496 U.S. 226 (1990) (plurality opinion).
56. Widmar v. Vincent, 454 U.S. 263 (1981). *See also* Country Hills Christian Church v. Unified School Dist. No. 512, 560 F. Supp. 1207, 1220 (D. Kan. 1983) (holding that school district must make facilities of district available to groups seeking to use them for religious services on terms equal to nonreligious groups, where facilities had become a "public forum" available for community use).
57. *Mergens*, 496 U.S. 226, 250.
58. *See* Edwards v. Aguillard, 482 U.S. 578 (1987); Epperson v. Arkansas, 393 U.S. 97 (1968); Wright v. Houston Indep. School Dist., 366 F. Supp. 1208 (S.D. Tex. 1978), *aff'd* 486 F.2d 137 (5th Cir. 1973), *cert. denied*, 417 U.S. 969 (1974); Peloza v. Capistrano Unified School Dist., 782 F. Supp. 1412 (C.D. Cal. 1992); McLean v. Arkansas Board of Education, 529 F. Supp. 1255 (E.D. Ark. 1982); Scopes v. State, 154 Tenn. 105, 289 S.W. 363 (1927).
59. *Epperson*, 393 U.S. at 103.
60. *Edwards*, 482 U.S. at 588.
61. *Id.* at 618 (Scalia, J., dissenting).
62. *Mozert*, 827 F.2d 1058 (6th Cir. 1987). For an extremely intelligent, sensitive analysis of *Mozert*, see Nomi Maya Stolzenberg, *supra* note 44.
63. *Smith*, 827 F.2d 684 (11th Cir. 1987).
64. *Mozert*, 827 F.2d at 1060. For a full account of the factual backdrop to *Mozert*, see Joan DelFattore, *What Johnny Shouldn't Read: Textbook Censorship in America* 13–75 (1992). An excerpt of her account of Mrs. Frost's beliefs is as follows:

[A]ll decisions should be based solely on the Word of God; using reason or imagination to solve problems is an act of rebellion. Everyone should live in traditional nuclear families structured on stereotyped gender roles. Wives should obey their husbands, and children their parents, without argument or question.

. . . [T]he United States has, since its inception been the greatest nation on earth. Any criticism of its founders, policies, or history offends God and promotes a Communist invasion by discouraging boys from growing up to fight for their country. Since war is God's way of vindicating the righteous and punishing the

wicked, anti-war material—and by extension, criticism of hunting or gun owner-
ship—is unpatriotic, disrespectful to God, and detrimental to the moral fiber of
American youth.

Pollution and other environmental concerns are humanist propaganda designed
to provide an excuse for government interference in big business and for international cooperation, either of which is capable of destroying this country. . . . International cooperation might lead to a one-world government, which would be the reign
of the Antichrist and bring about the end of the world . . .

Christianity—that is, Protestant fundamentalism—is the one true religion and the
religion on which the United States was founded.

Id. at 36–37. The author concludes that the objections to the public school curriculum in
Mozert were bound by the protesters' "total commitment to one religious and cultural
group, to the exclusion of globalism and multiculturalism." *Id.* at 37.

65. *Mozert*, 827 F.2d at 1062.

66. *Id.* at 1064.

67. *Id.*

68. *Id.* For discussion of whether granting an exemption from a general law—including a
compulsory education law—to a religious minority constitutes impermissible endorse-
ment of religion rather than a constitutional respect for religious pluralism, see generally
William P. Marshall, "The Case Against the Constitutional Compelled Free Exercise
Exemption," 40 *Case W. Res. L. Rev.* 357 (1989–90); Michael W. McConnell, *supra* note 39;
Douglas Laycock, "The Remnants of Free Exercise," 1990 *Sup. Ct. Rev.* 1; Geoffrey Stone,
"Constitutionally Compelled Exemptions and the Free Exercise Clause," 27 *Wm. & Mary
L. Rev.* 985 (1986); Mark Tushnet, "The Emerging Principle of Accommodation of Reli-
gion (Dubitante)," 76 *Geo. L.J.* 1691 (1988).

69. *Smith*, 827 F.2d 684, (11th Cir. 1987).

70. *Id.* at 686.

71. *Id.*

72. *Id.* at 693.

73. *Id.* at 694.

74. *Id.* at 692.

75. McCollum v. Board of Education, 333 U.S. 203, 255 (1948) (Jackson, J., concurring) ("If we
are to eliminate everything that is objectionable to any of these warring sects or inconsistent with any of their doctrines, we will leave public education in shreds").

76. *See* Mueller v. Allen, 463 U.S. 388 (1983). *Cf.* Committee for Pub. Educ. v. Nyquist, 413 U.S.
753 (1973) (holding invalid a New York statute that granted thinly disguised "tax benefits"
that were in effect tuition grants to parents of children attending private schools).

77. *See* Corporation of Presiding Bishops v. Amos, 483 U.S. 327 (1987).

78. *Mergens*, 496 U.S. 226 (1990).

79. Bowen v. Kendrick, 487 U.S. 589 (1988) (upholding as constitutional the Adolescent Family
Life Act).

80. Rust v. Sullivan, 111 S.Ct. 1759 (1991) (upholding requirement under Title X of the Public
Health Service Act that a grantee's abortion-related activity be separate from any family
planning activity that receives federal funds).

81. *See* note 54 *supra*. The Court granted certiorari in 1992 in a case that may shed considerable light on the matter. In Zobrest v. Catalina Foothills School Dist., 963 F.2d 1190 (9th Cir.
1992) *cert. granted* 113 S.Ct. 52 (argued Feb. 24, 1993) the Court will resolve whether the

Establishment Clause bars the state from providing an interpreter to a deaf student who attends a Catholic high school.

82. Thus, "children are the Achilles heel of liberal ideology." Steven Shiffrin, "Government Speech," 27 *UCLA L. Rev.* 565, 647 (1980).

83. Amy Gutmann, *supra* note 46, at 42.

84. *See* Steven Shiffrin, *supra* note 82; Mark Yudof, *When Government Speaks* 213–45 (1983).

85. A recent and highly controversial illustration of the extent of this power was the Court's decision upholding federal regulations—so-called gag orders—that barred recipients of federal funds from discussing the option of abortion with patients in any program that benefitted from federal money. The order is one that the Clinton administration has repealed. *Rust, supra* note 80.

86. Mark Yudof, "Library Book Selection and the Public Schools: The Quest for the Archimedean Point," 59 *Ind. L.J.* 527, 529–30 (1984). *See also*, Mark Yudof, *supra* note 84, at 213–45.

87. Amy Gutmann, *supra* note 15, at 42.

88. Tinker v. Des Moines School Dist., 393 U.S. 503, 506 (1969).

89. *Epperson*, 393 U.S. at 104 (1968) (quoting Shelton v. Tucker, 364 U.S. 479, 487 (1960) and Keyishian v. Board of Regents, 385 U.S. 589, 603 (1967)).

90. *See Tinker, supra* note 88.

91. *Id.* at 504.

92. *Id.*

93. *Id.* at 508.

94. *Id.* at 505 (quoting Burnside v. Byars, 363 F.2d 744, 749 (5th Cir. 1966)).

95. Bethel School Dist. No. 403 v. Fraser, 478 U.S. 675 (1986).

96. *Id.* at 678.

97. *Id.* at 687.

98. *Id.*

99. *Id.* at 681.

100. *Id.* at 683.

101. *Id.*

102. *Id.*

103. In the late 1980s and early 1990s, hundreds of colleges and universities enacted so-called hate-speech policies that made conduct, including speech conduct, by students that vilified another because of race, ethnicity, gender, or other group-based characteristics a disciplinable offense. The policies varied widely and were based on different theories of the nature of the offense and of the schools' interest in regulating the speech. They prompted a spate of law review articles that discussed at length the merits and dangers of such speech regulation. *See, e.g.,* Jack M. Balkin, "Some Realism About Pluralism: Legal Realist Approaches to the First Amendment," 1990 *Duke L.J.* 375; Richard Delgado, "Words That Wound: A Tort Action for Racial Insults, Epithets, and Name Calling," 17 *Harv. C.R.-C.L. L. Rev.* 133 (1982); Thomas C. Grey, "Discriminatory Harassment and Free Speech," 14 *Harv. J. of Law & Pub. Policy* 157 (1991); Thomas C. Grey, "Civil Rights v. Civil Liberties: The Case of Discriminatory Verbal Harassment," 8 *Soc. Phil. & Pol'y* 81 (Spring 1991); Charles R. Lawrence, III, "If He Hollers, Let Him Go: Regulating Racist Speech on Campus," 1990 *Duke L.J.* 431; Toni M. Massaro, "Equality and Freedom of Expression: The Hate Speech Dilemma," 32 *Wm. & Mary L. Rev.* 211 (1991); Mari J. Matsuda, "Public Response to Racist Speech: Considering the Victim's Story," 87 *Mich. L. Rev.* 2320 (1989); Rodney A. Smolla, "Rethinking First Amendment Assumptions About Racist and Sexist

Speech," 47 *Wash. & Lee L. Rev.* 171 (1990); Nadine Strossen, "Regulating Racist Speech on Campus: A Modest Proposal," 1990 *Duke L.J.* 484.

In June of 1992, however, the Court decided R.A.V. v. City of St. Paul, 112 S.Ct. 2538 (1992), a case that involved the prosecution of youths who burned a cross on the lawn of a sleeping African-American family, pursuant to an ordinance that made such action illegal because it was bias-motivated. The Court's ruling suggests that college campus regulations that make speech actionable for the content-specific reason that such speech conveys bias against people on the basis of race, gender, color, creed, or religion may be unconstitutional. Whether the Court would extend this principle to the elementary and high school setting, however, is far less clear, given *Fraser*. For an example of a state court case that upholds lower schools' power to regulate such speech, see Clarke v. Board of Educ., 338 N.W.2d 272 (Neb. 1983). *See also* Schmidt, "Speech Codes Tread Line Between Student Protection, First Amendment," XII *Educ. Week.*, Dec. 2, 1992, at 1, col. 2.

104. Hazelwood School Dist. v. Kuhlmeier, 484 U.S. 260 (1988).
105. *Id.* at 271.
106. *Id.* at 273.
107. Board of Education, Island Trees Union Free School Dist. No. 26 v. Pico, 457 U.S. 853, 857 (1982).
108. *Id.* at 858.
109. *Id.* at 857.
110. *Id.* at 867.
111. *Id.* at 868.
112. *Id.* at 870.
113. *Id.* at 874.
114. *Id.* at 875.
115. *Id.* at 878.
116. *Id.* at 879.
117. *Id.*
118. *Id.* at 907.
119. *Id.* at 914.
120. *Id.* at 909.
121. *See* Virgil v. School Board of Columbia County, Florida, 862 F.2d 1517 (11th Cir. 1989).
122. *See, e.g.*, Frances FitzGerald, *America Revised* (1979); Joan DelFattore, *supra* note 64; Henry Reichman, *Censorship and Selection: Issues and Answers for Schools* (1988); Stanley N. Wellborn, "As Drive to Ban Books Spreads in U.S.," *U.S. News & World Report* 66 (Mar. 8, 1982); Robert Lerner & Stanley Rothman, "Newspeak, Feminist-Style," 89:4 *Commentary* 54 (Apr. 1990); Frances M. Jones, *Defusing Censorship: The Librarian's Guide to Handling Censorship Conflicts* (1983); Stephen Arons, *Compelling Belief: The Culture of American Schooling* 38–74 (1983); Association of American Public Libraries, *Limiting What Students Shall Read*.
123. *See, e.g.*, Eric Rofes, "Opening Up the Classroom Closet: Responding to the Educational Needs of Gay and Lesbian Youth," 59 *Harv. Educ. Rev.* 444 (1989); D. Martin, *The Harvey Milk Off-Site High School Program* (The Hetrick-Martin Institute, Inc., 1991); Jan Goodman, "Out of the Closet But Paying the Price: Lesbian and Gay Characters in Children's Literature" 14 *Interracial Books for Children Bulletin* 13 (1983).
124. For an excellent illustration of the multiple meanings of "educational equality," see Christopher Jencks, "Whom Must We Treat Equally For Educational Opportunity to Be Equal?" 98 *Ethics* 518 (1988). *See also* David L. Kirp, *Just Schools: The Idea of Racial Equality in*

American Education 33–49 (1982). Competing constructions of equality consume a vast body of scholarship in law, philosophy, political science, and other disciplines. Among the more influential contemporary works are the following: John Rawls, *A Theory of Justice* (1971); Peter Westen, *Speaking of Equality* (1990); Joel Feinberg, "Noncomparative Justice," 83 *Philosophical Rev.* 297 (July 1974); Ronald Dworkin, *Taking Rights Seriously* (1977); Ronald Dworkin, "What Is Equality?: Part I, Equality of Welfare," 10 *Phil & Pub. Affairs* 185 (Summer 1981); Paul Brest, "In Defense of the Anti-discrimination Principle," 90 *Harv. L. Rev.* 1 (1976); Owen M. Fiss, "Groups and the Equal Protection Clause," 5 *Phil. & Pub. Aff.* 107 (1976).

125. Strauder v. West Virginia, 100 U.S. (10 Otto) 303, 306 (1879).

126. 163 U.S. 537 (1896).

127. *Id.* at 551.

128. 347 U.S. 483 (1954) (*Brown I*).

129. *Id.* at 495.

130. 349 U.S. 294, 301 (1955) (*Brown II*).

131. *See, e.g.*, Lynne Henderson, "Legality and Empathy," 85 *Mich. L. Rev.* 1574, 1593–1609 (1987).

132. *See, e.g.*, Herbert Wechsler, "Toward Neutral Principles of Constitutional Law," 73 *Harv. L. Rev.* 1, 34 (1959).

133. Derrick A. Bell, Jr., "*Brown v. Board of Education* and the Interest-Convergence Dilemma," 93 *Harv. L. Rev.* 518, 524 (1980). *See also* Derrick A. Bell, Jr., *And We Are Not Saved* 111–13 (1987); Derrick A. Bell, Jr., "Litigation Strategies for the 1970s: New Phases in the Continuing Quest for Quality Schools," 1970 *Wis. L. Rev.* 257, 290–92.

134. *See* Robert L. Carter, "The Warren Court and Desegregation," 67 *Mich. L. Rev.* 237, 243 (1968); Louis Lusky, "Racial Discrimination and the Federal Law: A Problem in Nullification," 63 *Colum. L. Rev.* 1163 (1963).

135. *See* Gerald Rosenberg, *The Hollow Hope* (1991) (arguing that the intellectual, social and legal impact of *Brown* was far less than that of civil rights statutes passed over a decade later).

136. *Brown I*, 347 U.S. at 493.

137. *Id.* at 493 (quoting McLaurin v. Oklahoma State Regents, 339 U.S. 637, 641 (1950)).

138. *Id.* at 494.

139. *See, e.g.*, Robert B. McKay, " 'With All Deliberate Speed'—A Study of School Desegregation," 31 *N.Y.U. L. Rev.* 991, 1017–38 (1956); Robert B. McKay, " 'With All Deliberate Speed': Legislature Reaction and Judicial Development, 1956–57," 43 *Va. L. Rev.* 1205, 1216–28 (1957); U.S. Commission on Civil Rights, *Survey of School Desegregation in the Southern and Border States 1965–66* (1966).

140. For an extended analysis of the Rehnquist Court's approach to race discrimination and its future direction, see Brian K. Landsberg, "Race and the Rehnquist Court," 66 *Tul. L. Rev.* 1267 (1992).

141. 112 S.Ct. 1430 (1992).

142. *Id.* at 1453–1454.

143. Washington v. Davis, 426 U.S. 229, 242–43 (1976). *See also* Village of Arlington Heights v. Metropolitan Housing Development Corp., 429 U.S. 252 (1977); Johnson v. San Francisco Unified School District, 500 F.2d 349 (9th Cir. 1974); Soria v. Oxnard School District, 488 F.2d 579, 585 (9th Cir. 1973), *cert. denied*, 416 U.S. 951 (1974); Husbands v. Pennsylvania, 395 F. Supp. 1107 (E.D. Pa. 1975); Oliver v. Kalamazoo Board of Education, 368 F. Supp. 143, 161

(W.D. Mich. 1973), *aff'd*, 508 F.2d 178, 181–82 (6th Cir. 1974), *cert. denied*, 421 U.S. 963 (1975); Arthur v. Nyquist, 573 F.2d 134, 142 n.15 (2d Cir. 1978), *cert. denied, sub. nom.* 439 U.S. 860.

144. As one commentator has observed, *Davis* represents the "taming of *Brown*." David A. Strauss, "Discriminatory Intent and the Taming of Brown," 56 *U. Chi. L. Rev.* 935 (1989). Strauss describes *Davis* as part of a more general and systematic taming process in law. "Great principles," he notes, "are announced in a form that is both vague and potentially far-reaching. Pressure then develops to change them by reducing them to something that is more clear and objective, and less threatening to established institutions."

145. Charles R. Lawrence, III, "The Id, the Ego, and Equal Protection: Reckoning With Unconscious Racism," 39 *Stan. L. Rev.* 317, 321–23, 331–39, 344–55 (1987).

146. Plessy v. Ferguson, 163 U.S. 537, 559 (1896) (Harlan, J., dissenting).

147. University of California Regents v. Bakke, 438 U.S. 265, 407 (1978) (Blackmun, J.).

148. *Id.*

149. *Id.* at 320.

150. *Id.* at 400–01 (Marshall, J., dissenting).

151. City of Richmond v. Croson, 488 U.S. 469, 488–90 (1989).

152. *Id.* at 524.

153. Affirmative action critics include the following: Alexander Bickel, *The Morality of Consent* 133–34 (1975); Thomas Sowell, *Civil Rights: Rhetoric or Reality* 13–48, 109–16 (1984); Shelby Steele, *The Content of Our Character* (1990); Stephen L. Carter, *Reflections of an Affirmative Action Baby* 7 (1991) (discussing the contradictions of affirmative action and describing it as a "mixed blessing"); Morris B. Abram, "Affirmative Action: Fair Shakers and Social Engineers," 99 *Harv. L. Rev.* 1312 (1986); Richard Posner, "The Defunis Case and the Constitutionality of Preferential Treatment of Racial Minorities," 1974 *Sup. Ct. Rev.* 1; Martin Schiff, "Reverse Discrimination Re-Defined as Equal Protection: The Orwellian Nightmare in the Enforcement of Civil Rights Laws," 8 *Harv. J. L. & Pub. Pol'y* 627 (1985); William Van Alstyne, "Rites of Passage: Race, the Supreme Court, and the Constitution," 46 *U. Chi. L. Rev.* 775 (1979).

154. Supporters of at least some forms of affirmative action include the following academics: Derrick A. Bell, Jr., "Bakke, Minority Admissions and the Usual Price of Racial Remedies," 67 *Calif. L. Rev.* 3 (1979); Paul Brest, "Foreword: In Defense of the Antidiscrimination Principle," 90 *Harv. L. Rev.* 1 (1976); John Hart Ely, "The Constitutionality of Reverse Racial Discrimination," 41 *U. Chi. L. Rev.* 723 (1974); Owen Fiss, "Groups and the Equal Protection Clause," 5 *Phil & Pub Aff.* 107, 147–70 (1976); Alan Freeman, "Racism, Rights and the Quest for Equality of Opportunity: A Critical Legal Essay," 23 *Harv. C.R.-C.L. L. Rev.* 295, 362–85 (1988); Kenneth L. Karst & Harold W. Horowitz, "Affirmative Action and Equal Protection," 60 *Va. L. Rev.* 955 (1974); Randall Kennedy, "Persuasion and Distrust: A Comment on the Affirmative Action Debate," 99 *Harv. L. Rev.* 1327 (1986).

155. *Croson*, 488 U.S. 469, 552 (Marshall, J., dissenting).

156. In *United States v. Fordice*, the Court held that race-neutral college admissions policies and student freedom to attend the institution of their choice may not satisfy a state's duty to dismantle a prior de jure segregated university system. 112 S.Ct. 2727 (1992). The Court thus is still willing, in some circumstances, to impose affirmative duties on a state to undo the effects of prior discrimination, even when the state has removed the legal barriers that first caused the discrimination. As such, the Court has not rejected entirely the notion that some ostensibly "neutral" policies may be traced to past intentional discrimination. *See*

also Green v. New Kent County School Board, 391 U.S. 430 (1968). As the Court has observed, "The Equal Protection Clause is offended by 'sophisticated as well as simple-minded modes of discrimination.'" *Fordice*, 112 S.Ct. at 2736 (quoting *Lane v. Wilson*, 307 U.S. 268, 275 (1939)).

157. Charles Fried, "*Metro Broadcasting, Inc. v. FCC*: Two Concepts of Equality," 104 *Harv. L. Rev.* 107, 109 (1990).

158. *See* note 153, *supra*.

159. *See* note 154, *supra*.

160. *See* Gary Peller, "Race Consciousness," 1990 *Duke L.J.* 758.

161. In the past several years, the debate over race consciousness as a vehicle for remedying past imbalances has been particularly vigorous among law scholars. *See* Randall Kennedy, "Racial Critiques of Legal Academia," 102 *Harv. L. Rev.* 1745 (1989); Scott Brewer, "Colloquy: Responses to Randall Kennedy's Racial Critiques of Legal Academia," 103 *Harv. L. Rev.* 1844 (1990); Gary Peller, "Race Consciousness," 1990 *Duke L.J.* 758; Duncan Kennedy, "A Cultural Pluralist Case for Affirmative Action in Legal Academia," 1990 *Duke L.J.* 705; Mari J. Matsuda, "Looking to the Bottom: Critical Legal Studies and Reparations," 22 *Harv. C.R.-C.L. L. Rev.* 323 (1987); T. Alexander Aleinikoff, "A Case for Race-Consciousness," 91 *Colum. L. Rev.* 1060 (1991); Neil Gotanda, "A Critique of 'Our Constitution Is Color-Blind'," 44 *Stan. L. Rev.* 1 (1991); David A. Strauss, "The Myth of Colorblindness," 1986 *Sup. Ct. Rev.* 99; Kimberlé Crenshaw, "Race, Reform, and Retrenchment: Transformation and Legitimation in Antidiscrimination Law," 101 *Harv. L. Rev.* 1331 (1988). *See generally* David A. Strauss, "Symposium, the Law and Economics of Racial Discrimination in Employment," 79 *Geo. L.J.* 1619 (1991).

162. For a discussion of the African-centered schools and their legal status, see Helaine Greenfeld, "Some Constitutional Problems With the Resegregation of Public Schools," 80 *Geo. L.J.* 363 (1991); Note, "Creating Space for Racial Difference: The Case for African-American Schools," 27 *Harv. C.R.-C.L. L. Rev.* 187 (1992). Smith, "All-Male Black Schools and the Equal Protection Clause: A Step Forward Toward Education," 66 *Tul. L. Rev.* 2003 (1992).

The Detroit experiment was struck down as unconstitutional because it excluded girls from the program. *See* Plaintiffs v. Board of Education of School District of City of Detroit, 775 F. Supp. 1004 (E.D. Mich. 1991).

163. *See, e.g.*, Tanya Neiman, Note, "Teaching Woman Her Place: The Role of Public Education in the Development of Sex Roles," 24 *Hastings L.J.* 1191 (1973); Sheila Tobias & Carol Weisbrod, "Anxiety and Mathematics: An Update," 50 *Harv. Educ. Rev.* 63 (1980); N. Frazier & M. Sadker, *Sexism in School and Society* (1973); *Gender in the Classroom: Power and Pedagogy* (S. Gabriel & I. Smithson eds., 1990); Comment, "Sex Discrimination: The Textbook Case," 62 *Calif. L. Rev.* 1312 (1974); Note, "Sex Discrimination in High School Athletics: An Examination of Applicable Legal Doctrines," 66 *Minn. L. Rev.* 1115 (1982); Karen L. Tokarz, "Separate But Unequal Education Sports Programs: The Need for a New Theory of Equality" 1 *Berkeley Women's L.J.* 201 (1985); Sheila Tobias, "How Coeducation Fails Women," in *Sex Differences in Education* 83 (S. Anderson ed., 1973); Susan Gluck Mezey, "Gender Equality in Education: A Study of Policymaking By the Burger Court," 20 *Wake Forest L. Rev.* 793 (1984); *And Jill Came Tumbling After: Sexism in American Education* (Judith Stacey et al. eds., 1974); *Gender, Class, and Education* (S. Walker & L. Barton eds., 1983).

164. For a history of coeducation in American public schools, see David Tyack & Elisabeth Hansot, *Learning Together* (1990).

165. 83 U.S. (16 Wall.) 130, 148 (1872). For an excellent discussion of the history and evolution of gender jurisprudence see, Deborah Rhode, *Justice and Gender* (1989).

166. *See* Weinberger v. Weisenfeld, 420 U.S. 636 (1975); Stanton v. Stanton, 421 U.S. 7 (1975); Califano v. Goldfarb, 430 U.S. 199 (1977); Craig v. Boren, 429 U.S. 190 (1976); Orr v. Orr, 440 U.S. 268 (1979); Caban v. Mohammed, 441 U.S. 380 (1979); Geduldig v. Aiello, 417 U.S. 484 (1974).

167. *See* Craig v. Boren, 429 U.S. 190 (1976).

168. 458 U.S. 718 (1982).

169. *Id.* Although the applicant could have enrolled in one of the coeducational programs farther from his home, he then would have been unable to also hold down a full-time job, which many female nursing students were able to do. Thus, the female-only policy imposed on males a burden that females did not bear. *Id.*

170. *Id.* at 729.

171. *Id.* at 720.

172. 450 U.S. 464 (1981).

173. *Id.* at 464.

174. *Id.* at 473.

175. *Id.* at 475.

176. The dissenting justices disagreed with this interpretation. They argued that the statute was based on a stereotypical, gender-based assumption that the male is always the culpable aggressor. If the true legislative purpose had been solely to deter illegitimate pregnancy, they reasoned, then there would have been no reason to exempt females. While the risk of pregnancy offers some deterrence for females, it obviously is inadequate to deter all teen pregnancies. Thus a gender-neutral rule would have served better the state's alleged purpose. Only if, as they believed was true, the act actually was based on an assumption that the male is the culpable aggressor would the exemption for females make sense. But this assumption was supported by no evidence other than "habitual attitude" and thus violated the male's equal protection rights. *Id.*

177. *See, e.g.,* Frances Olsen, "Statutory Rape: A Feminist Critique of Rights Analysis," 63 *Tex. L. Rev.* 387, 427–28 (1984).

178. *See generally Feminist Legal Theory: Readings in Law and Gender* (K. Bartlett & R. Kennedy eds., 1991); Susan Moller Okin, *Women in Western Political Thought* (1991 ed.); Deborah Rhode, *supra* note 169; *Feminism & Political Theory* (C. Sunstein ed., 1990).

179. Katherine Bartlett, "Feminist Methodologies," 103 *Harv. L. Rev.* 829 (1990).

180. Many of these differene theorists cite the famous 1982 study, *In a Different Voice,* in which Carol Gilligan suggests that girls' patterns of moral reasoning are different from, but not inferior to, boys'. When asked, for example, what a man should do if his wife is dying from a disease that could be halted with medication, and he cannot afford the drug, the boys were inclined to respond that he should steal the drug if the pharmacist would not give it to him for free. Life, the boys reasoned, is more valuable than property. Thus, the man has a moral right to steal the drug. The girls, in contrast, were inclined to respond by asking first whether all of the parties could sit down together and discuss the matter. Perhaps, they suggested, the man could make arrangements to pay for the drug in installments. And perhaps the pharmacist might come to appreciate the husband's dilemma. The girls approached the problem with what has been termed an "ethic of care," which differed from the moral reasoning approach of the boys but which, under traditional measures of moral reasoning, would wrongly be labeled less mature than the male method.

181. Catharine A. MacKinnon, *Toward a Feminist Theory of the State* (1989); Catharine A. MacKinnon, *Feminism Unmodified: Discourses on Life and Law* (1987).

182. *See, e.g.*, Audre Lorde, *Sister Outsider: Essays and Speeches* 41–42 (1984); Paula Giddings, *When and Where I Enter: The Impact of Black Women on Race and Sex in America* (1984); *All the Women Are White, All the Blacks are Men, But Some of Us are Brave* (G. T. Hull et al. eds., 1982); Regina Austin, "Sapphire Bound!" 1989 *Wis. L. Rev.* 539; Angela Harris, "Race and Essentialism in Feminist Legal Theory," 42 *Stan. L. Rev.* 581 (1990); *This Bridge Called My Back* (C. Moraga & G. Anzaldva eds., 1983); bellhooks, *Ain't I A Woman: Black Women & Feminism* (1983); bellhooks, *Talking Back: Thinking Feminist, Thinking Black* (1989); Judy Scales-Trent, "Black Women and the Constitution: Finding Our Place, Asserting Our Rights," 24 *Harv. C.R.-C.L. L. Rev.* 9 (1989); Kimberlé Crenshaw, "Race, Reform and Retrenchment: Transformation and Legitimation in Antidiscrimination Law," 101 *Harv. L. Rev.* 1331 (1988).

183. Patricia A. Cain, "Feminist Jurisprudence: Grounding the Theories," 4 *Berkeley Women's L.J.* 191 (1989–90); *This Bridge Called My Back, supra* note 182, at 107–64.

184. Craig v. Boren, 429 U.S. 190 (1976).

185. Jonathan Kozol recently described as "savage" the inequalities in education funding and services. He reports that urban, poor schoolchildren—a majority of whom are minority-race students—receive vastly inferior educations to those of their suburban, more affluent peers. Jonathan Kozol, *Savage Inequalities* (1991).

186. This link is a contested one. For discussions of the link between wealth and education, and various proposals for improving education finance equality, see John Coons, William Clune & Stephen Sugarman, *Private Wealth and Public Education* (1970); David L. Kirp, *Just Schools* (1982); Paul Brest, "Interdistrict Disparities in Educational Resources," 23 *Stan. L. Rev.* 594 (1971); Christopher Jencks, *Inequality* (1972); *On Equality of Educational Opportunity* (1966) (The "Coleman Report"); Paul Carrington, "Financing the American Dream: Equality and School Taxes," 73 *Colum. L. Rev.* 1227 (1973); James Guthrie, George Kleindorfer, Henry Levin & R. Stout, *Schools and Inequality* (1971); Kenneth Karst, "Serrano v. Priest: A State Court's Responsibilities and Opportunities in the Development of Federal Constitutional Law," 60 *Calif. L. Rev.* 720 (1972); Harold W. Horowitz, "Unseparated but Unequal—The Emerging Fourteenth Amendment Issue in Public Education," 13 *UCLA L. Rev.* 1147 (1966); Stephen R. Goldstein, "Interdistrict Inequalities in School Financing: A Critical Analysis of Serrano v. Priest and Its Progeny," 120 *U. Pa. L. Rev.* 504 (1972); Betsy Levin, "Current Trends in School Finance Reform Litigation: A Commentary," 1977 *Duke L.J.* 1099; Mark Yudof, "School Finance Reform in Texas: The Edgewood Saga," 28 *Harv. J. on Legis.* 499 (1991); Mark Yudof, "School Finance Reform: Don't Worry, Be Happy," 10 *Rev. of Litig.* 585 (1991); Note, "Unfulfilled Promises: School Finance Remedies and State Courts," 104 *Harv. L. Rev.* 1072 (1991); Michael J. Churgin, Peter H. Ehrenberg & Peter T. Grossi, Jr., Note, "A Statistical Analysis of the School Finance Decisions: On Winning Battles and Losing Wars," 81 *Yale L.J.* 1303 (1972).

187. An obstacle to the funding equalization movement, at least when based on federal constitutional grounds, is the 1973 decision of the Supreme Court, *San Antonio Indep. School District v. Rodriguez*, 411 U.S. 1 (1973). Here again, the Court refused to monitor state and local education decisions except in extreme cases.

    San Antonio involved a challenge of the state of Texas's scheme for apportioning public education monies. Like most jurisdictions, Texas relied on a combination of local property taxes and state contributions to finance public schooling. The Texas scheme resulted in per pupil expenditures that varied dramatically among the state's districts. For example, one district expended only $356 / pupil, while another expended $594 / pupil. The plaintiffs alleged that these disparities constituted a denial of equal education for those students who lived in property-poor districts and thus received lower per pupil expenditures than their peers in property-rich districts.

The Court rejected the argument that federal constitutional law required that the state equalize its per pupil expenditures on two grounds. First, the Court concluded that wealth-based classifications, unlike race-based classifications, are not inherently suspect and thus do not trigger strict judicial scrutiny. Rather, the Court will demand only that the state have a rational basis for wealth-based distinctions. In this case, moreover, the state funding scheme did not distinguish between rich and poor students; rather, the per pupil expenditures varied according to each district's ability to produce property tax revenues. In some cases, this meant that students from lower income families actually were the beneficiaries of higher per pupil expenditures because they lived in districts that could produce greater tax revenues due to commercial or industrial property within the district.

Second, the Court rejected the argument that education is a fundamental right, such that any disparity in education services must be supported by compelling justifications. The Court noted that the Constitution nowhere mentions education, despite education's undeniable link to intelligent exercise of the right to vote, to meaningful exercise of freedom of expression, and to economic success. Even if the Constitution were interpreted to guarantee each student a right to some *minimum* education, said the Court, nothing indicated that the Texas scheme fell short of such a baseline. Simply because some districts could afford to spend more per child and chose to do so did not mean that children elsewhere were being denied a constitutionally adequate education. The Court hinted that an absolute deprivation of education might be unconstitutional—a position it seemed to confirm in a subsequent case—but stated that a disparity in education resources was not. *See* Plyler v. Doe, 457 U.S. 202 (1982); Papasan v. Allain, 478 U.S. 265 (1986); Kadrmas v. Dickinson Pub. Schools, 487 U.S. 450, 466 n.1 (1988).

The practical effect of the 1973 case was to close the federal constitutional door on funding equalization lawsuits.

188. Dissatisfaction with the Court's approach and with the continued unequal pattern of school finance prompted extensive academic commentary. *See* authorities cited in note 186, *supra*. In some states, reformers convinced the courts or the legislature to revamp school finance schemes in ways designed to relieve the economic inequities. Examples of state court finance decisions are as follows: Serrano v. Priest, 5 Cal. 3d 584, 487 P.2d 1241 (1971); Serrano v. Priest, 18 Cal. 3d 728, 557 P.2d 929, 135 Cal. Rptr. 345, *cert. denied sub nom.*, 432 U.S. 907 (1977) (*Serrano II*); Robinson v. Cahill, 62 N.J. 473, 303 A.2d 273, *cert. denied sub nom.*, 414 U.S. 976 (1973); Horton v. Meskill, 172 Conn. 615, 376 A.2d 359 (1977); Board of Education v. Nyquist, 94 Misc. 2d 466, 408 N.Y.S.2d 606 (1978); Board of Education. v. Walter, 58 Ohio St. 2d 368, 390 N.E.2d 813 (1979), *cert. denied*, 444 U.S. 105 (1980); Buse v. Smith, 74 Wis.2d 550, 247 N.W.2d 141 (1976); Milliken v. Green, 390 Mich. 389, 212 N.W.2d 711 (1973); Thompson v. Engelking, 96 Idaho 793, 537 P.2d 635 (1975); Olsen v. State, 276 Or. 9, 554 P.2d 139 (1976); Shofstall v. Hollins, 110 Ariz. 88, 515 P.2d 590 (1973); Seattle School Dist. No. 1 v. State, 90 Wash. 2d 476, 585 P.2d 71 (1978); Edgewood Independent School District v. Kirby, 777 S.W.2d 391 (Tex. 1989) (*Edgewood I*); Edgewood Independent School District v. Kirby, 804 S.W.2d 491 (Tex. 1991) (*Edgewood II*); Edgewood Independent School District v. Kirby, 804 S.W.2d 491 (Tex. 1991) (*Edgewood III*).

189. Jonathan Kozol, *supra* note 185, at 73.

190. *See* Lau v. Nichols, 414 U.S. 563 (1974) (interpreting federal equal education statutes to compel districts to rectify language deficiencies caused by some students' inability to understand English); Martin Luther King Jr. Elementary School Children v. Michigan Board of Education, 451 F. Supp. 1324 (E.D. Mich. 1978) (construing federal law to cover language deficiencies where the home language is "Black English," as well as when the language is a foreign language such as Spanish or German). *See generally* Rachel Moran, "The Politics of Discretion: Federal Intervention in Bilingual Education," 76 *Calif. L. Rev.* 1249 (1988); Tyll van Geel, "Law, Politics, and the Right to Be Taught English," 83 *School Rev.* 245 (1975); Peter D. Roos, "Bilingual Education: The Hispanic Response to Unequal Educational Opportunity," 42 *Law & Contemp. Probs.* 111 (1978); Rachel Moran, "Bilingual Education as a Status Conflict," 75 *Calif. L. Rev.* 321 (1987); *From Shame to Struggle: Language Policy and Language Rights* (T. Kangas & J. Cummins eds., 1989); Kenji Hakuta, *Mirror of Language: The Debate on Bilingualism* (1986); Christine H. Rossell & J. Michael Ross, "The Social Science Evidence on Bilingual Education," 15 *J. of Law & Educ.* 385 (1986); *Advances in Bilingual Education Research* (E. Garcia & R. Padilla eds., 1985); Virginia L. MacDonald & Andrew F. MacDonald, "Cultural Literacy and English as a Second Language: A Perspective," 62 *The Clearing House* 314 (1989); Juan F. Perea, "Demography and Distrust: An Essay on American Languages, Cultural Pluralism and Official English," 77 *Minn. L. Rev.* 269 (1992).

191. *See* note 123, *supra*. *See also* Martha Nussbaum, "The Softness of Reason: A Classical Case for Gay Studies," *The New Republic* 26 (July 13 & 20, 1992) (discussing efforts to include gay studies in the curriculum at Brown University); Paul Schmidtberger, *The Right to Know Yourself: The First Amendment and the Suppression of Books on Homosexuality in Public School Libraries* (unpublished manuscript on file with author that discusses the importance of providing books on homosexuality to young people); "New Book Series for Gay Teen-Agers," *N.Y. Times*, Nov. 24, 1992, at B3, col. 3 (announcing Chelsea House Publishers proposed new series of books on gay topics for teenagers).

192. Gibson, "Gay Male and Lesbian Youth Suicide," in U.S. Dept. of Health and Human Services, Report of the Secretary's Task Force on Youth Suicide 3–110 (1989) (study showing that one-third of adolescent suicides are by young people struggling with their sexual identity).

193. This is debatable, however, and may be involved more as a tactical move to strengthen the claim that discrimination against gays is irrational, as well as to evoke sympathy for gays because they are "born with" their sexual orientation, than as a claim based on solid scientific data. *See* Janet Halley, "The Politics of the Closet: Towards Equal Protection for Gay, Lesbian, and Bisexual Identity," 36 *UCLA L. Rev.* 915, 920–22 (1989). *See generally* Warren J. Blumenfeld & Diane Raymond, *Looking at Gay and Lesbian Life* 85 (1988); Claudia A. Lewis, "From this Day Forward: A Feminine Moral Discourse on Homosexual Marriage," 97 *Yale L.J.* 1783, 1799 (1988); Richard Posner, *Sex and Reason* 85–110 (1992).

194. *See* Steven Lee Myers, "Schools Find That Diversity Can Place Values in Conflict," *N.Y. Times*, Oct. 6, 1992, A20, col. 1 (discussing some parents' objections to a New York City curriculum that teaches first graders to accept gay people); Joseph Berger, "Queens Schools Pressed to Teach About Gay Life," *N.Y. Times*, Nov. 17, 1992, at B12, col. 1 (discussing Queens school board's refusal to obey a 1989 resolution that required it to teach lessons that "view lesbians / gays as real people to be respected and appreciated"); Steven Lee Myers, "A School Board Avoids Meeting on a Gay Issue," *N.Y. Times*, Dec. 1, 1992, at A17, col. 6 (discussing continued defiance of Queens school board and describing the conflict over the "Children of the Rainbow" curriculum as "the most serious con-

frontation in Mr. Fernandez's three years as Chancellor over his power to mandate policy under the school decentralization law"); Steven Lee Myers, "School Board Out in New York Fight," *N.Y. Times*, Dec. 2, 1992, at A–1, col. 5 (reporting that Chancellor Hernandez suspended the defiant school board that refused to adopt the multicultural curriculum); Peter Schmidt, "Board Overrules Fernandez After He Tells Tales Out of School," *Education Week* 5 (Dec. 16, 1992) (discussing New York City School Board's decision to override Fernandez's suspension of the local school board over its refusal to adopt the multicultural curriculum). *See also* Richard Lacayo, "Jack and Jack and Jill and Jill," *Time* 52 (Dec. 14, 1992) (discussing controversy over proposed, nonrequired, public school readings designed to foster respect for gays and lesbians, including *Daddy's Roommate, Heather Has Two Mommies*, and *Gloria Goes to Gay Pride*).

6   TOWARD CONSTITUTIONAL LITERACY

1. Gerald Graff, "Teach the Conflicts," in *The Politics of Liberal Education* 57 (D. J. Gless & B. Herrnstein Smith eds., 1992). *See also* Gerald Graff, *Beyond the Culture Wars: How Teaching the Conflicts Can Revitalize American Education* (1992).

2. I rely on personal experience mindful of Sarah Lawrence Lightfoot's astute observation that academics have an unfortunate tendency to speak autobiographically when discussing the problems of American education. Sarah Lawrence Lightfoot, *The Good High School* 9 (1983). This discussion thus may display excessive interest in some aspects of education that matter much in law school settings but that matter less elsewhere. I believe nonetheless that the anecdotes on which I rely illustrate problems that have been documented in studies of students at *all* levels of American education. Indeed, my main point here is that the pervasiveness of these problems, even to the law school level, is striking evidence that Hirsch is on to something.

3. Some reports show gains, such that we may now have recovered the ground lost during the 1970s, though we have not yet pulled ahead. *See Crossroads in American Education* (NAEP, 1986). Reforms initiated in the mid-1980s were so widespread that by 1984–85, forty-one states had raised their standards for the number and types of courses they required for high school graduation. ETS Policy Information Center, *What Americans Study* 3 (1989). Thus, by 2002, law students will include mostly students whose education post-dates the education "lean years" of the 1970s. Then, only some of their teachers and older classmates will be remnants of this era.

4. U.S. Dep't of Education, *The Nation's Report Card: The U.S. History Report Card* 14 (1988).

5. U.S. Dep't of Education, *The Civics Report Card: Report of National Assessment of Educational Progress* (1990).

6. *Id.* at 7.

7. *Id.* at 8.

8. *Id.* at 9.

9. I should point out, with regret, that the law schools have taken no formal steps in reaction to this fact. In general, therefore, individual teachers either must adjust for the vast range of prior knowledge in the classroom—by explaining historical allusions or avoiding references to them—or talk over some students' heads. Although students can do quite well on law school examinations without this prior knowledge and can master the rules and their application to varying fact patterns, the process is for them more of an analytical puzzle isolated from a larger context than an historically situated inquiry.

10. Obvious exceptions would be people who have studied United States history or government in college or for whom this was a special focus. But, as studies of twelfth graders
indicate, even students who have taken some history and government courses as currently taught may retain very little knowledge of these subjects.

11. *See, e.g.,* R. Freeman Butts, *The Civic Mission in Educational Reform* 206 (1989) (noting that
textbooks remain the staple of elementary and secondary school civics).

12. Frances FitzGerald, *America Revised* (1979).

13. Arthur Schlesinger, Jr., *The Disuniting of America* (1990).

14. *See, e.g.,* Jean Anyon, *Ideology and United States History Textbooks, in Education and the State,
vol. II: Politics, Patriarchy, and Practice* 21 (R. Dale, G. Esland, R. Fergusson & M. Mac-
Donald eds., 1981) (critiquing the treatment of labor history from 1865 to World War II in
seventeen well-known secondary school United States history textbooks, on the ground
that they favored the interests of the wealthy and powerful social groups). *See also* William
A. Luker, Floyd H. Jenkins & Lewis Abernathy, "Elementary School Basal Readers and
Work Mode Bias," 5:2 *J. of Econ. Educ.* 92, 92–96 (Spring 1974); Council on Interracial Books
for Children, *Stereotypes, Distortions and Omissions in U.S. History Textbooks* (1977); Bal-
timore Feminist Project, *Sexism and Racism in Popular Basal Readers: 1964–1976,* (Racism
and Sexism Resource Center for Educators, 1976); Ruth Miller Elson, *Guardians of Tradition, American Schoolbooks of the Nineteenth Century* (1964); Hazel Whitman Hertzberg,
Social Studies Reform 1880–1980 (1981).

15. *See, e.g.,* Diane Ravitch, "Pluralism vs. Particularism in American Education," *The Responsive Community* 32, 34 (Spring 1991).

16. *See* Frances FitzGerald, *supra* note 12.

17. *See* Stephen A. Guardbaum, "Law, Politics and The Claims of Community," 90 *Mich. L.
Rev.* 685 (1992), for a helpful analysis of the disparate ways in which "community" appears
in legal and other theory. *See also* Jeremy Waldron, "Particular Values and Critical Morality," 77 *Calif. L. Rev.* 561, 582 (1989) (noting that "communitarians characteristically avoid or
evade the definition of 'community'").

18. Steven Shiffrin, "Liberal Theory and the Need for Politics," 89 *Mich L. Rev.* 1281, 1291 (1991)
(reviewing *Liberalism and the Good* (R. Bruce Douglass, Gerald M. Mara & Henry S.
Richardson eds., 1990)).

19. *Id.* at 1292.

20. This, warns Steven Shiffrin, would wrongly ignore the value of politics to realistic
assessments of "the kind of citizenry we want to promote and the forces that prevent us
from doing so." *Id.* at 1294.

21. *See* Richard Rorty, "Education, Socialization, and Individuation," 75 *Liberal Education* 2, 4
(Sept / Oct. 1989).

22. Indeed, we already tolerate numerous nationally administered achievement tests that
affect the sequence and content of public and private instruction. Admission to college,
graduate schools, and professional training programs is partly determined by performance on standardized tests, as is access to many occupations. Although the proposed
national education standards and the American Achievement Tests would have special
influence, they would join a well-occupied field of national education tests. Thus national
standards already influence an inexplicit national curriculum. Although the tests have
been severely criticized by some commentators, the criticisms have resulted in test
modification, not abolition. Schools, employers, and others continue to rely on them as
national measures of competency. As such, a national curriculum that makes explicit the

knowledge tested by these important measures actually may be fairer than the current system, which does not.

23. These common values are critical, not only to the contemporary discussions of a national curriculum, but also to the increasing pressure to deregulate schooling and permit vouchers to be applied to private school alternatives. Privatization of schooling, if unchecked by government regulation and common curricular standards, clearly could threaten our common values. No one has been more passionate in resisting this privatization and in defending public education as critical to maintaining our common values, than R. Freeman Butts.

   In Butts's view, "Achieving a sense of community is the essential purpose of public education." R. Freeman Butts, "The Public School: Assaults on a Great Idea," *The Nation* 16 (Apr. 30, 1973). Thus, he argues, public education not only should be preserved, it should inculcate *particular civic values*, rather than merely teach some civics knowledge. *See* R. Freeman Butts, *The Civics Mission in Educational Reform* (1989).

   Although other proponents of civics education disagree strongly with aspects of the Butts proposal, a surprising number agree that "civic responsibility" remains a useful cultural concept and that exciting civic consciousness is a proper governmental function. *See, e.g.*, Ehman, "The American School in the Political Socialization Process," 50 *Rev. of Educ. Research* 99 (Spring 1980); Morris Janowitz, *The Reconstruction of Patriotism* (1983); Richard Pratte, *The Civic Imperative: Examining the Need for Civic Education* (1988); *Civic Education: Its Limits and Conditions* (S. Douglas Franzosa ed., 1988); *Political Education in Flux* (D. Heater & J. A. Gillespie eds., 1981); Mary Jane Turner, "Civic Education in the United States," in *id.* at 49.

24. Amy Gutmann, *Democratic Education* 14 (1987).

25. *Id.* at 54.

26. *See* Hazel Whitman Hertzberg, *Social Studies Reform 1880–1980*, 123–26 (1981) (an excellent review of changes in social studies treatment of black history); Carter G. Woodson, *The Mis-Education of the Negro* (1933) (arguing that education of blacks is based on assumptions that promote white racism and rationalize oppression of blacks in the United States, such that black students find it difficult to break away from these assumptions and challenge the social structures that subordinate them); W. E. B. DuBois, *The Souls of Black Folk* (Vintage ed. 1990). Nathan Glazer & Daniel P. Moynihan, *Beyond the Melting Pot* (2d ed. 1970); Robert L. Gates, Jr., *Loose Canons: Notes on the Culture Wars* (1992); Jacques Barzun, *Of Human Freedom* (rev. ed. 1964); Beverly M. Gordon, "Cultural Knowledge," in *Civic Education: Its Limits and Conditions* 99 (S. Douglas Franzosa ed., 1988).

27. *See, e.g.*, Susan Douglas Franzosa, "The Education of the Citizeness," in *Civic Education: Its Limits and Conditions* 142 (S. Douglas Franzosa ed., 1988); Martha Minow, "Differences Among Difference," 1 *UCLA Women's L.J.* 165 (1991).

28. *See, e.g.*, Richard Rodriguez, "An American Writer," in *The Invention of Ethnicity* 3 (W. Sollors ed., 1989); Reed, Wong, Callahan & Hope, "Is Ethnicity Obsolete?" in *id.* at 226; Werner Sollors, *Beyond Ethnicity: Consent and Dissent in American Culture* (1986); Horace Kallen, *Culture and Democracy in the United States* (1924); Andrew M. Greeley, *Ethnicity in the United States* (1974); Edward Bok, *The Americanization of Edward Bok* (1920); Frederick Barth, *Ethnic Groups and Boundaries: The Social Organizations of Culture Difference* (1969); G. Devereux, "Ethnic Identity: Its Logical Foundations and Its Dysfunctions," in *Ethnic Identity: Cultural Continuities and Change* 42–70 (G. de Vos & L. Romanucci-Ross eds., 1975).

29. *See, e.g.*, Andrew Trusz & Sandra L. Parks-Trusz, "Will the Schools Rebuild an Old Social Order?" in *Civics Education: Its Limits and Conditions* 131 (S. Douglas Franzosa ed., 1988) (noting that, "As educational practice, civicism has stressed an idealized middle-class version of America"); Clarence Karier, "Business Values and the Educational State," in *Roots of Crisis* 6–26 (C. Karier, P. Violas & J. Spring eds., 1973); *Critical Pedagogy, the State, and Cultural Struggle* (H. J. Giroux & P. McLaren eds., 1989); Samuel Bowles & Herbert Gintis, *Schooling in Capitalist America* (1976); *Education and the State: Schooling and the National Interest*, vol. I (R. Dale, G. Esland, R. Ferguson & M. MacDonald eds., 1981).

30. *See, e.g.*, Nomi Maya Stolzenberg, " 'He Drew a Circle that Shut Me Out . . .': Assimilation, Indoctrination and the Paradox of a Liberal Education," 106 *Harv. L. Rev.* 581 (1993); Michael W. McConnell, "Religious Freedom at a Crossroads," 59 *U. Chi. L. Rev.* 115 (1992).

31. *See, e.g.*, Eric Rofes, "Opening Up the Classroom Closet: *Responding to the Educational Needs of Gay and Lesbian Youth,*" 59 *Harv. Educ. Rev.* 444 (1989); Jan Goodman, "Out of the Closet But Paying the Price: Lesbian and Gay Characters in Children's Literature," 14, *Interracial Books for Children Bulletin* 13 (1983).

32. I. B. Berkson, *The Ideal and the Community* 286 (1958).

33. *See* Reed, Wong, Callahan & Hope, *supra* note 28, at 226 (comments of Ishmael Reed).

34. *Id.*

35. Werner Sollors, *supra* note 28, at 31.

36. *The Invention of Ethnicity* xvii (Werner Sollors ed., 1989). *See also* Richard D. Alba, *Ethnic Identity: The Transformation of White America* (1990) (describing the diminishing significance of ethnicity among American whites of European ancestry and the increasingly voluntary nature of ethnic identification for members of these groups.

37. *See* Richard Posner, *Sex and Reason* (1992).

38. Werner Sollors, *supra* note 28, at 13.

39. *See, e.g.*. Mary Jane Turner, *supra* note 23, at 58.

40. John J. Patrick, "Education on the U.S. Constitution," No. 39 ERIC *Digest* (May 1987).

41. Hazel Whitman Hertzberg, *supra* note 26, at 139–40.

42. Stanley Fish, "The Common Touch, or One Size Fits All," in *The Politics of Liberal Education* 241, 248–49 (D. J. Gless & B. Herrnstein Smith eds., 1992).

Index

Toni Marie Massaro is Professor of Law at the University of Arizona Law School.

Library of Congress Cataloging-in-Publication Data
Massaro, Toni Marie, 1955–
Constitutional literacy : a core curriculum for a multicultural nation / Toni Marie Massaro.
p. cm.—(Constitutional conflicts)
Includes index.
ISBN 0-8223-1364-2 (cloth)
1. Education—United States—Curricula. 2. Education—Curricula—Law and legislation—United States. 3. Intercultural education—United States. I. Title. II. Series.
LB1570.M369 1993
375'.00973—dc20   93-10861 CIP